W9-BTT-425

EXPLORING
THE BOOK OF
DANIEL

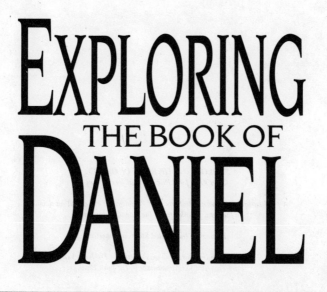

EXPLORING
THE BOOK OF
DANIEL

JOHN PHILLIPS
JERRY VINES

LOIZEAUX BROTHERS
Neptune, New Jersey

EXPLORING THE BOOK OF DANIEL
© *1990 by John Phillips and Jerry Vines*

*A publication of Loizeaux Brothers, Inc. A nonprofit organization devoted
to the Lord's work and to the spread of his truth.*

Printed in the United States of America

*Note to the reader: Part One was written by Dr. Jerry Vines,
Part Two and the Appendixes by Dr. John Phillips.*

Library of Congress Cataloging-in-Publication Data

Phillips, John, 1927-
Exploring the Book of Daniel/John Phillips and Jerry Vines.
p.   cm.
Includes bibliographical references.
ISBN 0-87213-988-3
1. Bible.   O.T.   Daniel—Commentaries.   I. Vines, Jerry.
II. Title.
BS1555.3.P45 1990
224'.507—dc20
90-31819
CIP

10 9 8 7 6 5 4

CONTENTS

FOREWORD

The publishers have honored me by their invitation to contribute a brief foreword to these studies on the book of Daniel. Only of the writings of Daniel did our Lord say, "Whoso readeth, let him understand" (Matthew 24:15).

Not many books on Daniel set forth clearly a logical continuity between the practical and the prophetic lessons in the twelve chapters of Daniel. John Phillips and Jerry Vines have put together their skills, through diligent and faithful study, guided by the Holy Spirit, to prepare this much needed study.

The history of the times in which Daniel lived is explained both typically and topically, showing how the characteristics of human nature remain unchanged. The reader will be challenged to total obedience by the behavior of Daniel and the three Jewish youths. Believers can obey God whatever the conditions and circumstances.

The exposition of the prophetic chapters presents a fresh contribution at such a time as this. Here the reader will see the sovereignty of God in his rule over gentile nations and the little nation Israel; the coming of the antichrist, his character and career. The climax of history will be reached with the return to earth of the Lord Jesus Christ.

This book should have a special appeal to all students of history and biblical prophecy.

LEHMAN STRAUSS

PREFACE

Some time ago I heard my good friend Dr. Jerry Vines preach a powerful message on the three Hebrew young men in the burning fiery furnace. It occurred to me at that time that he and I could profitably pool our knowledge and preaching specialties, team up, and write a book on Daniel.

Accordingly we divided up the book. Dr. Vines agreed to write on the first six chapters. He has brought to the exposition his skills as a pastor and evangelist, with special emphasis on the practical lessons of the book of Daniel. I have written on the last six chapters of the book, bringing to bear on these portions the results of some thirty years' study in the prophetic scriptures. I also have supplied the Introduction and Appendixes.

There was one area of overlap in our individual emphases that Dr. Vines and I agreed had to be commented on by each of us. Daniel 2 properly belongs in both a practical and a prophetical exposition. Dr. Vines's thoughts on that chapter are within the text and mine are included as Appendix 23.

Neither Dr. Vines nor I wanted to get into the soul-destroying, Bible-denying, Christ-rejecting theories of the so-called "higher critics"; other scholars have long since exposed their fallacies. We all, however, need to be informed about the work of such men as Charles Boutflower, Edward Pusey, Robert Dick Wilson, and Sir Robert Anderson, if only to have some defense against liberal attacks. We have put what information we deemed relevant along these lines in the Introduction and Appendixes to this volume.

JOHN PHILLIPS

INTRODUCTION

This commentary is not much concerned with the endless wrangles of liberal scholars nor with their destructive criticisms of the book of Daniel. Charles Boutflower summed up their skeptical and atheistic approach like this:

> The critics look upon the Book of Daniel as a religious novel resting upon a shadowy background of history, written about 164 B.C., in the troublous days of the Maccabees, and written with this noble intention, viz., to encourage the faithful in a time of persecution and to support them under very severe trials. Accordingly they see much in this Book that meets with their approval, and are fully awake to its literary beauties.
>
> But, all the same, it is in their eyes a mere work of the imagination, cleverly put together, but containing not a few historical inaccuracies, owing to its having been written some three or four hundred years after the times which it describes. To them, therefore, its great facts are pure fancies; its mighty miracles, mere feats of the imagination; its so-called prophecies, past history clothed with the garb of prophecy—a favourite practice in the apocalypses of the Pseudepigrapha.
>
> If this view of the matter be the correct one, the puzzle is, How did this Book of Daniel come to be included in the sacred Canon of the Old Testament? and how came it to be treated by our Lord Jesus Christ with such special honour?[1]

Enemies of the scriptures have brought up their heavy artillery against the book of Daniel because of "the minuteness of the predictions embracing even special events in the distant future."[2] Those critics have a god who is so small he cannot be permitted to foretell the future in accurate detail. They would rather hack the Bible to pieces than admit its supernatural character and acknowledge its author.

As Dr. Edward B. Pusey said:

> The book of Daniel is especially fitted to be a battlefield between faith and unbelief. It admits of no half-measures. It is either Divine or an imposture. To write any book under the name of another, and to give it out to be his, is, in any case, a forgery, dishonest in itself, and destructive of all trustworthiness.
>
> But the case as to the book of Daniel, if it were not his, would go far beyond even this. The writer, were he not Daniel, must have lied, on a most frightful scale, ascribing to God prophecies which were never uttered, and miracles which are assumed never to have been wrought. In a word, the whole book would be one lie in the Name of God. The more God, as we shall see, is the centre of the whole, the more directly would the falsehood come into relation to God. The book truly ascribes to God, that *He* gave wisdom to Daniel to interpret the visions of Nebuchadnezzar and Belshazzar; that *He* delivered the children from the burning fiery furnace and Daniel from the den of lions; that *He* revealed to Daniel things to come, the largest and the least, comprising successions of empires and Christ's Kingdom, with some exact dates and minute details. The miracles it implies, the prophecies it avers, to have been recorded by Daniel a contemporary.
>
> Either then we have true miracles and true prophecy, or we should have nothing but untruth. An apology for the supposed forger, such as those put out by some Germans[3] and lately in England, is utterly untenable and immoral . . .[4]

Here we must leave these blind leaders of the blind to their unbelief and to their obvious echo of the evil one: "Yea, hath God said?"[5] Let us turn instead to this great book, God-breathed by the Holy Ghost, this authentic and authoritative account of "Daniel the prophet" (as the Lord himself describes him) and hear his confident, "Thus saith the Lord."

---

1. Charles Boutflower, *In And Around The Book of Daniel* (London: Society for Promoting Christian Knowledge, 1923), p. 2.

2. Samuel Rollis Driver, *Cambridge Bible*, Daniel, Introduction, p. 66.

3. De Wette spoke of it as "the intelligent act of a patriot," Einl. 257. Zunz, an "enlightened" Jew, (Gottesdienstl. Vortr. d. Juden, p. 318 sqq. 405 sqq.,) and Lengerke, (15) excused it from habits of the times. Bleek did not seem to think such fraud needs excuse (Schleiermacher & Zeitschrift, iii. 250 ssq. 23). It was "necessary for his end, prophecy having ceased in

the time of the Maccabees" (1 Macc. ix. 27, iv. 46, xiv. 41.) Einl. p. 593.

4. Edward B. Pusey, *Daniel The Prophet* (New York: Funk and Wagnalls, 1886), p. 75. Acceptance of Pusey's stand against the higher critics does not mean endorsement of his theology in gereral.

5. See Appendix 1 for further discussions of Daniel's attackers by Sir Robert Anderson and Edward B. Pusey. Aslo see Appendix 18 for the remarkable defence of Daniel by Prof. Robert Dick Wilson.

PART ONE

Daniel
and His
Personal Friends
Daniel 1:1–6:28

It is difficult for people who serve in high-profile positions to go through their careers unscathed. We have witnessed this in American society. Prominent political and religious leaders have come under the searchlight of the media and have been publicly discredited when secret scandals in their lives have been exposed. Such revelations are bad enough when the guilty person holds high political office. They are worse when the person is a prominent evangelist or religious leader. Time and time again the public has been shocked to learn of marital infidelity, corruption, graft, and duplicity in individuals they have admired, trusted, and followed. The media has a heyday. The public eagerly waits for more details. The culprit retires from the scene in embarrassment and shame, volubly denying the charges or vowing revenge. On and on it goes. So it is that when a man stands in a position of prominence, when he is in a place where people can examine his life on a daily basis, it is hard for that man to escape various accusations.

For that reason the life of Daniel is one of the most unusual biographies in the Bible. Three times in this book he is called "greatly beloved" by God. Here was a man who spent almost his entire career, from the time he was a teenager until he was a very old man, in positions of influence and authority in highly visible public life. Yet there is not one record of anything against him.

We can put Daniel alongside Joseph in the Old Testament as an example to young and old of the ability of a person who knows the Lord, and who is living for the Lord, to serve in the public sector and maintain a testimony for the Lord Jesus Christ. It is God in the life of an individual who enables him or her to live a life well pleasing to God and beyond reproach. Daniel gives us a beautiful life on the pages of this book.

He also gives us an important book in the Bible. The book of Daniel is to the Old Testament what Revelation is to the New Testament. The two books go hand in hand. We cannot understand Revelation apart from Daniel, nor can we understand Daniel apart from Revelation.

Interestingly, the book of Daniel is one of the prime targets against which biblical critics launch their attack. They think they see in the book of Daniel the Bible's Achilles' heel. They believe that if somehow they can discredit this book the entire Bible will come tumbling to the ground like a house of cards. In the nineteenth century and later the so-called "higher critics," the destructive critics, set out to make a shambles of the book of Daniel. They picked up the arguments of an old infidel named Porphyry, who had attacked the book of Daniel centuries ago. They resurrected his arguments.

There are no new arguments against the integrity of the Bible. The agnostic liberal theologians of today are not coming up with anything new. Since the first century after the Bible was completed, there have been skeptics and infidels, critics who have cast aspersions on God's written word.

So the critics say, "The book of Daniel is a fictitious book, a historical romance. No man by the name of Daniel ever lived." Or, "The book of Daniel was not written when it purports to have been written. It was written some four hundred years later." Why would those critics make such an unsupportable claim? Because the book of Daniel has various prophecies that relate to times far ahead of Daniel's time, and the critics think such prophecy impossible. Remember, if the author of this book was writing about what had already occurred, as if he were predicting it, then the book is fraudulent.

The critics deny the supernatural in the Bible. Whenever they find anything supernatural, anything that defies scientific explanation, they cross it out and say it can't be true.

When we open up the Bible, we are opening a book that bears the imprint of the divine inspiration of a supernatural God. I believe in a God who created the universe, a God who is supernatural. If we have a supernatural God, then we have a God who can do supernatural things. The deist says God created the world, set it in motion, and then walked away from it and has nothing else to do with it. That is not true. This world was created by a personal God. He has not deserted it; He is vitally interested in it. When He so chooses, He can step into his own creation and alter laws that He himself devised.

I have a brother-in-law, retired from the navy and living in the Washington, D.C., area. He has a model railroad in his basement, with tracks and houses and engines and boxcars. He plays with them and has the best time you can imagine. It's his creation. He's the one who put it together. Anytime he so desires he can cut the power off or turn it on. He rearranges the cars, switches them on the tracks, makes them go backward or forward. He can do anything he wants to do anytime he wants to do it. That is what a miracle is—God doing what He chooses with his own creation. We call it "supernatural."

Liberals question the book of Daniel because it is a prophecy. Prophecy is history written ahead of time, God predicting what is going to happen in the future. We all are curious about the future. That is why people pick up their newspapers in the morning and read the daily "horrorscope." They want to know what that day has in store for them. That is why people go to psychics, why they buy books about astrology. They want to know the future. But psychics and astrologers do not know the future; it is not in the stars. But it is in the Bible. Only there do we have reliable information on what the future is going to bring. Only God can prophesy.

Remember what Jesus said about this. "And now I have told you before it come to pass, that, when it is come to pass, you might believe" (John 14:29). When Jesus speaks on a matter, that settles it. Thus Jesus has put his imprimatur on the supernatural.

We do not need to give much attention to the critics. Conservative scholars have answered all their accusations against the book of Daniel. This text stands as a remarkable demonstration of prophecy in our Bible: God predicting ahead of time what was going to be.

In the Olivet discourse, Jesus gave his own predictions concerning the end time. The only Old Testament book from which Jesus quoted in that Olivet discourse was the book of Daniel. He said, "When ye therefore shall see the abomination of desolation, spoken of by Daniel the prophet . . . " (Matthew 24:15). The critic says that Daniel is a forgery, a phony. Jesus says that Daniel is prophecy, and we take our stand with the Lord Jesus. It always amazes me how the critics seem to think they can tell the almighty what He can and cannot do. Jesus says there was a Daniel and Daniel was a prophet. That settles it.

I. A KING'S DAINTIES (1:1-21)

A. Daniel and His Destiny (1:1-7)

Let us look at young Daniel as he goes to the University of Babylon.

1. The Captivity (1:1-2)

These verses set before us the captivity of the nation of Judah, about which we read in 2 Kings 24 and 2 Chronicles 36. The nation of

Judah had been carried away captive from their land to the land of Babylon hundreds of miles away.

Have you ever been taken away from your familiar environs? Toward the end of World War II my father was drafted into the service. I was in the second grade. I remember the day I said goodbye to all my friends at school and with my mother moved to St. Petersburg, Florida, where my father was stationed, to a place I had never been before. I saw scenery I had never seen before, moved into a house I had not known before. I remember my first day in a strange school. Have you ever all of a sudden had to face that first day in a new school? Have you experienced that kind of fear and anxiety? Can you imagine what it was like for Daniel to be carried away captive to the land of Babylon when he was in his early teens? That is what the first two verses of chapter 1 are about.

a. *Jehoiakim and His Depravity.* Three kings are mentioned in these verses. Jehoiakim reminds us of the people's sin and failure. He was a godless man with no reverence for the things of God.

Two sins caused Judah to be carried away into captivity. One of those sins was disobedience to the word of God. God had told his people to give the land a sabbath rest every seventh year. In that year they were not to cultivate the land. But they disregarded God's word and for 490 years the land had no rest.

God says you cannot disobey his word and get away with it. How long will it take people to learn they cannot disobey God's word and escape? God is not playing games with us in the Bible. When God tells us to do something we must do it or pay the price. Think of it—490 years and no sabbatic years; seventy sabbatic years ignored. So God sent them into captivity for seventy years. God said, You are going to obey my word one way or the other.

Jehoiakim had no regard for God's word. When they brought him a scroll containing the written word of God, he took his penknife and cut up the pages of that scroll and threw them in the fire. Later on, instead of having a royal burial, Jehoiakim was buried outside the city, thrown on the city dump. He received "the burial of a donkey," the Bible says.

A second reason the Jews were carried into captivity was their departure from the worship of God, their departure into wholesale idolatry. They found a strange fascination with the idols of the pagan nations around them. Nothing could cure it.

Babylon was the center of idol worship; idolatrous religion had its origin there. Verse 2 refers to the land of Shinar, the old word for the land of Babylon. Nimrod, the tyrant, comes to mind, and visions of the tower of Babel. So when God allowed them to be taken into captivity to Babylon, He was sending them to the capital city of idolatry. "I can't cure you of your addiction to idols, so I'll take you to where they had their origin, back to the source, and there you can learn what idolatry is like. For seventy years you can experience those idols you so desperately want to serve."

After their years of captivity in Babylon they had no more desire for idol worship. To this day, the Jewish people are monotheistic in their worship. They worship only one God: Jehovah (Yahweh). Do you see what happened to them? God put them in the land of Babylon to learn to hate the false gods they had once loved.

We too had better be careful to what we attach ourselves; God may let us have our fill of it.

b. *Nebuchadnezzar and His Cruelty.* The second king is Nebuchadnezzar, the mightiest ruler on earth—a brilliant military strategist, a marvelous builder. But he was cruel. Young boys, the nobility and aristocracy of Judah, were torn from their homes, made eunuchs, and forced to serve their conqueror in a foreign land.

c. *Jehovah and His Sovereignty.* We may not discern the third king at first. "And the Lord gave Jehoiakim into Nebuchadnezzar's hands." At once we are reminded of the sovereignty of God. God is still on the throne.

Later on in this book, three times in one chapter, God says that the Most High rules in the affairs of men. God is the one who puts people in power, and God is the one who removes them. That is as true in America today as it was in Babylon and Judah in Daniel's day. God is still in control. In fact, Jeremiah called Nebuchadnezzar the Lord's servant. He was the temporal ruler; the Lord is the eternal ruler. God is in charge. That should bring us great comfort.

When I was in Washington recently, I became somewhat discouraged as I thought of some of the people who are running this country. If I didn't believe in a sovereign God, overcoming man's mistakes and man's self-will, I doubt if I could sleep at night. But I have no cause for worry. I can go to bed and drop off to sleep because "he that keepeth Israel neither slumbers nor sleeps." God is on the throne and He is going to stay awake.

2. The Captives (1:3-4b)

The word *children* is misleading. Don't get the idea these were infants. They were young people, teenagers, Judean youth.

a. *Their Nobility* (1:3). These were the elite of the children of Israel, "of the king's seed, and of the princes." They were the finest young people of the land.

Our country and our churches still have young people like that. These are the ones the devil wants the most—those with keen minds and promising futures. If the devil can corrupt them, he will go a long way toward destroying our land.

b. *Their Ability* (1:4a, b). Nebuchadnezzar had special requirements for those selected for public service in Babylon. They were to be people of outstanding ability, physically strong, "children in whom was no blemish," no defect. They were to be pleasing in appearance, healthy, and handsome. That's the kind of person the devil wants to destroy. Daniel and his friends were young, athletic, and strong.

Nebuchadnezzar's second requirement for public service was mental keenness. He wanted those who were quick to learn, those who were, so to speak, on the dean's list, the Phi Beta Kappa crowd.

They were also to be socially poised, "such as had ability in them to stand in the king's palace," young men who knew how to move in royal circles. They had to be cultured, an embarrassment neither to themselves nor to their superiors. These were the kinds of young people who were selected for special training by the king of Babylon.

3. The Crisis (1:4c-7)

Daniel and his friends were in a strange country, having been deported from their own land. They are the finest young people their nation could produce. They were of nobility and they had ability. They soon faced a crisis, however, because the king was determined to change them totally, to fit them for their careers in the public service of Babylon.

The crisis was threefold, a crisis similar to those every young person faces. God says, "Present your bodies a living sacrifice, holy, acceptable unto God . . . be not conformed to this world: but be ye transformed by the renewing of your mind" (Romans 12:1-2). We will be transformed, or we will be conformed.

Picture Daniel and his friends at the University of Babylon, with a three-year education and indoctrination program planned for them. Here we have a classic picture of brainwashing. We've read about men who underwent brainwashing when they were prisoners of war in North Korea. Loudspeakers were installed in their barracks, and incessantly, night and day, the political philosophy of communism was pounded at them. What was the purpose? To change their political outlook.

The original brainwasher is the devil. His purpose is to get us to believe his lies instead of God's truth.

a. *An Authority Crisis* (1:4c). They were to be enrolled in a curriculum that would indoctrinate them with Chaldean culture. Archaeologists have uncovered thousands of clay tablets that acquaint us with Chaldean life. They were to be subjected to the academic, philosophical, and religious ideas of a godless civilization, to pagan philosophies and evolutionary theories. They were to be taught astronomy, in which the Chaldeans excelled, and astrology, a highly developed Babylonian superstition. These young people were going to have an authority crisis. They were going to be taught that the philosophies and theories of Babylonian scholarship were truth, and that would be in direct opposition to what they had been taught at home.

There is always an authority crisis. Whom are we going to believe, God or the devil? Our young people go off to secular universities and at once face a secular mentality and a secular education. They walk into classrooms where all too often the professor's goal is to shake them from Christian faith, change the source of authority in their lives, remove them from the word of God, and get them to lean on the theories of men.

b. *A Morality Crisis* (1:5). They were to be well fed for three years, and at the end of that time they were to stand before the king. The king may have thought he was doing them a favor. He gave these students a three-year scholarship including room and board. They were to have opportunity to cultivate appetites for the very best that Babylon had to offer. Nothing was better than that.

This is the second crisis young people face: What is to be the source of our moral authority, the devil's theories or God's truth? The devil wants to change our appetites. He wants us to develop appetites for the things of this world instead of the things of God. He wants to give us a craving for gold instead of God, for the material instead of the spiritual. He wants us to be more interested in earth than heaven. We are subject to constant brainwashing, through the media, music, television, books, and magazines. We undergo constant pounding to give us appetites for the immoral ways of this world.

The purpose is given in the last part of this verse: "That at the end thereof they might stand before the king." The problem was that it was the wrong king. We must make up our minds which king we want to stand before.

When I was a boy, a man used to walk down the street wearing a big sandwich-board sign. On the front was written, "I am a fool for Jesus." People would look and laugh. Then they would look on the backboard. It said, "Whose fool are you?" We must make up our minds which king we intend to serve. We will either sell out to Jesus and stand before God's king or we will sell out to Satan and stand before the prince of this world's Babylon.

c. *An Identity Crisis* (1:6-7). The third crisis was spiritual. The purpose was to remove from these young men of Judah any vestige of devotion to the Lord. "Now among these were . . . Daniel, Hananiah, Mishael, and Azariah." Obviously there were more than four. Why are the others not mentioned? Was it because when pressure came, they caved in? When the testing time came, did they fail the test? Did they give in to the pressure because they would not pay the price, and so their names are not mentioned in God's Word?

We must make up our minds. We can go with the crowd and go off into obscurity or we can be like Daniel and his friends and be different. Young people who belong to a vital, live, Bible-preaching, soul-winning church have a tremendous advantage. They have a peer group who loves the Lord Jesus. When I committed myself to the Lord Jesus, I was the only Christian student in my high school, as far as I knew at the time. In fact, I was the only such young person in my youth group at church. Most of our church's young people were simply playing church. I didn't have anybody to stand with me.

I remember the night of the Junior/Senior Dance. I did not think that as a Christian it would be a good testimony for me to attend it. I went to the banquet, but when it came time for the dance, I left. Six teachers, some of whom were members of our church, stood at the door and tried to talk me into staying. I refused and went out by myself and drove away from that country club. I went to the little square of the county-seat town where I lived (it was probably about nine or ten o'clock by then). Although it was the place where all the young people came, not a single young person was there. As I drove up on that square, the devil said to me, "You've made a fool of yourself, haven't you? This Jesus business! This living for the Lord! Look at you, you haven't a friend left." But the devil is a liar. I did not hear an audible voice but it was just as if the Lord spoke to my heart. He said, "I'll tell you what, Jerry, you stood for me, and I'll stand for you. You've been a friend for me, and I'll be a friend for you."

All through the years I have had a glorious life being friends with Jesus. For every friend I've lost for Jesus' sake, He has given me a thousand in return.

Young people, dare to be different! Dare to be a Daniel. Never mind what the crowd does. Attend a class reunion later on in life and you'll see the crowd that used to laugh and make fun of you. You'll see some of them living with a fourth wife. They made fun of you because you belonged to an evangelical church, lived for Jesus, and tried to win people to the Lord. You will see their bloated, alcoholic faces. You will be glad, twenty years from now, that you stood for Jesus in your high school. Life somehow gives things a new dimension.

These Hebrew boys were different. Every one of their names is a form of the name of God, abbreviations of God—*el, elohim. Yah* is an abbreviation for *Yahweh* or *Jehovah.* Daniel means "God is my judge." Hananiah means "Jehovah is gracious." Mishael means "Who is He that is God." Azariah means "The Lord is help." Evidently they had parents who had faith in the Lord and who wanted to give their sons names with spiritual significance.

You can tell a lot about a society by the kind of names it gives to its children. There was a time in this country when parents named children after Bible characters. Now they are named after rock musicians and movie stars.

Behind the scenes something had taken place in the lives of these boys. There had been a revival in their land. A young king named Josiah one day found the Word of God. God spoke to him and there was a revival. It would be like the president of the United States one night in the White House browsing through the books in the White House library. He finds a copy of the Bible, opens it, and has a revival in his heart. The next day he goes on national television to say that God has moved in his heart and he wants to call the people of America to revival. He goes out with preachers and holds meetings and leads young people to Christ.

That would be no more dramatic than what happened in the days of Josiah. Under the leadership of the boy-king Josiah and of preachers like Jeremiah and Micah, they had a revival. Young people caught fire for God.

Wouldn't you like to see that happen in this land? See a revival that would rescue some of our young people? The misery a lot of them are going through is often a testimony to the sins and failures of their parents. Look at the suicide, alcoholism, sex, and all the other problems our young people face. These things are testimony to our society's sins. Oh, for an old-fashioned, Holy Ghost, sin-killing, Jesus-exalting, Bible-loving revival that would sweep thousands of young people into the kingdom of God! It could happen.

Nebuchadnezzar was not content to let these boys have names that reminded them of their faith in God. So he changed their names, and that caused an identity crisis. They changed Daniel's name to Belteshazzar ("Bel, protect my life"). The next one was changed to Shadrach ("I am fearful of god"). Then come Meshach ("I am despised before my god") and Abednego ("servant of Nebo"). You can see what they were doing. They were trying to remove from the minds and hearts and wills of these young men any commitment to God. In exchange they were offered the king's meat and wine, a place at the king's table. It was a small thing to give up—their old names. But big decisions ultimately rest on little decisions.

Have you made up your mind to live for Jesus? Pay the price. When you are older you will be glad you have lived for him.

B. Daniel and His Decisions (1:8-21)

Life is a series of decisions. We live on the basis of decisions we make, hundreds of them every day—what we intend to do, how we are going to respond to things. What we are today is the result of decisions we have made in the past. What we will be tomorrow will be determined by the decisions we make today.

Many of our major decisions are made while we are young. Most people decide for the Lord Jesus while they are young. We often make the decision for a life's partner when we are young, in our late teens or early twenties. We make decisions about our friends, and friends we make are often our friends for life. We decide what our vocation is to be, or where we will live.

Daniel was at a crisis time in his life. He was about to make the greatest decision he would ever make. Torn from his homeland and taken to a distant land, there he was in the king's palace. At once he had to make a decision.

In these opening chapters of the book of Daniel we find a series of tests for believers. In this chapter there is a test of the believer's walk; in chapter 2 there is a test of the believer's witness; in chapter 3 there is a test of the believer's worship. Every test of life is designed to help us make right decisions in life. So here was Daniel facing a decision. In 1:8 we see the decision Daniel made at the outset. He

"purposed in his heart that he would not defile himself with the portion of the king's meat." It was the right decision, praise God, and
he made it early on. It was a decision that transformed his life. From
that day to the end of his life he was a better man because of it.

Studying this decision of Daniel should give us encouragement
and instill conviction so that we too will make right decisions. We too
must decide to live for the Lord and be the kind of person He wants
us to be.

Daniel and his friends were called on to make a threefold decision.

1. A Heart Decision (1:8a,b)

"Daniel purposed in his heart" literally means Daniel "laid it upon
his heart." All real decisions are heart decisions. That is why the
Bible says, "Keep thy heart with all diligence; for out of it are the
issues of life" (Proverbs 4:23).

Daniel's Babylonian masters could change many things about
Daniel's life. They could change his homeland, diet, even his name,
but they could not change his heart. What we are in our hearts is
what we are, and nobody can change us in our hearts unless we let
them. Let us consider this heart decision.

a. *Individual* (1:8a). "But Daniel purposed in his heart." Daniel
made a decision in his own heart. It was something between him
and the Lord. It was made under tremendous pressure and was by
no means easy to make.

For instance, there was cultural pressure. Daniel was living in a
land where there was no concern for the authority of God's word.
The Babylonians laughed at the law of God and mocked the God
whom Daniel worshiped.

Our young people are living in a society, in an atmosphere, where
there is no respect for the authority of the word of God. Young people are under cultural pressure to make wrong decisions because the
word of God is not enshrined in the lives of worldly people.

Those who know Jesus must be ruled by a different standard. No
matter what the world says, what matters to Christians is what God
says. We do not get our standards from opinion polls; we get them
from the Bible. We don't look to see what the majority says in order
to decide what we are going to do. We make our decisions on the
basis of "thus saith the Lord." The world said to Daniel, "Daniel, go
along." God's word said, in effect, "Be not conformed to this world."

There was also peer pressure. As we have noted, only four young men are mentioned in this passage: Daniel and his colleagues. Probably there were several hundred boys involved in the events recorded here, but only four names are listed. Perhaps the others made up their minds to yield to Babylon, to do what Babylon told them to do. Those who just "go with the flow," those who decide to drift along where the current or the tide takes them, are never included in God's hall of fame.

We can imagine the conversation that went on in the dormitory, and the kinds of things that were said to Daniel as he refused the king's food and wine. One of his peers might have said, "Listen, Daniel, we're a long way from home. Nobody will know or care what you do here. We are off here by ourselves." Another might have said, "Come on, Daniel, it's just a little thing. It really doesn't matter." Another might have urged, "Now then, Daniel, let's not get legalistic about this. You can carry that kind of thing too far." Somebody else might have commented, "Daniel, it may not be strictly kosher, but it will give us an opportunity to witness. How can we win people if we offend them?" Peer pressure. Even if the majority of his peers said, "Go along," Daniel refused to be conformed to that pagan milieu.

There was also fear pressure, the pressure of circumstances and of consequences. Who knew what the king might do when he learned that Daniel refused to drink his wine and eat his meat? People did not go against the rules of the king of Babylon. Life was cheap there. Anyone who dared to defy the king would have to pay for it dearly.

There is a price to pay when we decide to say no to this world and yes to Jesus. There are times when the decisions we make will have enormous consequences. Our jobs might be at stake if we dare to say no for Jesus' sake. A young person might get a lower grade in a class because she or he takes a stand on an issue. Not every teacher is a Christian; I have known teachers to lower the grade of a young person because he dared to live for the Lord. We may not get that promotion at work. We may be excluded from a key group if we take a stand for Christ.

So, in spite of the pressures brought to bear on him, Daniel made his choice. There were solid, scriptural reasons why he did so. There was, for instance, the way the food was prepared. The Jewish people were told in the mosaic law how they were to prepare food. Probably some of these foods were prohibited by Leviticus 11; they were defiling and not to be eaten by Jews. In Babylon all wine was offered as a toast to the gods. All meat was offered in worship to Bel-Merodach or one of the other gods of Babylon. To eat such food meant a sacrifice of spiritual conviction. It meant acknowledging a pagan god. Daniel made up his mind to do what God wanted. There is abundant evidence in the book of Daniel that Daniel knew the scriptures.

I believe that Daniel had a daily quiet time. I believe there was a time every day when Daniel meditated on the truth of God and studied God's word. From that spiritual reservoir he drew convictions that enabled him to make a right decision when crises came.

Although the Bible does not give specific commands concerning all the issues we face in life, let me emphasize the importance of reading the Bible daily. Sometimes people say, "I've been reading my Bible, but I've not been getting much out of it." What they usually mean is they haven't been getting the feeling they want.

Is that *your* problem? Don't worry about the feeling; just keep on reading God's word, keep hiding it in your heart. You are storing in your heart the materials from which you construct convictions that will enable you to make right decisions at the right time. From that inner reservoir of God's word the principles will emerge to give you spiritual, scriptural guidance when decision times come.

Daniel made an individual decision. Everybody else was eating the king's meat but Daniel said, "Not I." Everybody was drinking the king's wine, but Daniel said, "I won't do it." He had the courage to say no.

Sometimes that is the most difficult word in the English language for us to speak. I challenge you to say it when you are in a difficult spot. Everybody is doing something questionable or sinful. You stand there and know what you ought to say, but that word *no* is hard to get out. But it is one of the most effective words in the English language.

Here's how it works. Your friends are all drinking. They urge you to join in. They tell you that a little drink is not going to hurt you. They threaten to ostracize you. But say no , and keep on saying it, and you will stay sober all of your life. You will never become an alcoholic. *No* is the most effective word in the English language. The same is true of drugs and sex. You say no and you will never become an addict. You say no and keep on saying no, and when you get married you will be pure. Young people, let me encourage you, in the power of Jesus, to use that word *no.* Make up your mind to make an individual decision to say no.

> You are starting, my child, on life's journey,
> Along the grand highway of life.
> You will meet with a thousand temptations,

Each city with evil is rife.
This world is a stage of excitement.
There is danger wherever you go.
But if you're tempted in weakness,
Have courage, my child, to say no.

Be careful in choosing companions.
Seek only the brave and the true.
Stand by your friends when in trial,
Not changing the old for the new.
When by false friends you are tempted,
The taste of the winecup to know.
With firmness, with patience and kindness,
Have courage, my child, to say no.

b. *Influential* (1:8b). Daniel stood all alone in this verse. Now read 1:10.
The prince of the eunuchs replied to Daniel and said, "For why should
he [the king] see your faces . . . ?" Do you see the impact of the phrase
"see your faces"? Daniel's decision was potentially influential.

What we decide will influence others. Every young person, every
businessman or woman, every housewife, every career person, every
one of us has a sphere of influence. The decisions we make are influential. They help determine the decisions that those in our sphere
of influence make. If we say yes, we may lead others into sin; if we say
no, we may lead others to do what God wants them to do.

My first night in college was at Mercer University in Macon, Georgia. The first drinking I ever saw I saw on the campus of that college.
I'm not criticizing my alma mater. I'm thankful for the education I
received there, for every teacher, for every dollar that was given to
me to make possible my education, but Christian colleges ought to
be different from secular colleges. There should be a higher standard of behavior and a reverence for the word of God far beyond
what one finds in a secular university. There was no homework my
first night on campus. When one of the boys said, "Let's just go and
look around town," six or seven of us jumped in a car. We stopped
at a restaurant and as we sat there one older boy said, "Let's have a
beer." I opened the door and stepped out of the car. They said,
"What are you doing, Vines?" I said, "I'm walking back to school. I've
come here to study to preach the gospel and I'm not starting my college education by taking my first drink of beer." They said, "All right,
Vines. Get in the car. If you won't drink, we won't drink." See my
point? Just one skinny youth from North Georgia—but when I made

an individual decision, it became an influential decision.

We would be surprised how many wrong things we could stop if we would have the courage to make an individual decision, if we would purpose in our hearts not to defile ourselves. We don't know who may be watching us to see if we as Christians are going to crumble under pressure. When we stand we may give others courage to stand under pressure too.

2. A Humble Decision (1:8c-16)

Daniel was an unusual man. He had hard, strong convictions but he handled them in a humble way.

a. *The Abstinence He Requested* (1:8c-10). The prince of the eunuchs, who was in charge of them, was named Ashpenaz (1:3). Daniel went to him and requested that he might not have to defile himself. Do you see the humility there? What a gracious attitude Daniel had.

We ought to take a stand, we ought to be firm, unyielding in our convictions, but we must be careful to be gracious and humble when we stand for those convictions. Often people who have strong convictions become hard, unyielding, and obnoxious in the way they hold their beliefs. They turn people away from the Christian faith and its standards by the rude way they express their views. One doesn't have to be a crank to have convictions. We can be sweet and kind in the way we hold them.

Notice that God was already working in this. God had already brought Daniel into favor with the prince of the eunuchs, who had a warm affection for him (1:9).

But the prince of the eunuchs did what most of us do. He made his decision in the light of how it was going to affect him personally (1:10). He said, "If I keep that king's meat and wine away from you, you might show it. You might look inferior to the others and I'll lose my head." Daniel's request was denied. Now what?

b. *The Alternative He Suggested* (1:11-16). Daniel said to Melzar (the word means "chief attendant," "the warden") that he would submit to a test. He said, "Put us to the test for ten days. Let us eat pulse (vegetables or grain). Let us be put on a strictly vegetarian diet for ten days. At the end of that ten days, check us out." Daniel had tremendous faith in God. He believed that God would honor his decision, and the prince of eunuchs agreed to the experiment.

Notice what happened. See what God did for those boys? He

affected the appearance and countenance of Daniel (and those who followed his lead) because they had the courage to have convictions, courage to be true to the Lord and not go along with the crowd. That is so important. Whom we serve will eventually show on our faces.

Ten days later they brought those boys in. They looked at their eyes, and their eyes were clearer than the rest of the boys. They looked at their faces, and their faces were more radiant than the rest of them. Their muscles were stronger and their posture was more erect. There was a difference in their countenance.

See that boy over there? That boy has decided to live his life for sin and Satan. Look at this boy here. He has decided to live for the Lord. That boy has decided to go along with the crowd, to adopt the customs and habits of the world. This other boy has decided, regardless of what the world does, to live for Jesus. The devil gets hold of one life and the Lord Jesus gets hold of the other. Follow them on down the road. Look at them ten or twenty years from now. See the face of the first one as the signs of sin have begun to make deep grooves in his face. See the guilt and emptiness in his eyes. That is what the devil does to a life. But the other one has a sparkle in his eye. Courage and conviction shine in his countenance.

It pays to serve the Lord. Daniel made a humble decision and God honored it.

3. An Honored Decision (1:17-21)

God says, "Them that honor me I will honor" (1 Samuel 2:30). Daniel's decision was an honored decision.

a. *Spiritual Revelation* (1:17). How did God honor Daniel and his friends? "As for these four children, God gave them knowledge and skill in all learning and wisdom." Learning is the acquisition of facts; wisdom is the ability to use those facts.

Those young men were studying difficult subjects at the University of Babylon. God honored their decision to be true to him by giving them learning and wisdom, knowledge and skill. He gave them discernment. They were able to take full advantage of their education. God allowed it to make sense.

The problem with secular education is that it leaves out the spiritual dimension. Secular education can teach a person how to build a great building, but not what to do with it. Secular education can tell a person how to have a healthier body, but not how to live in that body. Secular education can give a person a head full of facts, but it cannot give a heart of peace or build eternal relationships. God was at work with these boys.

It does not mean that if we live for the Lord, we won't have to study. Just because a person is a Christian doesn't mean he can waste his time before the test and then walk in on the day of the test, lay his head on the algebra book, and say, "Dear Lord, may the facts in this book be assimilated by my mind." It doesn't work like that. But if you study your hardest and pray your heart out, God will bless you.

We had a boy at school who really did study. We called him old Grady. Old Grady was a very spiritual fellow and also the manager of the softball team. He would say, "Brother Jerry, if the Lord leads, lay down a bunt." That's how spiritual old Grady was.

One of the subjects we took was Hebrew, and it probably was the hardest subject I ever took. The night before tests how diligently we would study. I know Grady studied. I saw him. He agonized over his Hebrew. He would come to me on the morning of the test. "Brother Jerry, the Lord knows I can't get this Hebrew, so I get on my knees after I've studied the night before the test and I say, 'Dear Lord, you know I can't pass this Hebrew. Show me the questions he is going to ask in the morning.' And He does it every test." Old Grady passed Hebrew.

Do your part, live for Jesus, and God will do his part. Do you want to be smarter than your teachers? Turn to Psalm 119. Every verse in Psalm 119 has reference to God's word. It is the longest chapter in the Bible and it is all about the Bible. Look at 119:97-99: "O how love I thy law! It is my meditation all the day. Thou through thy commandments hast made me wiser than mine enemies: for they are ever with me. I have more understanding than all my teachers: for thy testimonies are my meditation." In other words it is not enough just to know facts; we need to know Jesus and know how to put those facts together in a spiritual way.

b. *Royal Elevation* (1:18-20). Perhaps those young men were scared as they came in for their oral exams. We can imagine them perspiring. Their whole future was at stake, and now the time had come to defend their theses. The king himself was going to ask the questions. They were brought in, the king pondered their answers, and when the test grades were scored they finished at the top of their class. The king said, "I'm going to put you all in positions of royal authority." The Bible says they stood before the king. That means they had official positions in the imperial government of Babylon.

Moreover, "The king inquired of them." That means they were his counselors. We can be sure when he received counsel and advice from them it was ten times better than any other counsel.

c. *Personal Continuation* (1:21). We read, "And Daniel continued." Link that to 1:8, "But Daniel purposed in his heart."

Daniel lived through the remainder of the Babylonian empire and on into the empire of Persia. Think of all the in-fighting that goes on in high government circles. Think of all the attempts made by his jealous peers to sabotage his position. Think of the various changes of administration. When they were all gone, there was Daniel, still on top. The Bible says, "The world passeth away, and the lust thereof: but he that doeth the will of God abideth for ever" (1 John 2:17).

Note the reference to Cyrus, the first Persian emperor. It was he who wrote the decree that released the Jews from bondage and allowed them to return to their land. The first chapter of Ezra tells about that. It's possible that Daniel's last official act was to prepare the papers releasing his people from Babylonian bondage.

Decide now in your heart to live for Jesus. God might use you one of these days to be the means of setting a multitude free from the captivity of sin.

II. A KING'S DESTINY (2:1-49)

A. The Dream and Its Consequences (2:1-30)

On the morning of April 14, 1865, Abraham Lincoln was gathered with his advisers and cabinet, discussing implementation of his plan for reconstruction of the Union of states. During the hours in the morning while they were working, Abraham Lincoln told them about a recurring dream. This dream came at a crucial time in the war. In his dream he saw himself on board a singular, indescribable vessel that was moving rapidly to an indefinite shore. They talked about the dream that morning, but nobody knew what it meant. That night Abraham Lincoln went to Ford's Theater and was shot by John Wilkes Booth. Before another day had ended, he was in eternity.

The vessel was his own life. The dream he had was a warning of what was soon to take place. He was about to embark for the shores of eternity. Little did he imagine that the dream had personal meaning for him, and very important meaning, too, for the nation.

Sometimes dreams convey messages to us. That was especially so in Old Testament times. (See Appendix 22.)

1. The King and His Distress (2:1-3)

Nebuchadnezzar, king of Babylon, the mightiest empire in the world, was the greatest of all its kings. More is said in the Old Testament about this particular pagan ruler than any other. He too received a recurring dream; God seems to have given this dream to Nebuchadnezzar on several occasions. Through it there was to be given to Nebuchadnezzar a message from God for himself and also a message for the kingdoms of the world, from his day all the way down to the coming of the Lord Jesus. God has a message for all of us in these passages of scripture.

a. *His Disturbance* (2:1). Nebuchadnezzar, a mighty ruler, was disturbed. The prophecies of Jeremiah refer to Nebuchadnezzar as "God's servant." Such a phrase does not mean that Nebuchadnezzar was saved, but that God used him as an instrument of his will. God used Nebuchadnezzar to carry out his plan for his people, the nation of Judah.

Nebuchadnezzar thought he was building a magnificent empire for himself. Actually he was building a school to which God sent his chosen people for seventy years to teach them lessons they would never forget. Daniel 2:29 tells us what Nebuchadnezzar was thinking about the night he dreamed his dreams. Scripture says, "As for thee, O king, thy thoughts came into thy mind upon thy bed, what should come to pass hereafter." Nebuchadnezzar was like other world rulers who go to bed at night and wonder what the future holds for their countries.

We would all be wise to think about the future. It is not enough for us merely to live; we must live with reference to the future. People are foolish who do not learn from the lessons of the past. They are also foolish if they do not give thought to the things that lie ahead in the future. This great leader did what many people do. He took the cares of the day to bed with him and they became his companions for a troubled night. We who know the Lord should put our burdens on him (though sometimes it is hard to do that).

When I had my first church at the age of eighteen I was active in reaching people for the Lord and building church attendance. I was on the go day and night. One day I walked into the house of some of our members and collapsed right there on the floor. I'll never forget what the doctor later said to me: "Young man, I want to give you some advice as you begin your ministry. You take care of the day shift and you let the Lord take care of the night shift." Good advice—not that I have always followed it. It is so easy to take our problems and burdens to bed with us, isn't it?

Nebuchadnezzar was evidently thinking about things, and he began to dream. The use of the plural indicates recurring dreams. These dreams would come and go, and although he was not able to remember the things he had dreamed, his spirit was troubled. He was disturbed by his dreams but he couldn't recall the details.

We can all get apprehensive about the future. When we read of what is taking place in the world, what a dangerous place it is becoming, it makes us fear for the future of our children. We too are disturbed.

b. *His Demand* (2:2-3). When Nebuchadnezzar gave an order, it was carried out immediately. The wise men of Babylon were hauled out of bed. The various classes of wise men are listed to show us that the king was so disturbed by his dream that he wanted all his experts, all his keenest advisers, to be present. They wasted no time obeying the summons that came over the palace hot line. These were the brains of the empire, men who were supposed to have the answers, who could solve riddles.

One of their specialties was the interpretation of dreams. They had turned dream interpretation into an exact science. They had books about dreams, with the meaning of dream symbols. Give them some of the details of a dream and they would draw out more information until they had it all. Then they would take those symbols, go to their books, and interpret the dreams.

But answers to some of life's problems cannot be discovered in such a mechanical way. Some enigmas in life are not solved by reference to textbooks. There are inconsistencies in life that do not fit the norm. Many problems we face deal with personalities, and personalities do not always do what they are supposed to.

These men thought they had the answer in the books. They were the intellects, the wise men, of their day. They may have made fun of Daniel and his friends. They may have scoffed at those Bible-believing Jews who, for reasons they could not fathom, had been placed on the king's advisory staff.

Things operate much the same today. Several years ago I read in an Atlanta newspaper about a furor at the University of Georgia. There was a chemistry professor there, Dr. Fritz Schaefer, who had come from the University of California at Berkeley where he had been on the faculty. This man has a Ph.D. in chemistry and has been nominated for two Nobel prizes in chemistry. What was the problem, since he was eminently qualified? Wasn't he doing a good job? He was doing a magnificent job and was popular with students.

The problem was that this professor had had an experience with the Lord Jesus Christ some years before and was giving lectures outside class on creation and on the resurrection of the Lord Jesus Christ. Other professors on that campus were disturbed, because here was an outstanding scientist who believed the Bible, who believed in the creation of the universe, someone who believed in the resurrection of Christ. That upset his unbelieving colleagues.

2. The Scholars and Their Dilemma (2:4-13)

From this point in Daniel through 7:28, the text is in Aramaic, not Hebrew. The Jews in the court of Nebuchadnezzar would speak in the official language, which was Aramaic. Also note that this prophecy was specifically addressed to gentile nations. So God used a gentile language.

The king's advisers arrived and in Aramaic asked him to tell them his dream. But the king had forgotten its details (2:5). Others translate his response as this: "The order from me is sure." That is, he was warning them of the certain consequences if they failed. "If you will not make known unto me the dream with the interpretation thereof, you will be cut in pieces."

King Nebuchadnezzar was a typical tyrant. How would you like to have been in his cabinet? Not only would they themselves be dismembered, but their homes would be converted into public garbage dumps. Those were the penalties. But there were also promises: If they were able to interpret the dream, they would receive gifts and rewards and great honor.

a. *Their Ignorance* (2:4-9). The wise men began stalling for time, but the king was getting suspicious of his advisers and saw through their little game. He was growing impatient and angry.

Note the ignorance of the men who were supposed to have all the answers. The intellects of this world can tell us a lot of things, but they cannot tell us the answers to the basic problems and questions of life. They can tell us how to exploit our every passion and desire, but they can't tell us how to deal with the resulting problem of guilt. They can tell us how to synthesize chemical compounds and work out mathematical equations, but they cannot repair a broken heart.

b. *Their Arrogance* (2:10-13). If they didn't have the answer, well, nobody else did either. They thought wisdom originated and died with themselves. But there was a man in that kingdom named Daniel to whom God had already given supernatural ability to understand visions and dreams. They had forgotten he even existed. The professionals thought they were the only ones who knew anything.

Most of the time we don't want to admit that we don't know an answer. I heard about a young doctor who had just opened his practice. When his first patient came in, he examined him but had no idea what was wrong. He racked his brain, thought back through all his medical training. He couldn't even guess what was ailing the man, but he didn't want to admit it. Finally he looked at the fellow very seriously and said, "Well, sir, have you ever had this before?" The man said, "Yes." "Well, you have it again," the doctor replied. We don't like to admit it when we don't know the answers.

The wise men of Babylon were so arrogant that they said, "There's not a man on earth who knows this." The intellects of our day may think there aren't answers to many of the great questions of life, but there are.

Everybody needs answers to three questions: Who am I? Where did I come from? Where am I going?

Some people have found the answers to those questions. When a person is born again and the Holy Spirit comes into his or her heart, that person has access to a wisdom from above. That wisdom is beyond anything found in a textbook. A janitor sweeping the steps on a college campus, if he knows Christ, knows more about life and how to live it than the arrogant professors who walk by him will ever know.

Remember what Jesus said: "I thank thee, O Father, Lord of heaven and earth, because thou hast hid these things from the wise and prudent, and hast revealed them unto babes. Even so, Father: for so it seemed good in thy sight. All things are delivered unto me of my Father: and no man knoweth the Son, but the Father; neither knoweth any man the Father, save the Son, and he to whomsoever the Son will reveal him" (Matthew 11:25-27).

Some things come only by divine revelation, things that only God in heaven can give to us. The Babylonian professionals said, "Nobody can do what you ask. No king has ever asked anything like this." And they added, "There is none other that can show it before the king, except the gods, whose dwelling is not with flesh" (2:11). What an amazing admission. Here were men supposedly in touch with the gods, yet by their own statement they revealed themselves as frauds.

Naturally the king was furious. He commanded that all the wise men of Babylon be destroyed, and Daniel and his friends were included in that group. As soon as the decree was signed, the king's officers went after Daniel and his friends.

3. The Prophet and His Desire (2:14-30)

a. *His Promise* (2:14-16). When Arioch, the royal executioner, arrived at Daniel's door, Daniel discovered what was in store for himself and the others. Notice how calm Daniel was.

If we want to know what we really are like, we will find out when a crisis comes. Courage is developed in crisis, but we will never be calm in a crisis unless we have prepared ourselves in times of calmness. Daniel asked Arioch why the king's decree was so hasty, and Arioch told him.

Evidently Daniel had access to Nebuchadnezzar's oval office. Now he went in and asked the king to give him time; then he promised to give him the dream's interpretation.

b. *His Prayer* (2:17-18). Daniel went back home to his companions and said in effect, "Let us go to God in prayer. Let us desire the mercies of the God of heaven."

That is the basis on which we can pray. We cannot go into the presence of God to pray on the basis of personal merit. We have access to God on the basis of his mercy.

Notice how Daniel talked about God. He called him "the God of heaven," an expression that is almost exclusive to the captivity books. It occurs nine times in the book of Daniel, six times in the book of Ezra, and four times in the book of Nehemiah. The first time it occurs is in 2 Chronicles 36, where it makes reference to the captivity. During the captivity God was known as "the God of heaven." Why?

When Judah turned away from the Lord, Ezekiel saw a vision of the glory of God departing from the earth. Ezekiel saw that glory, the shekinah glory cloud which had rested on the mercy seat, as it lifted up from the holy of holies and moved over to the threshold of the temple door. Then it moved from the temple to the mount of Olives on the east of the city. Finally it departed back to heaven and for a period of time (until Jesus came) there was no glory of God on earth. God was "the God of heaven."

By using this title, Daniel recognized that Judah's sin had put them in their captive condition. So Daniel and his friends prayed for the mercies of the God of heaven.

We can do one of two things when trouble comes into our lives: we can panic or we can pray. The Bible says, "If any of you lack wisdom, let him ask of God" (James 1:5).

Daniel and his friends were young, but remember, some of the prayer meetings that have shaped the history of the Christian church were begun by young people. Many revivals were begun by young people who came together and called on God. Perhaps Daniel's friends stayed up all night and prayed. Daniel evidently had so much confidence in God that he went to bed. Daniel seems to have received assurance in his heart that the answer was on the way. And the secret was revealed to him in a night vision. What assurance! The Lord gave to Daniel the dream he had given to Nebuchadnezzar, detail by detail.

God answers prayer. And the same God in heaven who answered the prayer of Daniel is still in heaven, waiting for us to pray and bring our burdens to him.

c. *His Praise* (2:19-23). Before rushing off into the presence of the king, Daniel spent time in the presence of God: "Daniel blessed the God of heaven. Daniel answered and said, Blessed be the name of God for ever and ever: for wisdom and might are his." Then follows one of the most magnificent expressions of praise and thanksgiving in the Bible (2:21-23).

Praise without prayer is presumption; prayer without praise is ingratitude. Prayer plus praise will tear down strongholds of the devil. Find a Christian who knows what it is to pray, what it means to thank God and praise God when the answer comes, and you have a force for God on this earth.

So Daniel went back to Arioch, the chief executioner, and said, "You don't have to kill anybody. God has given me an answer from heaven."

d. *His Proclamation* (2:24-30). Arioch hurriedly took Daniel to the king. It was an emotional moment. Things were moving quickly.

But look at Arioch. He rushed into the presence of the king and said, "I have found a man." That was not so. How true to life—someone always wanting to take credit. Did Arioch have that reward in mind (2:6)? So Daniel stood before the king and dared to issue a proclamation.

The first three chapters of Daniel are a series of tests for believers. We have the test of a believer's walk in chapter 1, and the tests of a believer's witness in chapter 2. Daniel now had the answer to the dream. What an opportunity for him to take some credit to himself.

"Well, can you interpret the dream?" Nebuchadnezzar asked. Then Daniel spoke: "The secret which the king hath demanded cannot the wise men, the astrologers, the magicians, the soothsayers, show unto the king; But there is a God in heaven." He was saying, "Your majesty, you have been looking in the wrong direction for your answer. You have been looking here, there, and everywhere, and did not get it. I want to point you in the right direction. There is a God in heaven!"

Do you think there are no answers to your problems? There is a God in heaven. Do you think your present dilemma is hopeless? There is a God in heaven. Do you think you have a burden so heavy it cannot be lifted? There is a God in heaven. Lay hold of that fact.

Daniel said, "There is a God in heaven who reveals secrets." There is a God in heaven who will answer our prayers. There is a God in heaven who will meet our financial needs. There is a God in heaven before whom we can bring our wayward children. There is a God in heaven who will save us and deliver us from sin. There is a God in heaven.

B. The Dream and Its Contents (2:31-49).

In the remaining verses of this chapter we have the account of how God revealed the meaning of the king's dream to Daniel and how Daniel interpreted that dream to Nebuchadnezzar. Imagine the excitement when Daniel came into the presence of the king. The wise men of Babylon were under the death penalty because, in their human wisdom, they were not able to explain or give the correct interpretation of the dream. Now Daniel came in with the answer.

This passage is one of the fundamental passages on prophecy in the Bible. The Bible contains a great deal of prophecy, especially about the coming of the Lord Jesus. All Old Testament prophecy concerning the first coming of Christ was fulfilled exactly as written. But there are other prophetic portions of the Bible that have yet to be fulfilled, telling of things that have not yet come to pass. We are confident that, in the providence of God, they will come to pass. When God speaks, we can be sure that it will take place. God does not lie.

If we grasp the basic truth of this prophecy in Daniel 2, we have the key to God's entire prophetic program. Someone has said that this is the ABC of prophecy and the book of Revelation is the XYZ of prophecy. But we cannot get to the XYZs until we understand the ABCs.

In this image about which Nebuchadnezzar dreamed, God

revealed his plan for the gentile world powers from the time of Nebuchadnezzar to the coming of the kingdom of Jesus Christ on earth.

1. Prophetic Truth (2:31-45)

Daniel had already given Nebuchadnezzar an indication of what he
was going to say: "There is a God in heaven that revealeth secrets,
and maketh known to the king Nebuchadnezzar what shall be in the
latter days" (2:28). He continued: "As for thee, O king, thy thoughts
came into thy mind upon thy bed what should come to pass hereafter" (2:29). Note the two phrases, "the latter times" and "what shall
come to pass."

a. *The Image Described* (2:31-35). Then Daniel described the image
about which Nebuchadnezzar had dreamed. "Thou, O king, sawest,
and behold a great image." The wise men had not been able to
reveal even that much. We can imagine the king nodding with
approval as Daniel began to remind him exactly what he had
dreamed.

The image was a large one, a massive image. Its "brightness was
excellent," because of the different metals of which it was composed.
It had a dazzling luster. As it towered before the king its form was
terrible, instilling fear and awe. By now the king knew that Daniel
was on the right track, that Daniel's God had indeed revealed to him
exactly the vision he had seen. Daniel continued to describe the
image. It had a head of fine gold, its breasts and arms were of silver,
its thighs were of brass, and its legs were of iron. The feet of the
image were part iron and part clay.

Notice first of all the deterioration of that image. Daniel 2:39 says,
"And after thee shall arise another kingdom inferior to thee." The
Aramaic word translated "inferior" literally means "downward from
thee," "earthward to thee" (see Appendix 5). There was a decline
in value as the metals moved from gold at the top to silver, brass,
iron, and on down to clay at the bottom.

There was also a decline in weight. It began with gold and ended
with clay; the image was top heavy. It rested on a worthless foundation.

Everything pictured here implies declining. It is declining in
value, declining in weight—just the opposite of the theory of evolution. Evolution says that things begin with mud and get better and
better. The theory of evolution is that man is improving, and civilization is progressing. Man goes from mud to gold. God says that
man goes from gold to mud.

Everywhere we look in civilization and nature we find that what God says is true. Things do not progress upward in life; they have a tendency to decline downward. Leave horses to themselves and there is a tendency for them to become scrub horses. We have rose bushes in our garden, and we cannot just leave them alone. If we do, instead of having beautiful roses, all we will have will be very poor petals and a lot of leaves. The tendency is downward. Leave nature to itself, leave man to himself, and the drift is always downward.

Mankind was created by God and placed at the apex of God's creation on earth. Because of sin, man fell and his trend is downward. That is why the good news of the gospel is so wonderful. Jesus has broken into that downward spiral. He came into the world as God's perfect man. Now, when we have a new birth experience, the Lord Jesus Christ reaches down, catches us on that descent, saves us, puts the Spirit of God in us, and starts us upward so that we can become more and more like him.

The Lord Jesus himself gave us insight into the meaning of this prophetic image. Talking about the end times, He said, "And they shall fall by the edge of the sword, and shall be led away captive into all nations: and Jerusalem shall be trodden down of the Gentiles, until the times of the Gentiles be fulfilled" (Luke 21:24). Note the phrase, "the times of the Gentiles." Contrast that phrase with another phrase, "the fulness of the Gentiles" (Romans 11:25). These are not the same. "The fulness of the Gentiles" has reference to the completion of the mystical body of Christ in the salvation of lost souls today.

God is taking out of the world a people for his name. God is saving people out of the gentile world. Of course, Jews are being saved too, but not in large numbers. God's primary goal in this age is to take out of the gentile world a people for his name.

One of these days "the fulness of the Gentiles" will be completed. One of these days the last soul will be saved and the heavenly Father will signal to the angel Gabriel. Gabriel will take his trumpet off the battlements and will begin to blow it. The Lord Jesus will "descend from heaven with a shout, with the voice of the archangel, and with the trump of God: and the dead in Christ shall rise first: Then we which are alive and remain shall be caught up together with them in the clouds, to meet the Lord in the air: and so shall we ever be with the Lord." That is what is meant by "the fulness of the Gentiles."

Jesus was, however, talking about "the times of the Gentiles." That is what we have in these verses in Daniel. That is the ultimate meaning of this dream of Nebuchadnezzar. He saw a panoramic view of gentile world power from the days of the Babylonian empire until the final days of gentile power and to the time when the Lord Jesus Christ will establish his kingdom on this earth.

In his dream, Daniel said Nebuchadnezzar next saw a stone "cut without hands" that came and smote the image on its feet. Then the stone became a great mountain filling the entire earth (see Appendix 6).

We can be sure that by this time Nebuchadnezzar was getting more than a little interested. Daniel had done what none of the other wise men could do.

b. *The Image Discussed* (2:36-45). Daniel then began interpreting the king's dream. "Thou, O king, art a king of kings: for the God of heaven hath given thee a kingdom, power, and strength, and glory. And wheresoever the children of men dwell, the beasts of the field and the fowls of the heaven hath he given into thine hand, and hath made thee ruler over them all. Thou art this head of gold."

According to Deuteronomy 32 it was God's intention that the nation of Israel should ultimately govern the nations of the world, that Jerusalem should be the center of dominion and power on earth. But Israel failed to live up to its destiny. Because the Hebrews were not faithful to God, they were carried into captivity. Later, when the Lord Jesus presented himself as their king, they rejected him. God's plan, that Israel should rule the nations and Jesus Christ be the king who would rule on earth, was spoiled. When Israel rejected God's perfect plan, however, God turned to gentile nations and gave them the dominion and power He had intended for Israel.

It was to this king, Nebuchadnezzar, and the Babylonian empire, that God delivered world dominion at that time. It was a gift of God.

What we are reading here was prophecy in the days of Daniel, but it is now history. That is exactly what happened. Babylon was the first great gentile power from the prophetic standpoint, and Nebuchadnezzar was its king.

Note the emphasis on gold. When the Greek historian Herodotus went to the city of Babylon ninety years after the reign of Nebuchadnezzar, he was astonished. He had never seen a city so full of gold. Babylon's temples, chapels, and even utensils were made of gold. Everywhere he looked was gold. Isaiah 14:4 called Babylon "the golden city." Just exactly what God said Nebuchadnezzar would do, he did. He established a mighty monarchy, a mighty empire of gold. It lasted until Belshazzar died under the judgment of God. When that happened, gentile world power was passed on to another king-dom.

The second kingdom corresponded to the breasts and arms of sil-ver. Daniel 8:20 expands on this prophecy and makes it clear that the next kingdom would be the Medo-Persian empire. That is why the image had two arms. They were made of silver, Daniel explained, because the second kingdom would be inferior to the first; it would not have the autocratic strength enjoyed by Nebuchad-nezzar. It would lack central control. Still, it would be a very wealthy empire, as the symbol of silver indicates. The Persians had a broad and efficient system of taxation, so the empire accumulated vast hordes of silver. The kings of Persia had almost unlimited resources with which to conduct their battles and military expeditions.

Then a third kingdom, this one of brass, would rule. Again Daniel 8:21 tells us specifically that the next world empire would be Greece. The young general Alexander and his brazen-coated sol-diers made short work of the Persian empire. Greek soldiers wore brass armor. They had brass helmets, breastplates, shields, and swords. It is said that after Alexander conquered the known world he wept because there were no more worlds to conquer.

Then Nebuchadnezzar's attention was directed to the fourth empire, a kingdom "strong as iron: forasmuch as iron breaketh in pieces and subdueth all things: and as iron that breaketh all these shall it break in pieces and bruise." Here was a picture of an empire, relentless in its advance, one that would subdue everything in its path. When we read these verses, we can almost hear the tramp, tramp, tramp of marching feet, the iron legions of Rome. The Roman empire subdued everything in its path.

At the same time the Roman empire was a mixture of strength and weakness. Rome was strong militarily, but it was also marked by internal decay (clay). In time, Rome fell from within; it collapsed upon itself.

Edward Gibbon's famous history, *Decline and Fall of the Roman Empire*, documents the empire's decay and collapse. When we read of what caused Rome to fall, and then think of contemporary Amer-ican history, we discern a frightening parallel. Unless we have a revival in America, unless we come back to God in this land, unless professing Christians repent of their sin and worldliness, and put the Lord Jesus Christ before everything else in their lives, our country is as doomed as ancient Rome was. That empire collapsed from within, and so will we.

Between Daniel 2:41 and 42 there is a gap, as is often true of Bible prophecy. Sometimes between one verse of scripture and the next, a Bible prophecy will leap over hundreds of years.

We find a graphic picture of that in the words of the Lord Jesus. He was in the synagogue of his home town while quoting from Isaiah 61. He stopped right in the middle of the verse. Then He said, "This day is this Scripture fulfilled in your ears," but He said nothing about the rest of the verse. Why? Because right in the middle of a verse in Isaiah 61 was a gap of centuries between two statements.

Just so, there is a gap here. Although the Roman empire came to an end, in many ways its institutions, its system of government, its laws, its jurisprudence, have lasted to this very day in the European nations and their former colonies.

In Daniel 2:42 we come to the end times, to the "latter days" just before the return of the Lord Jesus. Evidently the Roman empire is to be revived. Verses 42 and 43 describe a futile attempt to combine autocratic rule (iron) with a people's democracy (clay).

Daniel said, "They shall mingle themselves with the seed of men: but they shall not cleave." Iron and clay do not mix. He continued with a reference to "the days of these kings" (referring back to the ten toes of the image), to the time when the Roman empire will be revived.

There have already been attempts to revive that empire. Napoleon tried and failed. So did Mussolini. In the last days, however, there will be a European federation of nations corresponding to the ancient Roman empire. It will be a ten-kingdom alliance, headed eventually by the antichrist.

The European Common Market may herald the near fulfillment of this scripture. It is interesting that the European Common Market came into existence by the Treaty of Rome in 1957. The number of members fluctuates but that is not the important thing. The important thing to know is that at the end times there will be some such coalition, some kind of military, political, and economic union of European powers that will revive the Roman empire, and with it that final gentile world power depicted here in Daniel. But it will fail in the end because it will be a mixture of iron and clay.

Daniel moved on to the end: "In the days of these kings," at that time, drastically, the God of heaven will set up a kingdom that will never be destroyed. The end-time Roman empire will not be succeeded by other gentile empires, as was the case with Babylon, Persia, and Greece. It will be replaced by Christ's kingdom, which "shall break in pieces and consume all these kingdoms, and it shall stand for ever" (2:44). This refers to the millennium reign of Jesus Christ on the earth. The Lord Jesus will come and smash gentile world power just as the image was smashed by the stone. The kingdom of Jesus will be established on this earth.

None of this was fulfilled at the first coming of the Lord Jesus. Here we have a picture of the messiah coming suddenly, decisively, to reign, and when He comes He will end gentile power absolutely and forever. It will be like chaff in the summer wind. This is described further in Revelation 19:15, the theme of which is the return of Jesus to this earth: "And out of his mouth [talking about the Lord] goeth a sharp sword, that with it he should smite the nations: and he shall rule them with a rod of iron." These things will happen when Jesus comes back and He puts down all the nations.

We are left in no doubt as to the meaning of the stone in Daniel 2:45. The Bible interprets the Bible. Follow carefully this symbol of the stone throughout the Bible, beginning with Genesis, and it is evident that "the stone" refers to the Lord Jesus Christ himself.

He was the supernatural stone, the stone made "without hands." He came to earth the first time, born of a virgin, but with no human father. He had a heavenly father.

Jesus was also the stumbling stone. When He came into this world, He was a stumblingblock to the nation of Israel. His own people rejected him.

He was also the smitten stone. In the Old Testament, when the children of Israel had no water, they came to Moses and complained. God told Moses, "Smite that stone, and when you do, the water will begin to flow." That verse can refer to Jesus, for He is our rock of ages.

> Rock of Ages, cleft for me,
> Let me hide myself in thee.
> Let the water and the blood,
> From thy wounded side which flowed,
> Be of sin the double cure,
> Save from wrath and make me pure.

Jesus is our smitten stone, smitten on Calvary for our sins.

He is also the salvation stone. He is referred to as "the stone which the builders disallowed [rejected], the same is made the head of the corner" (2 Peter 2:7; cp. Acts 4:11-12). "Neither is there salvation in any other," Peter added in his Acts sermon. Jesus is that salvation stone.

We cannot be neutral about the Lord Jesus. Salvation through Jesus Christ is not an optional matter. We either come to Jesus for salvation or there is no salvation for us at all. Jesus said, "Whosoever shall fall on this stone shall be broken, but on whomsoever it shall fall, it will grind him to powder" (Matthew 21:44).

We can come to the Lord Jesus in repentance and trust him as personal Savior. When we do that, He crushes us, takes away our sin, and makes new creatures of us. Reject him and the day will come when He will fall on those who have rejected him and crush them in judgment.

Then, too, He is the sovereign stone. This stone, the Lord Jesus, is going to fill the entire earth one of these days. He is to rule and reign over all the earth.

2. Personal Triumph (2:46-49)

When Nebuchadnezzar heard all this, he was awestruck.

a. *Respect Given to Daniel* (2:46-47). When the text says that "he worshiped Daniel," we must qualify that with the next verse where he acknowledged that it was Daniel's God to whom credit belonged. Nebuchadnezzar was giving respect and reverence to Daniel, acknowledging that Daniel was the messenger of the eternal God, the revealer of secrets. This is like what we read in Revelation 3:9: "Behold, I will make them of the synagogue of Satan, which say they are Jews, and are not, but do lie; behold, I will make them to come and worship before thy feet, and to know that I have loved thee."

The Lord says to us: "Just be faithful to me and I'll take care of things. One of these days your enemies will acknowledge that you are mine."

Boys and girls, be true to the Lord! Business men and women, be true to the Lord! College students, live for Jesus! Let them laugh at you and make fun of you if they wish. You keep being true to the God of heaven and one of these days the scoffers will have to acknowledge that you are God's person.

b. *Rule Given to Daniel* (2:48-49). Daniel wanted to make sure his friends also came into the good of his triumph. They had been his prayer partners in all of this. They were set over the affairs of the province of Babylon, but Daniel sat "in the gate of the king." God elevated him. That means he was in charge of all the wise men. He managed all of Babylon.

If Daniel had never purposed in his heart, when the temptation came to eat the king's meat and drink the king's wine, if Daniel had just gone along with the crowd, we would never have heard anymore about him. But because Daniel purposed in his heart that he would not defile himself, God promoted him to be prime minister of Babylon.

After you come to Jesus, the way is always up.

III. A KING'S DEMANDS (3:1-30)

A. They Would Not Bow (3:1-12)

In this chapter we have the familiar account of the three Hebrew young men who were cast into a fiery furnace because they would not worship the image of gold which the king had erected. This passage not only pulsates with drama but is a thrilling account of courage and faith. Here we have three "profiles in courage." These young men are immortalized in the halls of the heroes of faith in Hebrews 11. It says, "Through faith [they] . . . quenched the violence of fire." In Daniel 2, Nebuchadnezzar had acknowledged that the God of heaven is the true God. He seemed to have taken a step in the direction of the Lord, but now we discover that Nebuchadnezzar's faith was short-lived. In repudiation of everything God had revealed to him, he erected this image of gold in honor of himself.

Daniel 3 is a test of the believer's worship. We discover here what it means to take a stand for the Lord and refuse to compromise with the gods of this world.

1. Construction of the Image (3:1)

This magnificent image of gold was ninety feet high and nine feet wide, a mammoth of a thing. Archaeologists, excavating about six miles southeast of the city of Babylon, have found ruins which they believe might be the foundation of this image. Everything Nebuchadnezzar did was lavish and done with flair. No expense was spared. The image seems to have been constructed of wood, overlaid with gold.

There seem to be several reasons why the king constructed this image.

a. *Deification of Nebuchadnezzar.* Nebuchadnezzar was an able general who reigned forty years and never lost a battle. Now, God said to him through Daniel that he was the golden head of the image he had seen in his dream. Like so many world rulers, he was not satis-

fied to be just the head. He wanted to be the entire image. Nebuchadnezzar could have claimed: "*Mine* is the kingdom, and the
power, and the glory, for ever."

So, out on the plain of Dura, away from the gods of the city and
the temples dedicated to other gods, Nebuchadnezzar constructed
this huge image to himself. It was a tangible contradiction of what
God had revealed to him—that he would have a magnificent kingdom, but it would pass away and be replaced by other empires. Nebuchadnezzar made the common mistake of thinking he could go
contrary to God's word. He had the idea he could mandate history
for himself. So the image seems to have been constructed as an act
of deification of Nebuchadnezzar.

b. *Glorification of Man.* This was an image of a man, but it was
grotesque—a size and appearance not uncommon in that day. Others had made grotesque images of men and given them dimensions
all out of proportion in order to magnify the greatness of man. What
we are reading about here is an ancient version of what we might call
secular humanism, the attempt to deify man, the belief that man can
solve all his own problems. In these days of scientific achievement
and technological skill, there is a modern tendency for human beings
to think they can solve all their problems by their own ingenuity.

In the construction of this image, however, even unknown to the
king and the builders, there is a revelation by God of man's total failure. The image had the number six stamped upon it. It was sixty
cubits high and six cubits wide. The number six in the Bible is the
number of man. It was on the sixth day that God created man. Six
is the number of man's failure. Man never quite gets there. Six
comes short of seven, the number of divine perfection. Man is always
a little bit short.

The image in the Old Testament is a preview of one revealed in
the New Testament. Revelation 13 predicts that at the end time the
antichrist will construct an image. It will be an image to Mr. Trinity
of Failure himself, the man whose mystical number is 666.

Man is a failure. We cannot reach up to God, but He has reached
down to us. The Lord Jesus, God's perfect man, came and died on
a cross that we might be saved.

c. *Unification of Religion.* The image was also to be an object of worship. This was a skillful move on the part of a king who was trying to
consolidate his empire and unify its many provinces politically. He
understood that one of the best ways to unite people politically is to

unite them religiously. It was mandated politically that all persons were to fall down and worship this golden image.

This, too, points us to the last days. When the image of the antichrist is set up in the end time, it will be as an object of worship. The entire world will be required to worship it. There will be a one-world religion. Tyrannical government always wants to make religion a tool of the state. Ecumenism, the synthesis of all religion, is a politically skillful move for a world leader.

I do not get excited about making all denominations one. The Lord spoke to me from Psalm 119:63 several years ago and showed me the basis of fellowship for all believers, regardless of what denomination: "I am companion of all them that fear thee, and of them that keep thy precepts." If a person loves Jesus and believes the word of God, it makes no difference to me if he or she is Baptist, Methodist, Presbyterian, or whatever. Those who love the Lord Jesus, who have received him as Savior and who love God's word and believe it and obey it, are in fellowship together. It doesn't matter what label you put on it.

I am suspicious of ecumenism to bring about religious union in the world. If you can take two tomcats and tie their tails together, you have union, but you don't have unity. There is no need to unify believers; they are already unified. We are all one in Christ.

2. Dedication of the Image (3:2-7)

After the image had been constructed, the king called for a dedication ceremony.

a. *A Powerful Order* (3:2-3). All the leaders from the provinces were to come for the dedication ceremonies, and in those days when the king said, "Come," everybody came. We are told of all the different leaders who were to come.

Imagine what it was like on the plain of Dura. Hundreds, perhaps thousands, of leaders were gathered there, all in their official robes and military uniforms. What a sight it must have been. They were being interviewed on "Good Morning, Babylon!" They were waiting to have their picture taken with the king.

b. *A Paid Orator* (3:4-6). Next a herald, the paid announcer of the king cried aloud. He was probably the king's chaplain, on his payroll, an apostate preacher. His job was to say what the king wanted said.

Preachers have to be careful when they get orders from the government about what they are to preach. Many a preacher has ceased to be a prophet when he became a politician. Preachers ought to take a stand and have a right to vote for whom they want in office. But we have to be careful when as children of God we are dealing with the political world.

This hired preacher of the king announced that when everyone heard the sound of the music playing it was the king's command that they fall down and worship the image of gold.

You cannot command worship. Worship is something that comes spontaneously out of the heart. It must be in spirit and truth. You can force people to get down on their knees in front of images of gold, but you can't force them to worship it if they don't want to.

They had an orchestra there with every imaginable instrument. The herald said, "When the orchestra begins to play, that is the signal for all of you to fall down before the golden image."

Music is a powerful medium. Aristotle said that music has the power to form character. Music can be used to worship God, but music can also drag people down toward hell. A great deal can be learned about a society by the kind of music it chooses. Wherever we find depraved music we will find a society filled with permissiveness and immorality. Music reflects the spiritual and moral condition of a society.

We use music in our churches to lift up Jesus, to touch hearts and prepare us for worship. Do you love music that honors the Lord Jesus?

c. *A Pathetic Ordeal* (3:7). Then the king's herald added, "To help you make up your minds, the king has a burning fiery furnace ready for dissenters." Could the people see this furnace, see the flames leaping out of it and hear the flames crackling? If so, it really helped them make up their minds. So the music began to play and people fell to the ground by the thousands. That is, all but three.

3. Repudiation of the Image (3:8-12)

It's not easy to go against the crowd. When everybody is doing something, it is not easy to be a nonconformist. Many of us boast about being nonconformists, but most of us are very conformed. Remember all the fads you went through in high school? I remember when Argyle socks were in. I thought them the ugliest socks ever, but I wore them because all the boys at school did. It is difficult to go against the majority.

a. *Consternation of the Majority* (3:8-11). The three dissenters soon paid
for it: "Wherefore at that time certain Chaldeans came near, and
accused the Jews" (see Appendix 4). The word *accused* literally means
"to eat the pieces of." It suggests malicious intention. The
Chaldeans' design was to denounce these Hebrew young people and
discredit them before the king. So they went to the king and told
him that some prestigious Jews would not bow down to his image,
specifically naming Shadrach, Meshach, and Abednego.

b. *Determination of the Minority* (3:12). Thus, unconsciously, the world
pays tribute to people who have convictions. There were the thousands in the dust. Here were three young Hebrews, a decided minority over there on the radical right, who dared to stand up for what
they believed.

It's that way at the office. Do people get upset when somebody is
telling dirty jokes? When almost everybody is gambling on the football games? No. So why do they get upset with a Christian who refuses to go along with it? Why is it that in high school they get upset with
the few young people who will not conform to the fashions of the day,
who won't go to their dances, and who won't drink with the majority?
What is it that upsets people in the few who refuse to bow down?

It is because people are not satisfied to be in sin themselves; they
want to drag others also into sin. Eve took the forbidden fruit, ate
it, and gave it to her pushover husband. From that time, fallen man
has always been a pusher. He is not content to go to hell by himself;
he wants to drag as many people with him as possible. He takes pleasure in others who do such things (see Romans 1:32).

Make up your mind that you are not going to bow. Join the
minority with convictions.

The three Hebrew young men said they were not going to do it.
Remember, they had been through a pre-captivity revival led by the
boy-king, Josiah, under the preaching of Jeremiah. During that
revival they had developed convictions that now stood them in good
stead when the test came.

Churches must be interested in their young people, have youth
camps, discipleship programs, and strong church-training programs.
Preachers must preach against sin, preach about having convictions.
They must do something for today's young people that will stay with
them on the college campus and in the business world. Young people, make up your minds now to serve the Lord Jesus and not to bow
down to the images of gold in this world. Make that commitment
now, and when the testing time comes, you will "be strong in the

Lord, and in the power of his might" (Ephesians 6:10).

The world said to these young Hebrews, "Bow down, you stupid fools." They said, "We will not bow down." They refused to be just like everybody else.

When I became pastor of a church some years ago I was asked to speak to the deacons and tell them what I expected of them. I believe that deacons are to be the spiritual leaders of the church and that they should be men of God. At that first deacons' meeting I spoke to them about Bible standards for deacons. Before I said it, I thought, "There is no need for me to say this; they know this." However, I went ahead and said, "I don't think a man who is a social drinker ought to be a deacon. Would you agree with that? I don't think a deacon ought to have a habit he couldn't recommend to a sixteen-year-old." One of the deacons present was also a Sunday school teacher. In fact, his father had been pastor of that church for twenty-four years. He was a lawyer and had the largest law firm around, located in a whole suite of offices in the largest building in town. He walked up to me after the meeting and said, "If that's what you expect of a deacon, I guess I'll just have to resign tonight." I patted him on the back. I thought he was joking. Then I looked at him and saw he wasn't kidding. He said, "I'm a social drinker and I don't intend to quit. I teach Sunday school in this church. I'm a deacon in this church. I'm a trustee of this church, but if you don't believe people who are social drinkers ought to be deacons, I'll just resign." I said, "Sir, I'll accept your resignation."

Can you imagine the shock waves that sent over the church? Here was a brand-new preacher, a young upstart from the clay hills of North Georgia, and here, at the first deacons' meeting, the big shot in the church resigned. Later this deacon decided to put pressure on me and make me bow down, just as he had made other preachers bow down. He called me to his private club on the top floor of the building where his offices were located. He fed me a good meal. (I ordered the most expensive thing on the menu. I figured if this was going to be my execution meal I might as well have a good one.) When the meal was over, he looked at me and said, "Now listen, preacher, many men who have been leading this church for years drink. You can't build a church if you don't let men serve who are social drinkers. You won't have enough leadership. You will tear this church up if you insist on that kind of standard."

I don't take any credit for what happened, because I was scared to death. I give Jesus all the glory and all the honor and all the credit. I looked that man right in the face and said, "I want you to know,

first of all, that I love you. But I have a few convictions. I don't have
enough convictions. I don't have all the convictions I ought to have,
but I have a few, and I want you to know that the world will crumble
and fall before I'll ever surrender those convictions."

Well, that church did not die. It grew as it had never grown
before. We don't have to compromise. We don't have to bow down
to the gods of this world.

Be true to Jesus. Be faithful to him and He will bless you. Make up
your mind while you are young to stand for Jesus regardless of the cost.

B. They Would Not Bend (3:13-18)

The three Hebrew young people who so resolutely refused to bow
to the king's golden image precipitated a religious and political crisis. Look at these three young men who arrayed themselves against
the mightiest empire on earth. The drama that follows is thrilling.

1. Attitude of the King (3:13-15)

Later on this same king of Babylon went mad. Here we can detect
the beginning of the kind of emotional upheaval which showed that
something was wrong in his life.

a. *Anger* (3:13). "Then Nebuchadnezzar in his rage and fury . . ."
That is the second time such a thing is recorded. We read before
that "the king was angry and very furious" (2:12). Here was a man
who had no control over his emotions, a man who could not handle
his anger.

There is a proper place for anger. The Bible says we are to be
angry, and sin not (Ephesians 4:26). But this king was expressing
sinful anger, anger filled with fury, violent anger. He was livid with
rage at the three young Hebrews. He took their defiance as a personal affront. When he gave orders he expected everyone to obey.
Nobody ever dared defy the king of Babylon. He could take their
lives in a moment.

This world's Babylon always has its images of gold and it always
demands that we bow down to them. This chapter, particularly,
warns God's people not to capitulate to the tendencies and trends
of this world. The Bible says, "Love not the world" (1 John 2:15). It
warns of the insidious pressures of the world. The world wants us
to go along with its fashions and follow its customs. It is its purpose
to make us like everybody else.

The J. B. Phillips paraphrase of Romans 12:2 is tremendous. Instead of "Be not conformed to this world," J. B. Phillips puts it, "Don't let the world around you squeeze you into its own mold." That is exactly what the world wants to do. This world wants all to have the same standards—its standards; all accept the same beliefs—its beliefs; all go to the same places—its places; all do the same things—its things. It wants to make us products of its assembly line. When an individual dares to be different, this upsets the world and it gets angry. We see here, then, the anger of the world against three people who were not willing to go along with it.

b. *Amazement* (3:14). These three young men were brought before the king. "Is it true?" he said in amazement. He could hardly believe his ears. He could not believe that anybody was foolish enough to defy him. One word from Nebuchadnezzar, and men fell prostrate before him. He had the idea that everybody had his price.

Many persons do have their price. Some people will compromise their convictions for a very small price. But some people in this world are not for sale.

Let me remind you about Charles Spurgeon. He was brought up in England and called to preach at an early age. In his early twenties he became pastor of a church in London, and so many people came to hear him they had to move out of the building in order to expand. By the time the expansion was completed so many people were coming they had to build an even bigger place. For many years Spurgeon preached to five thousand people at a time. They would pack the building out on Sunday morning and pack it out again on Sunday night. Spurgeon used to beg his members to stay away on Sunday nights so that lost people could get in.

Here in America, at the same time Spurgeon was preaching in London, P. T. Barnum was in the circus business. His job was to get a crowd too, to fill up his tent. He heard about the young preacher Spurgeon who was drawing such great crowds of people and he wired an offer to him to come over to America and speak in his tent. He wanted Spurgeon to draw big crowds for him. P. T. Barnum offered him an enormous amount of money to come and speak at his circuses. Spurgeon wired back one verse of scripture: "Read Acts 8:20." Here's what that verse says: "Thy money perish with thee, because thou hast thought that the gift of God may be purchased with money." Praise God for a man who has that kind of conviction.

c. *Antagonism* (3:15). The king of Babylon tried diplomacy. We can see him as his expression changed. He was going to try a different approach to bend these young men to his will. He was used to bending the wills of others. We can hear the changed tone of his voice as he said, "Young men, I'm going to do the generous thing. Perhaps you did not understand the imperial command; I'm going to give you one more chance. I'll have the orchestra play again and if, when the tune is played, you get down on your knees and worship the image, all will be well." If they wouldn't bow, he would make them bend. Be like everybody else. Go along with the crowd. Bend, don't be different. However, there was also a warning: "If you don't do it, you will be put pronto into the burning fiery furnace."

That is what the world always does. If we refuse to bend, it has its furnaces to put us in. It has its furnaces of scorn and laughter. One of the most effective tools the devil has with young people is laughter. Nobody likes to be laughed at. Everybody wants to be one of the crowd. So, when we refuse to yield to pressure, refuse to go along, make up our minds we are not going to drink, not going to sacrifice our purity, there are always those who will scorn.

I remember hearing about Harry Ironside, the great Bible teacher. When as a young man he was unsaved his mother would talk to him about coming to the Lord. Young Ironside would say, "Mother, I know I need to be saved and I would like to be saved, but I'm afraid if I get saved the boys will laugh at me." His mother used to say, "Harry, just remember one thing. Your friends can laugh you into hell, but they can never laugh you out of it."

"Who is that God that shall deliver you out of my hands?" the king demanded. In that statement the battle shifted. What the king did not realize was that he had moved the focus of the battle. Now, the battle was not between the king and the young men; it was between the king and the God of heaven. "Who is that God?" he was saying. "I don't believe such a God exists. There is no God who can deliver from my burning fiery furnace." But just because the king did not know of such a God did not mean there was no such God.

People may not know about the God of heaven, but that does not change the fact that there *is* a God in heaven—the God who created fire, a God who can turn it up or turn it off at will. There is a God in heaven who can deliver, a God who has power over the powerful of this earth. Let the infidels laugh. These young men had been taught and trained that there is a God who is real, a God who works on behalf of his children.

2. Answer of the Hebrews (3:16-18)

They were under tremendous pressure. Nebuchadnezzar was in for a big surprise. He was about to hear such words as had never been heard in the corridors of his palace before. Notice what their answer was.

a. *Courage* (3:16). "O Nebuchadnezzar," they said, "we don't have to take time to think up our answer. We don't have to have a meeting. We don't have to study the matter to decide what we are going to do. We are not careful to answer thee in this matter." They had already made up their minds a long time ago. They knew to whom loyalty belonged. They knew that in the ten commandments God had given a specific command: "Thou shalt not make unto thee any graven image." That commandment forbade the worship of an image. Idolatry was specifically forbidden. These young men already had their answer embedded deep in their hearts. It was an answer of courage.

Picture these young men standing there in front of that king. The king was putting on them all the pressure that the power of his office could wield. Their knees may have been knocking (after all, they were only human), but their hearts were firm. They looked that king in the eye and perhaps with a sweet smile said quietly, "O king, we will not bow down to your image of gold." That was courage.

It is wonderful to see people with the courage of their convictions. A theologian named Athanasius, who lived many centuries ago, was fighting heresy in his day. The Roman emperor Theodosius summoned Athanasius to appear before him. The emperor brought the pressure of his office to bear on the theologian. He wanted him to relinquish his stand against a popular heresy of the day. The emperor, however, could not get Athanasius to compromise. Finally Theodosius said, "Athanasius, don't you understand? The whole world is against you." Athanasius looked back at him and said, "Then Athanasius is against the whole world." Pressure did not move him.

My grandfather was an old-fashioned country Baptist preacher. I have his picture in my billfold. I carry it with me all the time just to inspire and encourage me. He died at the age of eighty-four. Every time I open up my billfold it reminds me to have the courage of my convictions as he did. He had a conviction about picture shows on Sunday. He believed that the Lord's day should be a holy day, a different day. When they started opening the movie house on Sunday in our little country town, he was upset about it. He went down to the courthouse and took out an injunction to force them to close the theater. The son of the man who owned that movie house was my best friend and the man who owned the place was the state legislator. He was the most powerful man in the county and was he angry! My grandfather lived in a little four-room white-frame house. The legislator lived at the country club, and owned a big mansion. He was Mr. Powerhouse in that part of the state. When he walked into the governor's office, he was used to getting anything he wanted. He was accustomed to people doing whatever he wanted them to do. The very idea of a nobody Baptist preacher closing up his movie house on Sunday!

One Sunday afternoon, he drove down to my grandfather's house, knocked on the door, and introduced himself. He tried to reason with my grandfather. He tried everything a politician knows how to do, but Grandfather would not budge. Finally, in exasperation, that movie owner looked at my grandfather, shook his finger in his face, and said, "Old man, I'll starve you to death." My grandfather said, "You'll have to starve God almighty first!" That was courage. Later that man came back to my grandfather's house, broke down, and cried. He said, "Preacher, you know my father was a Methodist preacher. He's dead and in heaven now, and if he knew the way I was living, it would break his heart. Preacher, pray for me."

b. *Confidence* (3:17). These young Hebrews had a God who could do something, a God of power, a God who was *able*. God is able to save to the uttermost. God is able to do "exceeding abundantly above all that we ask or think." There are no limits to the power of God.

Sometimes God delivers us out of the fire. Sometimes He delivers us through the fire.

Don't be afraid to take a stand for the Lord. God will bless you for it. God will deliver you.

c. *Commitment* (3:18). They said, "God is able to deliver us from the fiery furnace if he wants to, but if not . . ." Are you prepared for the "if nots" of life? Some people will serve the Lord as long as He does what they want him to do. But what if God doesn't do what we want him to do? The question is not, *can* God do something; the question is, *will* God do something? Sometimes God will deliver us from the fiery furnace, and sometimes He will let us go through the fiery furnace.

In Acts 12 we read of two apostles, James and Simon Peter. James was killed by the king; Simon Peter was delivered by God. We do not understand why God did not save both of them. It is great faith that says, "God will deliver." It is greater faith that says, "If God does not deliver, we will still serve him and still be faithful to him."

Are you prepared to serve Jesus even when things do not work out the way you think they should? God can deliver, but if not . . . God can heal, but if not . . . God can move in this situation, but if not . . . Service for the Lord Jesus Christ should not be contingent on the pleasantness of the circumstances.

Remember Job. Although Job loved the Lord, and was true and faithful to him, nothing seemed to work out in his life. He lost all his wealth, he lost his family, his friends deserted him, his wife urged him to curse God and die. Yet in spite of everything, Job said, "Though he slay me, yet will I trust him."

These young men believed in an afterlife. They did not have as much light on the subject as we do, but they believed in it. Look at what they said, "Our God whom we serve is able to deliver us from the burning fiery furnace, and he will deliver us out of thine hand, O king." They were saying, "We may go into that fiery furnace and die. So what! We will then be in a land where you can't touch us." They believed in another world, in an afterlife.

One of these days the battle will be over. Then it will matter whether or not we stood for the Lord Jesus. Then it will be all important whether we were faithful to the Lord in difficult circumstances. If Jesus is your Savior and you love him, He is worth suffering for, He is worth standing for. Let me encourage you, whichever way it goes, if God delivers, or if He doesn't seem to, make up your mind not to bow, not to bend, to the devil's image of gold.

C. They Would Not Burn (3:19-30)

The names of Shadrach, Meshach, and Abednego are mentioned thirteen times in this chapter. It is as though God was so proud of them that He was shouting their names down the halls of heaven.

I see a beautiful prophetic picture in all this. The fiery furnace symbolizes the time of great tribulation, when God's wrath will be poured on this earth. Daniel, being absent, pictured those of God's believers who will be raptured before the great tribulation begins. The three Hebrew young men foreshadow the Jewish people who will go through the great tribulation. God will walk through the fire with them and when it is over they will come out purified, ready to receive their messiah, the Lord Jesus Christ.

In this study we shall look at this chapter from a very practical point of view. We shall see three young men who would not burn.

Their refusal had precipitated a crisis. We can imagine how the crowds began to gather, everyone scrambling to get front seats. The king now had no choice. His command had been defied and his authority was now in question. The king had been painted into a corner, so to speak. Now he had to punish them; he had to do what he had threatened to do.

Some lessons can be learned only in the furnace experiences of life. Are you in the furnace right now? God's people experience all kinds of furnaces. Maybe it is a family furnace. Or maybe your furnace is a deep personal problem. I don't know how to define your furnace experience, but remember, some lessons can be learned only in the furnace.

1. Persecution (3:19-23)

For instance, there is the lesson of persecution. God's people will encounter persecution along the way.

a. *The King's Fury* (3:19-20). We have already seen that this king had an uncontrollable temper. Now, for the second time in the chapter, we are told that he was "full of fury."

Nothing is more terrible than for a person not to be able to control his temper. I was reading recently about the coach of the basketball team at Indiana. This coach has a problem with his temper. He had just lost his temper again and he not only had to apologize to the fans but the university had to rebuke him.

It is a serious thing not to be able to control your temper. There is no bigger loser on earth than the person who loses his temper. That person does things he would not think of doing under other circumstances. He makes an absolute fool of himself. He is embarrassed when it is over. It is a terrible thing when we do not know how to control our tempers.

The only one who can give us power to handle a violent temper is the Lord Jesus Christ. Let Jesus take control. Ask him to control your temper for you.

But this king did not know the Lord. He had no personal experience with him. God had not come into his life. So he was beside himself with anger. It was written all over his face.

The face often mirrors the emotions of the soul. You can usually tell what a person is experiencing by his face. We sometimes talk about "a poker face," referring to a person who has so learned to control his facial expressions that we cannot tell what he is thinking, but most of us cannot put on that poker face. We mirror our emotions in our faces, expressing wonder, disappointment, admiration, glee, mischief.

The king commanded that the furnace be heated seven times hotter than it normally was. That is a reminder of the fact that for us who are Christians, trying to live for the Lord, the experiences of life will be more severe than they are for others. We may have more difficulties now that we are saved than we had before. Then we were just going along with the stream; now we are going against the stream, so we experience more difficulties than ever before. "Turn the heat up," the king said. "Turn the heat up," the devil may say, as he looks at our lives.

They then bound those three young men up in all of their clothing. Evidently they were still in their official robes, the uniforms of their office, which would add fuel for the fire.

Are you dressed for the furnace? If you know the Lord and are living for him, you had better be prepared—because persecution will come into your life sooner or later. Christians in today's world need to have a suit of heavenly asbestos in their wardrobes.

b. *The King's Furnace* (3:21-23). We have to slow down and focus on this passage because it is so familiar to us. We must not miss the drama. That furnace was so hot that even the king's men, assigned to throw them in, could not withstand the tremendous temperature. They were consumed, burned up, just throwing those boys in.

How the devil must have been gloating. We can hear him: "Now see what you've done, fools. You have gone overboard on religion. You have refused to compromise just a little and now you are going into the fire—where you deserve to go." So they hurled those boys into that furnace like chips of wood into a glowing Vesuvius.

What is the lesson here? There are furnace experiences in life, and sooner or later we are going to be immersed in them. It may be the furnace of criticism. If you are successful, people will criticize you. If you are not successful, people will criticize you. There will always be a critic somewhere, somebody to pass judgment on what you are doing. It may be the furnace of isolation. No one understands, and no one cares enough to try to help. Maybe you are going into the furnace of intimidation. You are feeling put down and threatened.

Whatever it is, God's people know what it is to be persecuted. We must not be disturbed or frightened. The Bible has told us that suffering will come. Peter says, "Think it not strange concerning the fiery trial which is to try you" (1 Peter 4:12). Jesus said, "They persecuted me, and they will persecute you." The closer we get to our Lord, the more of the mud they throw at Jesus will land on us.

Let me share a promise with you that might not be so exciting as some of the others. God promises, "Yea, and all that will live godly in Christ Jesus shall suffer persecution" (2 Timothy 3:12). That's not one of the more pleasant promises, but it's a promise. You say, "I'm a Christian and I'm not being persecuted." Look at the promise. In other words, make up your mind you want to live like God, be like God, do what He would do in life, and you will suffer persecution. If you are not being persecuted, it may mean you are not living a godly life.

The furnace experiences, the persecutions, that come to believers are good for us. God purifies us through such times. He uses persecution to purge the impurities in our lives, to get out the sin that creeps in. Sometimes He puts us into the flames of persecution to burn away things that ought not to be in our lives, but sometimes He does it to put us to the test. Sometimes God allows the little furnace to get us ready for the big furnace.

Think, for instance, of Jeremiah. People were making fun of him, laughing at him, mocking his preaching. Jeremiah told the Lord about it. The Lord said to Jeremiah, "If you have run with the footmen, and they have wearied you, what will you do with the swelling of the Jordan?" (see Jeremiah 12:5). God's sermon to Jeremiah was, "Cheer up, Jeremiah, it's going to get worse!" God allows the little furnaces, and when we come through the fire greatly improved, then God says we are ready for a big furnace. The size of the furnace is a compliment to your faith. God says, in effect: "I have enough confidence in you to believe that you can stand this kind of persecution and to come out stronger for me." So, God says, "I have chosen thee in the furnace of affliction" (Isaiah 48:10).

2. Preservation (3:24-28a)

Now comes the lesson of preservation. These boys wouldn't burn! We are in the realm of a miracle. It is impossible for a person to be thrown into a fiery furnace and not be incinerated. Yet the Bible says that these boys wouldn't burn. Who created the universe? God. That being true, who created fire? God. Cannot the God who created fire take three young men and make them fireproof for a little while?

I have no trouble with the miracles of the Bible. There is one verse of scripture which, if you really believe it, will resolve all problems you may meet in the rest of the Bible. Genesis 1:1 says, "In the beginning God created the heavens and the earth." If that statement is true, if God is the creator of the heavens and the earth, then surely, such a God can preserve three of his people in a fiery burning furnace for a few moments of time.

They walked on hot coals unharmed. They washed their faces and hands in bowls of fire and were not scorched. We are in the presence of a miracle of God.

Here we learn two things about the preservation of God's people in times of trial.

a. *By the Presence of God* (3:24-25). Notice what happened. These three young men were thrown into the burning fiery furnace. The king looked into that furnace and was astonished, startled. We can imagine the king rubbing his eyes and looking again into those flames. The young Hebrews were unbound! He said, "Did not we cast three men bound into the midst?" They assured him that was so. He said "Lo, I see four men loose, walking in the midst of the fire." God was keeping his word. He had said, "When thou walkest through the fire, thou shalt not be burned; neither shall the flame kindle upon thee" (Isaiah 43:2). He has promised preservation in those times when we go through life's fiery trials.

That furnace had become a microwave oven. A microwave oven is an amazing thing. Its fire is selective. It cooks some things, but not others. The flames in this fire became selective flames. They did not burn the boys but, according to scripture, the bonds that bound them were burned off by the flames of the furnace.

There we see the lesson of preservation. God lets us go through the furnace in order to set us free from things that have been binding us.

I was reading the life of Martin Luther recently. That great theologian came to understand the truth that "the just shall live by faith." He had been bound by religious dogma, taught that he had to earn his salvation. Oh, how he suffered! He went through the furnace of persecution and affliction. But the fires burned away the things that bound him and set him free to be the man of God that his heavenly Father intended him to be.

Think, too, of John Wesley, the father of Methodism. John Wesley wanted to preach in the pulpits of the land, but his doctrine was so different and his message so contrary to that of the religious establishment that the authorities closed the pulpits to him. He thought he was being deprived, but God knew something Wesley did not know. God knew that the people were not in those churches. The masses were not coming to those churches. So John Wesley, banned from the pulpits of the Anglican churches, went outside the church. John Wesley, his brother Charles, and George Whitefield, all fiery evangelists, began to preach in the open air where the people were, and thousands were won to Jesus Christ. The flames of persecution simply loosed them from the ropes that bound them.

That fiery experience you are going through is going to be used by God to unbind you one of these days. God will take that fire and use it to rid your life of those things that hinder you from being everything you ought to be.

Further, they were unharmed: "And they have no hurt" (3:25). Nebuchadnezzar expected them to be burned to a cinder, writhing in anguish. But instead, he saw them walking in victory. They were walking in that fire completely unharmed. He saw the saints of God preserved by the presence of God. The Bible says he saw not only the saints of God, he saw the Son of God. He said, "Didn't we throw only three men in there?" He was assured that was so. "But I see four men," he exclaimed. In the actual Hebrew text Nebuchadnezzar said, "One is like unto a son of the gods." That was the only way this pagan king knew how to describe what he saw. He had no spiritual vocabulary, so he used the language of paganism to describe a spiritual reality that was beyond his ability to understand.

We know what he saw. He did not see a son of the gods; he saw the Son of God, the Lord Jesus Christ, walking with those faithful believers in that furnace of fire.

We call that an Old Testament theophany—an Old Testament manifestation of the eternal Son of God, the Lord Jesus Christ. Jesus did that from time to time. He walked with Enoch, and together they walked right on into glory. He feasted with Abraham. There were times when Jesus in his preincarnate state took human form and walked with his children through times of deep trial.

Down here on earth, people who saw the situation into which those three young men had gotten themselves must have thought, "Aren't they fools?" But the Lord Jesus in heaven stepped off his throne, strode through the battlements of heaven, descended the starry staircase to earth, assumed human form, walked over to that furnace, opened up the door, went inside, and said to the fire, "Cool it!" And the fire lost its heat.

Now it's time for a lesson in mathematics. How many went into the fiery furnace? Three. When the king counted them, how many

did he count in the fiery furnace? Four. When the king commanded them to come out of the fiery furnace, how many came out?
Three. Where was the fourth man he saw in the fire? He was still
there. That means that when you go through the furnace of fire the
Lord Jesus Christ is already in there waiting for you. He will be right
there and He will walk with you through the trial.

> When through fiery trials thy pathway shall lie,
> My grace, all sufficient, shall be thy supply.
> The flames shall not hurt thee; I only design
> Thy dross to consume, and thy gold to refine.

b. *By the Power of God* (3:26-28a). The king again called for all his officials. When they arrived, those pagan Babylonians likewise became
witnesses to the power of God. The scientists and experts examined
them and what did they find? On their bodies the fire had no
power! Not a hair of their heads was singed; they didn't even smell
like smoke.

When Jesus performs a miracle, He doesn't do a partial miracle;
He does it properly. When Jesus gave hearing to people who
couldn't hear, He didn't heal one ear and leave the other ear deaf.
When Jesus healed blind eyes, He didn't make just one eye whole
and leave the other blind. When the crippled man was healed by
the power of God in Acts 3, the Bible says that the Lord gave him
perfect soundness. That means God does a total job.

If you will come to the Lord Jesus Christ, He will do all that is
needed. He will forgive you of your sins. He will put them as far
from you as the east is from the west. He will cast them into the
depths of the sea. He will remember them no more. He will put
them behind his back. He will cover them as with a thick cloud. He
will put them under his blood and you will be perfectly justified. It
will be just as if you had never sinned.

3. Promotion (3:28b-30)

There is also the lesson of promotion.

a. *The King Praises God's Person* (3:28b-29). The astonished king promoted those young men, but first he praised God.

b. *The King Prospers God's People* (3:30). Maybe he gave them an
increase in salary. Maybe he expanded their official responsibilities
and gave them better living quarters. Through that pagan king, God

brought them to a place of promotion as a result of that fiery furnace experience. I believe that God never effectively uses a person until that person has experienced suffering in her or his life. The pathway to glory is always the pathway of suffering. You may be going through the furnace right now, but remember that the pathway of suffering is your pathway to promotion.

"And he shall sit as a refiner and purifier of silver" (Malachi 3:3). What a picture of God—as a silversmith. A silversmith takes a crucible and puts silver into it. Then he turns the flame on the crucible and heats the silver until it turns to liquid. The silver goes to the bottom and the impurities rise to the top. Then the silversmith takes a skimmer and removes the impurities. He carefully regulates the fire. His purpose is not to destroy or ruin the silver, but to refine and purify it. He keeps up the process until nothing is left but pure silver. How does the silversmith know when his job is completed? When he looks into the silver and sees the reflection of his own face, he knows that the refining work is finished. It is time to take the silver out of the fire.

You may be going through the fire. You say, "When is it all going to be over?" Jesus is getting the impurities out of your life. When He sees the reflection of his face, when He sees Christlikeness in you, when He sees your life becoming more and more like his, then He will take you out of that fire and He will promote you and use you in ways you never dreamed possible.

IV. A KING'S DISCOVERY (4:1-37)

Let me tell you about an astonishing booklet. It is about the size of a gospel tract. This booklet, published in Russia, describes the personal testimony of a well-known Russian leader who for years acted more like a beast than a man. He says that he was out of his mind, spiritually insane. Now he claims to believe that there is a God in heaven. He has yielded himself to that God, he says, and he intends to serve him for the rest of his life. He calls on all the world's people to hear what God has done in his life.

You don't believe a word of that? You are absolutely correct. It is not true at all. It is only an imaginary vignette. It would be an amazing thing if any Soviet leader should experience a genuine Christian conversion and come to know Jesus Christ as Savior.

What we read in Daniel 4 is almost as incredible.

A. Introduction (4:1-3)

Here we have an official Babylonian document recording the conversion experience of Nebuchadnezzar, who was one of the cruelest monarchs of history. In this tract he told us what God did in his life. He gave evidence in this testimony that he had experienced conversion. Here is the account of a man who came to know God in a personal way, and who was so thrilled about it that he not only wrote his personal testimony but instructed that it be sent out to all the nations of the known world.

The beginning of his account is somewhat reminiscent of a Pauline epistle. He wanted all the peoples of the world to read it. He said, "Peace be multiplied unto you," the way Paul often began his letters. This is the language of a converted man. He was overwhelmed by the greatness of God. He said that the greatness of God was beyond his ability to understand. He was overwhelmed at God's mercy, which had reached down into his wicked life and touched him. Psalm 66:16 says, "Come and hear, all ye that fear God, and I will declare what he hath done for my soul." That describes what Nebuchadnezzar provided for us in this chapter.

Here we have the remarkable spiritual history of a human soul in the hands of God. The same God who saves the poor and lowly is able to save the high and mighty. No one is beyond the reach of our sovereign God. No man can shut God out of his life or put himself in a position where God cannot speak to his soul.

B. Proclamation (4:4-36)

1. Reception of the Dream (4:4-18)

Everything that God told Nebuchadnezzar was going to happen in his life took place as God said it would.

a. *The King's Dread* (4:4-9). Nebuchadnezzar was in his magnificent palace, evidently in bed asleep. He had subdued nation after nation, never lost a battle, but now his battles were over. His official affairs were moving smoothly. He was a man experiencing personal peace as far as his kingdom was concerned. But Nebuchadnezzar's security was a false one. That night he received a dream that filled him with dread and terror.

God has a way of getting to us. At this point in time, Nebuchadnezzar was probably not afraid of much. He was certainly not afraid of any of the surrounding nations. No threat could alarm him. It would be hard to frighten a man like King Nebuchadnezzar. When lightning fell, he was not worried. What did he care that there might be a God in heaven who could throw lightning bolts? It is very difficult to disturb a man like this or make him afraid.

b. *The King's Dream* (4:10-17). Yet one night the eternal God sent
into the heart of Nebuchadnezzar a dream that shook his peace of
mind and security. The king was never the same again.

Disturbed by the dream, he called for the wise men of the kingdom, as he had done in the past. They were just as unable to give
answers to the questions in his heart as they had been before.

Nebuchadnezzar made the mistake most people make. He kept
going to the wrong place to get answers. People who do not know
the Lord do not know where to go when they have problems. So
they go to an unsaved psychiatrist, or tune into a talk show host, or
consult a lawyer or politician.

"But at the last Daniel came in." Probably Daniel came last on
purpose. Most likely he timed his arrival so that he would be the last
seer to come before the king. Remember, Daniel had been working
for Nebuchadnezzar a long time. He was a man of God who had
won the respect of this pagan king. Probably Daniel had witnessed
to King Nebuchadnezzar many times through the years. But Nebuchadnezzar was too big for God. (Some people are like that.) I
imagine there were many times when Daniel prayed on his knees
before God, "O God, I know it would be a miracle, but do something
for this wicked king that I serve. Somehow get hold of his heart and
save him. Lord, what a testimony it would be if King Nebuchadnezzar got saved!"

Vance Havner used to say that some of his sermons were like time
bombs—sometimes they didn't go off until a long while later. One
of Daniel's time bombs was about to go off. One of his prayers was
about to be answered.

When Daniel came in, the king told him he knew that the spirit
of the holy gods was in him. Three times in this chapter we are told
that the spirit of the holy gods was in Daniel. That was a pagan way
of saying that God was evident in Daniel's life.

If the Lord is in our lives, people will know it. We won't have to
tell them. We won't have to wear a sign claiming that God is in residence. The king recognized that Daniel was God's man, one who
knew how to get hold of God in prayer. When people are in trouble
they often want to find somebody who knows how to get in touch
with God. They may make fun of us when things are going smoothly, but when life falls apart, it's a different story.

In his dream, Nebuchadnezzar saw a tree, great in height (see
Appendix 7). It grew, it was strong, its leaves were fair, and it bore
much fruit. It provided food for all. The beasts of the field found
shade beneath it. In his dream the king saw a "watcher" or a "holy

one" come down from heaven (4:13), which is probably a description of one of God's angels.

The angel came with a terrible pronouncement: The tree was to be cut down. It was destined for a fall. Its stump, however, would be preserved. So, though it looked dead, life was still there. In other words, the tree would come back to life—there would be a restoration.

Now note what struck terror into the heart of Nebuchadnezzar. The dream moved from the impersonal "it" (talking about the tree) to "his" (talking about Nebuchadnezzar). Nebuchadnezzar received the stunning news that the tree represented *him.* "Let his heart be changed from man's, and let a beast's heart be given unto him; and let seven times pass over him" (that is, seven years). The king understood that in some mysterious way God was speaking to his heart.

2. Revelation of the Dream (4:19-27)

a. *Daniel's Astonishment* (4:19). The king then asked Daniel to interpret this dream and Daniel was silent for an hour. Here was the preacher in an audience with the king and for one solid hour he had not one word to say. Can you imagine a preacher standing before a congregation and saying nothing for a full hour? It is even more remarkable that the king did not interrupt Daniel's contemplative silence.

At the end of the hour, the king said, "Daniel, don't let the dream trouble you, don't let the interpretation frighten you." Then Daniel answered, "I have some bad news to tell you O king." Daniel was experiencing what every true-hearted preacher of the word of God experiences. There are times when God lays a happy message on a preacher's heart. For example, it is a joy to preach about heaven and the wonderful future God has promised us.

But sometimes God puts a different kind of message on the preacher's heart. There are times when he has to deal with sin in the lives of people. He must come down hard. There are times when the faithful preacher has a message that weighs his heart down. This is why sometimes the Old Testament prophets called their message "the burden of the word of the Lord."

Will Daniel water down his message because it is unpleasant? Will he tone it down so as not to be offensive to the king?

Too much of that kind of subterfuge is going on in pulpits these days. Some preachers, because they fear the faces of men, have watered down the truth of God's word. As a result, multitudes are not brought face to face with their lostness, sinfulness of heart, desperate need of the Lord Jesus, and their peril of going lost to eternity. There are preachers today who would fill hell with flowers and do not tell people the truth. Daniel was not that kind of man.

b. *Daniel's Assessment* (4:20-27). The interpretation of the dream must have had the same impact on Nebuchadnezzar as Nathan's word did on King David. David had hidden sin in his heart. He thought nobody knew, but God knew, and He sent Nathan the prophet, who said four words that changed David's life forever: "Thou art the man." David discovered that God knew what had been going on in his life.

Daniel's five words shook the world of Nebuchadnezzar: "It is thou, O king." You are the man. Then Daniel told the monarch what was going to happen to him.

Through Daniel God now said to Nebuchadnezzar: "King, because you have not recognized that it is I, the most high, who really rules over human affairs, I am going to turn you into an animal. I am going to put you out there with the animals. You are going to have the heart of an animal, and your lifestyle will be that of an animal." There are mental disorders in which an afflicted person thinks he has become an animal. That condition has given rise to all kinds of legends, and also jokes.

We have, for instance, the werewolf legend. When I was a boy the popular horror movies were werewolf movies. Lon Chaney was the werewolf, and he was scary. When the full moon came out, Chaney would turn into a werewolf. His fingernails would elongate, hair would grow all over him, his teeth would lengthen, and so on.

God, however, promised Nebuchadnezzar that he would be restored. Daniel gave one more faithful witness to this man. He was to stop sinning and live righteously; he was to show mercy to the poor.

That is the Old Testament equivalent of what we have in the New Testament. All persons need to repent of their sins, believe on the Lord Jesus Christ, and bring forth fruits worthy of repentance. Daniel was simply saying, "O king, you need the Lord in your life."

3. Realization of the Dream (4:28-36)

Everything God says comes to pass eventually. If it's in God's word, you can mark it down; it will surely take place.

a. *Sudden Condemnation* (4:28-33). Twelve months went by and nothing happened. Fear had doubtless subsided in Nebuchadnezzar's heart—the way it does when a lost person is brought under the convicting power of the Holy Spirit, is shaken to his foundations, but walks out. The impression of God fades as months pass. The conviction dies away.

God was giving that pagan king space to repent, because God is merciful. For an entire year Nebuchadnezzar had the opportunity to repent and thus avert the judgment of God. But it did him no good.

One day when he was walking around his palace in Babylon he said in effect: "What a city! What a palace! I built it, and it's mine, all mine!" Babylon occupied twenty square miles and had two gigantic walls to protect it. Wide avenues bisected the city. It had a processional street a thousand yards long. It was beautified with enameled brick depicting lions, dragons, and bulls. It had a banquet hall that would seat ten thousand people.

The city was famous for its hanging gardens, one of the seven wonders of the ancient world. One of Nebuchadnezzar's queens was homesick for the mountains of her homeland, so he constructed magnificent hanging gardens for her on the top of the buildings. From a distance the city of Babylon looked like a luxuriant tree-covered mountain. So Nebuchadnezzar boasted, "I have done it all." In his heart there was no willingness to acknowledge that God in heaven had given him all that he had.

While those words were still in the king's mouth, a voice from heaven spoke. Like a thunderbolt, judgment fell. The kingdom departed from him.

It is a warning for everyone. You keep saying no to Christ, keep on rejecting God's merciful appeals to your soul, and one day God's judgment clock in heaven will strike the judgment day for you. It may come while the wrong words are in your mouth.

One moment Nebuchadnezzar's mind was as clear as anyone else's. His eyes were sharp and steady. Then, within the hour, his mind became confused, his heart became the heart of a beast. We can almost see him as he ran out of the palace and began to make sounds in the streets like an animal. He tore the clothes off his body. We can see him rush deep into the thickets of the Euphrates. In time his hair grew long and his nails became like bird's claws. He had become a mad man.

Evidently his counselors took care of his kingdom during that time. Perhaps Daniel supervised it as the king's custodian. Imagine what people must have said. "Is he sick? He hasn't made a public appearance in months. Somebody said he's dead and they just don't want to tell us; they are afraid there will be a rebellion." Then rumors began to circulate: "Somebody said he's been seen in the thickets of the Euphrates, that he goes around on his hands and knees. His body is covered with hair. I've heard that the king has turned into an animal."

God can bring us down. A person can make fun of the gospel all he wants. He can laugh at the claims of Jesus Christ and think himself very important. But all God has to do is touch one cell in that person's brain and he will become a babbling idiot.

Now is the time to be saved. Who knows if you will have the sanity of mind to receive the Lord Jesus Christ as your Savior tomorrow?

How many opportunities have you had to be saved? Maybe you have been rejecting Jesus Christ for years. What makes you think God has to give you another opportunity to receive Christ? One of these days you may be like a vegetable. Prayer won't do you any good. Witnessing won't do you any good. Preaching won't do you any good. There is a God in heaven who controls human affairs.

b. *Sweet Salvation* (4:34-35). People return to sanity when they begin to look up. "I will lift up mine eyes unto the hills, from whence cometh my help. My help cometh from the Lord" (Psalm 121:1). It is a great day in anyone's life when they stop living like an animal and start living like a human being, when they look up toward heaven to the God who can change anyone's life.

There is hope for a man or woman who will look up to heaven. You don't have to have the words to say. You don't have to have the proper spiritual vocabulary. But you have to want to be saved. All you have to do is "look unto him, all the ends of the earth" and you will be saved. The Bible says, "Whosoever shall call on the name of the Lord shall be saved (Romans 10:13). When Nebuchadnezzar lifted his eyes to heaven, his sanity returned.

That is what happened to the prodigal son. He was living like an animal. Have you ever stared into the face of a hog? The prodigal son did. He was living with the hogs. Finally, the Bible says, "he came to himself." Then he said, "I will arise and go to my father."

Nebuchadnezzar's understanding returned. We hear him praising God, honoring "him that liveth for ever" (4:36). His reason returned and he was reestablished as king. He was changed. He was saved. Only God can do that in a life.

c. *Swift Restoration* (4:36). With the words, "those that walk in pride he is able to abase," Nebuchadnezzar walked off the pages of scripture. The last we see of this pagan king is a thoroughly converted man praising God with all his heart and soul.

C. Conclusion (4:37)

I believe we will meet Nebuchadnezzar in heaven. We will walk right up to him and say, "Bless your heart. It's a joy to meet you. I read your salvation tract down there on earth. What a conversion you had!"

If you have had a conversion experience, you should be able to tell it. If God has changed your heart and given you a new one, if He has taken away that old beast heart of yours, taken away cruelty from your life, taken away your old sin and lust, don't you think you should be able to give a testimony? If you cannot do anything else, do what Nebuchadnezzar did—write a letter to someone about it. Put it in a booklet and pass on the news.

If God could save Nebuchadnezzar, He can save you.

V. A KING'S DOOM (5:1-31)

In this chapter we have the initial fulfillment of the prophecy given to Nebuchadnezzar. The head of gold is replaced by silver in the image. The Babylonian empire is now swept away by the Medo-Persian empire.

The mention of Belshazzar in this chapter was once used by liberals to deny the accuracy of the Bible (see Appendix 16). At the turn of the century there was a movement in rationalistic biblical scholarship called "higher criticism." According to its approach, the Bible must be viewed as any other book. There is no room for the supernatural or for miracles. Therefore, if a statement in the Bible is unsupported by secular history, or if some name is given that is unknown to scholars, it is assumed that the Bible is in error. For many years there was no historic evidence of the existence of a king of Babylon named Belshazzar. Liberal critics pounced on the Bible and claimed to have found an error. "The Bible," they said, "is not historically credible."

Archaeology proved those critics wrong. There was indeed a man named Belshazzar and he did rule as king of Babylon. Belshazzar's father was Nabonidus, who, though he was the rightful king of Babylon, was not interested in ruling (see Appendix 9). He was an archaeologist, far more interested in historical research than in presiding over a kingdom. So, because he was constantly on the move, and to ensure that the kingdom be adequately administrated, he appointed his son Belshazzar to be his co-regent. That is why King Belshazzar said that anyone who could read the writing on the wall would be made the *third* ruler in the kingdom.

That, too, was a mystery to those critics. Why would the king say that? Whatever "modern scholarship" did not know, the Holy Spirit made no mistake. He knew that Nabonidus and his son Belshazzar were joint rulers of Babylon.

Whenever you find something in the Bible you do not understand or something not corroborated by secular history, just be patient. God will always vindicate his word. The Bible says, "Let God be true and every man a liar."

Between chapter 4 and chapter 5 a period of about twenty-three years transpires. Daniel was now an old man. Although a captive from his native land, he had served faithfully in the kingdom for almost seventy years. He was probably in his late eighties. Belshazzar was now ruling over the city of Babylon. His father had been captured by the Medes and the Persians, and most of Babylonia had fallen. All that remained to be conquered was the city of Babylon itself.

Belshazzar was convinced that the city was impregnable. Vast sums of money had been invested in its defense. Babylon was designed to withstand any kind of assault. A massive double wall, over three hundred feet high and eighty-seven feet wide, had been built around the city. Several teams of chariots could run abreast on the top of that wall. Over a hundred towers had been strategically placed around the wall to provide surveillance and cross-fire. Under the wall and running diagonally through the city was the Euphrates River, so there would be no water shortage. Enough food had been stockpiled to last twenty years. Moreover, the citizens could grow more food inside the wall.

Belshazzar believed he was absolutely secure. Like a sleeping lion with a spider weaving its web around him, he was oblivious to his imminent danger. So much so, he was enjoying a night of revelry.

A. Dissipation (5:1-9)

1. A Great Feast (5:1)

It was a night of dissipation. Belshazzar was hosting a thousand of his lords and other officials. Archaeologists have discovered several banquet halls in the ruins of Babylon, all of tremendous size—able, indeed, to seat ten thousand people at a time. Such a crowd must have been present the night Belshazzar gave this tremendous feast. The king, his wives, and his concubines were all there. We can picture them with rings on their fingers, bracelets on their arms, dressed in their finest robes and opulent jewels. The atmosphere was filled with the fragrance of perfume.

Music, dancing, drinking, all kinds of debauchery (see Appendix 10)—it all sounds so up-to-date. Almost everywhere we turn in America today, alcohol is prevalent. The Bible condemns the use of liquor. It says, "Wine is a mocker, strong drink is raging: and whosoever is deceived thereby is not wise" (Proverbs 20:1). Alcohol is a deceiver. The chief goal of the liquor industry is to deceive you into believing there is nothing wrong with their products, that alcohol is great.

Many of those brought up in alcoholic families can testify to that truth. They have experienced the reality of Proverbs 23:29-35: "Who hath woe? who hath sorrow? who hath contentions? who hath babbling? who hath wounds without cause? who hath redness of eyes? They that tarry long at the wine. They that go to seek mixed wine. Look thou not upon the wine when it is red, when it giveth his colour in the cup, when it moveth itself aright."

Were you brought up in a home where liquor was a cause of constant contention? Have you seen your mother beaten by a drunken father? Were you as a child brought up by a father who hurt you without cause, though he would never have done it if he had been sober?

"At the last it biteth like a serpent, and stingeth like an adder." The Bible compares liquor to a poisonous snake. It says that in the end it is just as poisonous as the bite of a snake.

The Holy Spirit continues, "Thine eyes shall behold strange women, and thine heart shall utter perverse things." When a person is under the influence of liquor, there are other things that accompany his intoxication—sexual immorality for instance. Drunkards say perverse things, things they would never say if they were not inebriated.

"Yea, thou shalt be as he that lieth down in the midst of the sea." That is a description of seasickness. The Holy Spirit says that a drunkard makes himself sick. How absurd it is to get drunk and then boast of having had a good time.

The Spirit of God likens a drunkard to a man "that lieth upon the top of the mast. They have stricken me, shalt thou say, and I was not sick; they have beaten me, and I felt it not: when shall I awake?" In other words, the drunkard wakes up the next day feeling he has been beaten up, but without any knowledge of what happened. He can't remember where he has been. He has wounds and marks on his body but does not know what caused them.

But then he says, "I will seek it yet again." That is the ultimate horror of alcohol. In the end it takes control of its victim.

When a nation succumbs to the deception of liquor, when its leaders habitually drink alcoholic beverages, it is headed for ruin. A nation addicted to alcohol is a nation ready to fall.

When Belshazzar drank that wine he became brave with the false courage of alcohol. He wanted to make a gesture to defy the enemy army outside his walls. His wild party in itself was intended to send them a message: "We're not scared of you." Now that he was drunk, he wanted to defy God.

When Nebuchadnezzar took Judah captive he also took some of the sacred temple vessels from Jerusalem to Babylon. Perhaps they were on display to remind the world of the superiority of the gods of Babylon over the God of the Jews. Perhaps Jewish captives would take their children to see those golden vessels. Did they say, "Children, those vessels came out of the temple, the house of the God of the universe, the God we serve and love"?

Belshazzar was getting cocky. In his drunken condition he decided to do something he might not have had the nerve to do when sober. He decided to defy the God of heaven.

2. A Great Folly (5:2-4)

The king ordered that the vessels taken from the temple be brought. Then they drank their wine out of those sacred vessels. That was sacrilegious. They were making light of holy things.

That is where we are in America today. People are mocking sacred things. They are ridiculing the name of the Lord, using the name of Jesus Christ in vulgar profanity. The name of God is taken in vain. The Lord's day is a thing of the past. It began as "the holy sabbath," then it became "the sabbath," then it was simply "Sunday." First it was "the Lord's day," now it's just "the weekend," just another day. The Lord expects us to dedicate at least one day to go to his house and to study his word. Unless there is an absolute emergency, it would be far better for us to do our buying and selling some other day than on the Lord's day.

So there they were drinking from sacred chalices and praising the gods of gold and silver, brass, iron, wood, and stone. They were challenging God, and this time God took up the challenge.

That phrase "the same hour" means "suddenly" (5:5). Right

there, in the midst of their revelry, something happened that caused the music to die down, the singing to cease, and the drinking to stop. Every eye was riveted on the mysterious fingers of a man's hand writing on the wall (see Appendix 11).

3. A Great Fear (5:5-9)

Perhaps somebody said that the king was having delirium tremens. Perhaps someone said that the writing was just some hieroglyphics that had not been noticed before. But what about that eerie hand? We can be sure it happened exactly as the Bible says it did. The hand of God wrote on the wall.

Had God's finger ever written before? Yes, in the days of the exodus, in the land of Egypt, when the plagues came. The magicians of Egypt said, "This is the finger of God." Did it happen in New Testament times? Yes, "I do miracles by the finger of God. I cast out devils by the finger of God" (see Luke 11:20).

The king was alarmed. His countenance was changed, and he began to shake all over. He was in such mental anguish that he began to cry aloud. Literally it means that he shrieked.

Of what was the king so afraid? Why did he interpret the writing as a supernatural message? Why did he not interpret the writing positively to mean, "This is a sign that we are going to win against the Medes and Persians who surround us"? We always interpret things according to our consciences, don't we?

Take the case of Adam and Eve in the garden of Eden. When they sinned, the Bible said they clothed themselves with fig leaves. Then they heard the voice of the Lord God walking in the garden in the cool of the day and they ran and hid. Why were they afraid? They interpreted the visit of God according to their consciences. When Herod (who had killed John the Baptist) heard of the mighty ministry of Jesus he said, "This is John the Baptist come back from the dead." He interpreted the unknown according to his conscience.

A telephone call will scare some people to death. A knock at the door will frighten some people because they interpret everything unknown according to their consciences. It has been said that "conscience makes cowards of us all."

So the king did next what the lost always do. He sent for the wise men and asked them the meaning of the handwriting. But all the experts together could not read it. Spiritual things cannot be discerned by those who are unspiritual (1 Corinthians 2:14). Spiritual things have to be revealed by God.

This world does not have the answer to human problems. For instance, in a comprehensive and interesting feature article in *Time* magazine about the problem of alcohol, there was not a single solution. No remedy at all. Drunkenness is a sin and the only one who has the answer to the sin problem is the Lord Jesus. If you are lost, if you are an alcoholic, the only hope for you is Jesus. You need to come running to the Lord Jesus while the handwriting is still on the wall, before judgment falls.

B. Revelation (5:10-28)

The bankruptcy of the wise men of Babylon brings us to the next point. It was a night of revelation. The queen came in. This is probably a reference to the dowager queen, the grandmother of Belshazzar, the widow of King Nebuchadnezzar. There was no word for "grandfather" in this language. So when "father" is mentioned, it may mean that Belshazzar was the grandson of Nebuchadnezzar.

The queen mother took in the situation at a glance. She addressed the king: "O king, live for ever." This was an interesting statement, for he was not going to live the rest of that night. This was Belshazzar's last day on earth. His life was now in the final countdown; he had but a few hours to live.

Belshazzar was like many other people who refuse to face the fact that they are going to die. Dr. Bob Jones, Sr., once said that the thought that gripped his heart, as no other thought had gripped it, was the thought that one hundred years hence he would be somewhere in eternity.

A hundred years from now and all of us will be somewhere in eternity. We are not going to live forever. "It is appointed unto men once to die," the Bible says (Hebrews 9:27). Foolish indeed is the person who gives no regard to the affairs of eternity. Where will you be one hundred years from now if you should die tonight?

1. Daniel's Reputation (5:10-12)

The queen mother told Belshazzar about a man in that kingdom, Daniel, "in whom is the spirit of the holy gods." That was the reputation of Daniel.

God had been with Daniel all through the years of his captivity. As a young man he had made up his mind to be true to God, and God had honored that commitment. Now he was an old man. All through the many years of his life, Daniel had been faithful to God.

Probably he was now retired, and known only by reputation. But the queen mother recalled the impact that Daniel had on her deceased husband, King Nebuchadnezzar. Her description was a pagan way of saying that God was in the life of this man.

How wonderful it would be if it could be said of us that the spirit of the holy God were in us. Wouldn't it be great if people could see so much of Jesus in our lives that we would be known as people in whom God lived and through whom God worked?

Daniel had knowledge, understanding, the ability to interpret dreams, untangle hard sentences, and dissolve doubts. The word *doubts* here means "knots." Daniel could solve knotty problems. Here was a man of God who was able to answer the questions that trouble people. Up until now, before the crisis came, the king and his cronies had no time for Daniel.

Many times God's people are ignored by this world. They just need to bide their time. The crisis will come. People will want to know the answers to the riddles of life. They will look for somebody able to get in touch with God.

In the little town where I was brought up, there was an automobile dealer who had no regard for the things of God. I remember him making fun of our pastor, laughing at him and ridiculing him. He called him "that old Bible-thumping, hell-fire and brimstone preacher." Then one day this prosperous car dealer went to the doctor and found out he had terminal cancer. Whom do you think was the first person that man called to come see him?

This world may not be interested in you right now, but it may get interested in you one of these days.

2. Daniel's Separation (5:13-16).

Then, and only then, was Daniel brought in before the king. Daniel was not at the feast. He was not there when the partying was going on. He may have received an invitation (because his name was still on the list of Babylonian notables) but declined it. As you recall, Daniel dared to separate himself from the worldliness and debauchery of the kingdom in which he lived. No doubt some people would have said: "Daniel, how do you ever expect to win the devil's crowd if you don't mix with them? You don't have to drink any liquor; you can just get a soft drink. You can drink your lemonade while they drink their alcohol, and everything will be fine." But Daniel believed that God meant what He said: "Come out from among them, and be ye separate, saith the Lord" (2 Corinthians 6:17). Daniel was a separated man.

Perhaps pressure has been placed on you to go to this or that drinking party. If you decline you might offend some people, but if you go you offend the Lord. Whom are you willing to offend? If Daniel had been at that drunken feast and had compromised his testimony, do you think they would have looked to him that night? No. They wanted somebody they knew to be different, somebody in touch with God.

It must have been something to see when Daniel, that grand old man of God, came walking in. What a contrast he made to the wine-sodden, dissipated crowd. There is supposed to be a difference between God's people and the world's people.

3. Daniel's Proclamation (5:17-28)

The king began with flattery and then made a tremendous offer: "If you can read the handwriting on the wall and tell me what it means, you can be the third ruler in the kingdom." In essence he was saying, Daniel, here's your chance to get enough money to help you through your retirement years. Daniel's answer? "Give your presents and your playthings to somebody else. I am not for sale."

Daniel refused the king's bribe, but he did read the writing. Those halls had never heard a sermon like Daniel preached that night. Imagine an old-time preacher being invited by accident to one of those White House dinners and giving them an old-time sermon, preaching about sin and hell and eternity and heaven and Jesus. I admire a man who is willing to preach fearlessly, who is not intimidated by his audience. That is the kind of man Daniel was.

Daniel's proclamation began with a history lesson. He recounted the history of King Nebuchadnezzar and reminded Belshazzar of that remarkable document in chapter 4—how his grandfather had come to the realization that the true God was the God of heaven and that this God rules in the affairs of men. Then he turned on Belshazzar: "You have not learned the lesson of history."

ᴠ Somehow we never seem to read the spiritual realities behind history. The Bible says the wicked, and all the nations that forget God, shall be turned into hell. America is due for judgment. We are already under judgment. America has ridiculed the things of God. In many schools the name of Jesus cannot be mentioned. We cannot put the ten commandments on the walls of our schools. People guilty of sodomy march by the hundreds of thousands to the capital of our nation and their so-called "lifestyle" goes unquestioned by this nation. No country that turns from God can survive.

Belshazzar had failed his history test, so Daniel gave him a theology lesson. He accused him of serving gods who could not hear him when he prayed, who could not answer him in his need. He reminded Belshazzar about the God who held his breath in his hands.

The person who ignores the God whose hands control his breath is a fool. It is foolish not to become acquainted with the God of heaven.

Then Daniel gave Belshazzar a spelling lesson. He explained what was written on the wall. (See Appendix 11.)

Why could Daniel read that while nobody else could? It was his Father's handwriting!

MENE: That first word simply meant "numbered." God was saying to this wicked king, "Your number is up."

The whole universe is built on numbers. Every material substance is made up of a certain number of chemical elements. Music is built on numbers; a certain number of vibrations determine every note in the musical scale. The life of each of us is made up of numbers—months of the year, days of the month, hours of the day, minutes of the hour, seconds of the minute. The Bible says, "So teach us to number our days, that we may apply our hearts unto wisdom" (Psalm 90:12).

Your days are numbered by God. The very day we are born we begin to die. How many more days are there in your life? In mine?

What Belshazzar did not know was that his days were numbered and now they were finished. The hourglass of his life was running out. He was down to hours, not days. Soon it would no longer be hours but minutes. At that very moment the army that had been laying siege to Babylon for more than two years was about to invade the city.

TEKEL: Belshazzar had been weighed on God's scales and had come up wanting.

I once knew an old man who enjoyed talking to preachers. He thought he had it all figured out. He said to me, "Now preacher, this is the way I think it is. When you come to die there is going to be a big scale out there. On this side of the scale all of the good you have ever done will be placed. All the bad you have done will be put on that side of the scale. If the good outweighs the bad, then you will get into heaven." I would quote this verse to him: "Thou art weighed in the balances, and art found wanting."

If you think you are going to accumulate enough good on one side of the scale to get you into heaven, you don't stand a chance of getting there. When you are laid on God's scales you always come up wanting. Put America on the scales of God and America is found wanting. Put your family on the scales of God. Put your personal life on God's scales. Only one thing can balance the scales in your life to God's satisfaction and that is the blood of the Lord Jesus Christ. You need to get Jesus on the scales.

C. Condemnation (5:29-31)

PERES: The night of revelation became a night of condemnation. It was just as though the king did not hear a word Daniel had said. He was filled with debauchery, unbelief, sacrilege, and blasphemy. This faithful man of God had just told him his days were numbered, judgment was at the door, yet he went ahead and put all of the finery on Daniel as though he were going to live on forever. He was oblivious to the message of judgment that God had brought him.

1. It Came Suddenly (5:29-30)

Outside, the engineers of Cyrus the Persian had been secretly preparing a channel to divert the flow of the Euphrates River. That very night the canal was finished and the waters diverted. Swiftly the river Euphrates subsided and the army of the Medes and the Persians came stealing into Babylon along the river bed. Perhaps the guards at the gates were so drunk that they did not know what was taking place.

2. It Came Significantly (5:31)

In a matter of moments enemy troops were in the banquet room where Belshazzar was. That night he was slain; he lost his kingdom and his life. When judgment was upon him, he paid no heed to the warning of God.

Will you heed the warning of God? God is speaking to you. How many times has He spoken? How many warnings has He sent? Maybe it was a close call in an accident. Maybe it was in a service of some kind that your heart was moved by the Spirit of God. You have been putting it off. Today may be your moment of decision; your opportunity has come. You may never have another.

VI. A KING'S DISMAY (6:1-28)

This chapter stands as a monument to the keeping power of God. The Bible says that those who belong to the Lord are "kept by the power of God" until the day of salvation. God has committed himself to his children so that nothing can permanently harm them. No weapon formed against them shall prosper.

Daniel was a prophet statesman. He endured all through the years and through the changing of kingdoms. Administrations came on the scene and passed away. In the midst of epoch-making changes, Daniel prospered and survived.

D. L. Moody was one of the most remarkable Christian men of modern times. He was a lay preacher, mightily used of God to proclaim the gospel and win thousands to Jesus Christ. He established the Moody Bible Institute, which to this day is a monument of faithfulness to the word of God. He was a man of remarkable vision, energy, and Holy Ghost anointing. When D. L. Moody died, they put this text on his tombstone: "The world passes away, and the lust thereof: but he that doeth the will of God abideth for ever" (1 John 2:17).

That could have been the epitaph of Daniel's life too. The world and its lusts, its kingdoms and its powers, all passed away, but Daniel continued on.

A. The Decree of the King (6:1-9)

Darius was now over Babylon. Prophecy had been fulfilled. The Babylonian head of gold had been replaced by the silver arms of the Medes and the Persians. Darius organized the kingdom into 120 provinces with princes placed over each of them. Over those provinces and princes he installed three presidents. Over them, he put Daniel.

1. Promotion of the Prophet (6:1-3)

Daniel was selected to be prime minister, so to speak, preferred by the king, before all others. Thus, in Darius's reorganization of the former Babylonian empire Daniel played a preeminent role.

Think what that meant. Daniel was no longer a young man. We have followed Daniel all the way from the days when as a teenage boy he purposed in his heart to be true to God. Now we come to the concluding years of his life. By now he was in his nineties. At a time when a man should be slowing down, Daniel was placed as the number one minister of state, under the king. As the New Testament puts it, though the outward man was perishing, the inward man was renewed day by day. "An excellent spirit was in him." The Spirit of God was at work in the life of this man.

Wouldn't you like to be like that when you reach old age? Who wants to become cantankerous, bitter, cross, obstinate, difficult to get along with? I like the story of the eighty-year-old man who got married and bought a four-bedroom house near an elementary school. Be an optimist like that. God can use us regardless of our age. We need not be put out to pasture just because we are a little older. When a person retires from secular employment, that simply means he or she can now work fulltime for the Lord.

Some of the most remarkable people in history have been elderly. William Gladstone was prime minister of Great Britain at age eighty-three. Michelangelo did his immortal *Last Judgment* at age eighty-nine. John Wesley, the founder of Methodism, was still preaching many times a day at age eighty-eight. Thomas Edison was still inventing at age ninety. J. C. Penney was engaged in his business at ninety-five. Ronald Reagan at seventy-seven was still president of the United States, exhibiting the exuberance of his personality.

Daniel's success and prosperity, however, made him the object of jealousy. It is the strongest warrior who is the object of the enemy's arrows. It is the ripest fruit that is pecked by the birds. When people are really doing something, amounting to something, they can expect to be objects of jealousy on the part of their peers. Daniel was no exception.

2. Persecution by the Princes (6:4-5)

The green-eyed monster of jealousy reared up its head. Why were the princes jealous of Daniel? He was where they wanted to be, even though he would soon be off the scene. He had saved their nation. He had lived a pure life before them and had done nothing but good, yet they hated him. The godliness and the beauty of his life were a daily condemnation of the corruption of their lives.

Daniel became the object of an official government investigation. They sought to find some reason to charge him with wrong. They put a detective on the job. They had private investigators dig into Daniel's past life, but they could find nothing against him at all. His life was above criticism. That was a remarkable testimony.

Our lives should be like an open book. Let them put private investigators to work on us if they want to. Our lives may not be perfect and there may have been times when we disappointed people, when we have failed to be all that a Christian ought to be, but we should have no guilty secrets. We should try to be the same everywhere.

What if somebody put a private investigator to work on your life? Would he find you pious on Sunday and living inconsistently on Monday? We should so live as never to bring dishonor to the name of Jesus.

The investigators reported back and said, "We have not come up
with anything. This man Daniel has not one single thing about him
that is wrong." Then the conspirators said, "There is only one place
we can get anything on him, and that is in his spiritual life." The
Bible says, "But they could find none occasion nor fault; forasmuch
as he was faithful" (6:4). Can God write that in the books of heaven
about us?

Daniel had the reputation of loving the Lord, a reputation for
being a praying man. Daniel had religious convictions that were different. They knew that three times every day he could be seen on
his knees before an open window, praying to the God of heaven,
with his face toward Jerusalem. That was the only thing for which
they could fault him.

So, since they could find no dirt on Daniel, they decided to work
on a weakness in the character of Darius. Darius was a brilliant man,
but he knew he was a brilliant man. He was a magnificent administrator, and he knew he was a magnificent administrator. Darius was
puffed up with pride. Darius sometimes thought he was more of a
god than he was a man. So Daniel's foes said, "Let's get Darius to
sign a decree." When a decree was written into the laws of the
Medes and the Persians, it was unalterable. They therefore went to
King Darius and asked for a law that would prohibit making a
request of anyone except him for thirty days. Anyone found breaking this law would be thrown into the lions' den.

3. Pronouncement from the Palace (6:6-9)

"King Darius, god for a month"—that title appealed to his pride. He
liked the idea: to think that for thirty days nobody could pray to any
God, only to him. The decree was signed.

That was a serious matter. Think of it. Thirty days, and no sick
person could call on the God in heaven to heal. Thirty days, and no
brokenhearted mother could pray for her wayward child to come
back to the Lord. Thirty days, and no sinner could call out to the
God of heaven for forgiveness. Thirty days, and no prayer could go
up to God.

If that kind of law were passed in America, it would not bother a
great many people at all. Some people go for thirty days at a
time—they go month after month—with never a prayer to God.
There are even people who claim to be Christians who for weeks
never bow the knee to God in prayer.

How can a person be saved and never talk to his or her heavenly

Father? How can a person claim to know Jesus and never talk to him in prayer? Thirty days, and no prayer—such was the decree of the king.

B. The Devotion of the Prophet (6:10-17)

See the calmness of Daniel, of this man who had been living for the Lord all along. He had been trusting God all through the years. We can almost see him as he goes to an upstairs room in his house. We can almost hear him as he sings one of the Hebrew hymns.

If we live for Jesus when we are young, and start proving him, and go on proving him all the way through life, when we get to our latter years and crises come, we will be able to trust him then. We don't have to panic. We don't have to be afraid.

1. Commission (6:10)

Daniel had a decision to make. He had some alternatives to consider. He could have rationalized the situation. He could have said, "Thirty days is not very long. I've been praying all my life. I'll omit it for just thirty days, and then start up again afterward." Or he could have said, "It is a little presumptuous of me to open up my window for everybody to see. That is showing off, opening that window for everybody to see." Or he could have said, "I don't have to pray out loud. God can hear me whether I pray out loud or not." He could have said, "I can go down to the basement and pray there just as well as I can in front of that open window." Or he could have said, "I can pray in the privacy of my bedroom."

But he took none of those options. He went straight to his open window. He was not ashamed of the Lord. A den of lions would not shut him up or scare him.

Look at his prayer life. Look what an example of prayer he is. He had a place for prayer. He prayed toward Jerusalem. There was a passage in the Old Testament that if the Jews found themselves in captivity and if they would pray toward the promised land, toward the city of Jerusalem, and toward the temple, acknowledging their sins, then God would hear his people and restore them from captivity (2 Chronicles 6:36-39). He "kneeled upon his knees"—that's posture in prayer. (We do not have to kneel in prayer, but sometimes it helps to humble the position of the body in order to humble the heart.) He was obeying Psalm 55:17, where the psalmist said, "Evening and morning, and at noon, will I pray." He had a posture in prayer. He had a period for prayer. He had a purpose in prayer. He "prayed, and gave thanks before his God, as he did aforetime."

Let us make up our minds to be praying Christians.

> Satan trembles when he sees
> The weakest Christian on his knees.

2. Conspiracy (6:11-13)

These men found Daniel praying. We can hear them as they went running back, "We caught him praying!"

Has anybody ever caught you praying? Have your children ever caught you praying? I believe that it would make a lasting impact on them if they did.

I knew a layman in Georgia who was used mightily of God to win people to the Lord. He used to say that when he was a backslidden boy, away from God, running from the Lord, when he would come in late at night, he had to go by his parents' room to get to his own. Many a night, he said, as he would go by that room he would hear his mother praying, and he would hear her say his name. One night his mother's prayers caught up with him.

Well, they caught Daniel praying, and they ran to King Darius with the terrible news. They confronted the king with his decree: "You know what you said, O king. Now you have to throw Daniel into the den of lions."

3. Consternation (6:14-17)

Darius knew he was caught. He realized he had been duped; his pride had been his downfall. He spent all that day trying to undo his immutable law. He put all his lawyers to work to find a loophole in the law. How could Daniel be delivered?

It was all in vain. There was nothing he could do except have Daniel taken and cast into the den of lions. Was it possible that Daniel's God could deliver him in that impossible situation?

We can picture Satan gloating at Daniel's predicament: "Old man, you've made your final, fatal mistake. You have slipped through my fingers all these years, but I've got you now. You have been an extremist, you have gone too far, and now you are ending up as a late-night snack for those big cats."

C. The Deliverance of the Lord (6:18-28)

1. Misery in the Palace (6:18)

Now the narrative switches to King Darius. He spent a miserable night in the palace. He could not sleep. He passed the night fasting. Musical instruments were banned from before him. That night the king himself was in the tooth and paw of a lion he could not tame. His accusing, guilty conscience roared. All through the night he wondered what had happened to Daniel.

Early the next morning he rushed to the den, afraid that all he would hear would be the growling of the lions awaiting their breakfast, their appetites whetted by the human meal they had had during the night. Grieving, he called out to Daniel, "Did the God you serve deliver you?"

2. Miracle in the Den (6:19-23)

From down in the den of the lions a voice replied, "My God hath sent his angel, and hath shut the lions' mouths, that they have not hurt me." In heaven, the Lord had called to one of his specialist angels, his lion-taming angel. He said, "One of my servants is about to be thrown in a lions' den down there on planet Earth. This is your area of expertise. Go down there and see to it that those hungry cats do not lay a single tooth or claw on my faithful man Daniel."

I don't have any problem believing that. The Bible says it. God sent one of his angels. There was Daniel, down there in the lions' den. As he hit bottom, a lion growled. The angel said, "Don't you touch that man." Another one growled. "Shhh, let's make this a quiet night. This man needs a good night's rest. He's in his nineties!" Perhaps Daniel simply went over to a lion, said, "Hello, Leo," then lay down beside him and put his head on the now purring lion's gorgeous mane, while the lion's tail swished away the gnats and mosquitoes.

3. Meaning of the Passage (6:24-28)

You may get in a lions' den, but in God's good time He will bring you out. I was in a meeting at Boca Raton several years ago. One of the trustees of the church was very sick. The song leader got up that night and said, "Someone asked me today how our brother was getting along. I told him he is doing much, much better. They said,

'You mean he's getting well?' I said, 'No, he died today.'" You may get in the lions' den of sickness, but if you die, you will be much, much better off. God will have taken you out of the lions' den.

In the last part of this chapter, the enemies who had Daniel thrown in the lions' den were thrown in themselves, with their families. Lost person, you are going into a den of lions, too, one of these days, but there will be no God to resurrect you. You will face the judgment and there will be no Savior to plead your case for you. The decision is yours. It is either Satan, the roaring lion, or Jesus, the lion of the tribe of Judah. Which will it be? Will you be destroyed or delivered? It depends on what you do with Christ.

PART TWO

Daniel and His People's Future

Daniel 7:1–12:13

The first six chapters of Daniel are concerned with Daniel and his personal friends and are essentially historical in character. The remaining chapters are concerned with Daniel and his people's future, are mostly prophetical in character, and can be summarized in pairs: two coming dictators (7—8), two critical delays (9—10), two complete disclosures (11—12).

I. TWO COMING DICTATORS (7:1–8:27)

A. The Coming of Antichrist (7:1-28)

The two coming dictators who first loom up before us are each described as a "little horn," though the little horn of chapter 7 is not the same person as the little horn of chapter 8. In chapter 7 the person so described is antichrist; in chapter 8 the person described is Antiochus. Antichrist is associated with the final stage of the Roman empire. Antiochus is associated with the final stage of the preceding Greek empire. Antiochus has already come and gone now, so we in the twentieth century can study his story in the light of history. The antichrist has not yet come, so we are confined to prophecy for information about him.

1. Introduction to the Vision (7:1-3)

a. *When Daniel Dreamed* (7:1). This vision came to Daniel in "the first year of Belshazzar, king of Babylon." Chronologically it belongs between Daniel chapter 4, which deals with the humbling of Nebuchadnezzar, and chapter 5, which deals with the overthrow of Belshazzar. No wonder Daniel showed such contempt for the promised gifts and promotions of Belshazzar when asked by him to read the writing on the wall. Daniel had known for some time that the Babylonian empire was to be replaced on the world stage by the Medo-Persian empire. Belshazzar had no largess to bestow.

Belshazzar was the eldest son of Nabonidus and heir to the throne of Babylon. His father was emperor; he was prince regent. Nabonidus lived in virtual retirement at Tema; Belshazzar ran things from Babylon. Though Nabonidus actually reigned for seventeen years, he took little interest in his empire for the last ten of them. During this period Belshazzar was commander-in-chief of the army and, for all practical purposes, in charge of the country.

Nabonidus had come to the throne on the time-honored expedient of murdering his predecessor, the boy-king Labashi-Marduk, grandson of Nebuchadnezzar, rightful heir, and the last of his line. Belshazzar was about twenty at that time. The title "king" given to him in this chapter is more than a courtesy title. It was a real one. He was king of Babylon; his father was king of the Babylonian empire and for at least five years, at the close of the reign of Nabonidus, Belshazzar reigned along with his father as full co-regent.

The glory of Babylon had already begun to fade by the first year of Belshazzar. Powerful forces were abroad in the world. Weak rulers were on the Babylonian thrones. Nabonidus had succeeded in alienating the powerful Babylonian priesthood and, in any case, was more interested in antiquarian pursuits than in ruling an empire. Belshazzar was a profligate.

From the time of Nebuchadnezzar's death until the coming of Cyrus the Persian (when Daniel was again catapulted back on center stage) the aging prophet seems to have lived in retirement. Certainly Belshazzar did not know him. For Daniel those years were years of rest, study, meditation, and prayer.

b. *What Daniel Dreamed* (7:2-3). The vision of this chapter must have awakened memories of Daniel's youth, when he was first brought before Nebuchadnezzar to interpret that king's dream of a great image. The vision of the four great beasts and the dream of the great image had much in common.

Both visions were concerned with the course of gentile world power down through the ages, the chief difference being one of perspective. The heathen monarch envisioned such power as something glorious, something to be put on a pedestal and worshiped. The saintly Hebrew prophet saw gentile world power as something bestial and dreadful to behold. Nebuchadnezzar saw the gentile world empire as a vast human image, well-proportioned, intelligent, godlike, and splendid. The substance, the strengths, the scenarios, were varied, but the symbol was one complete whole. Daniel saw the differences between the empires, saw their true characters as seen by the eye of God. Nebuchadnezzar, the first world emperor, mostly saw things that concerned the beginning and ending of gentile world power: the head of gold, the feet and toes of the image, and the smiting stone from heaven. The saintly prophet saw all four empires but was most impressed with the final features of gentile world power, when all its abuses would come to a head in the person of a terrible antichrist. He saw, too, the essential differences between the empires, for the beasts were "diverse one from the other." Moreover, although the empires succeeded one another in the inevitable march of history, Daniel saw them all at once, the way God sees the passing events of time.

Daniel saw first *the striving winds* (7:2), or "the four winds of heaven" as they "strove upon the great sea." The geographic location is significant. In the case of Nebuchadnezzar's vision it was Babylon that was important. The world empires of scripture became world empires as they seized and held Babylon. World rule, originally intended for the Jews, in the providence of God, was now vested instead in Nebuchadnezzar, the first Babylonian king, the first king to conquer Jerusalem and hold it in bondage to gentile power.

Thus began "the times of the Gentiles" (Luke 21:24). This significant period is destined to last until the reign of the antichrist, to the end-time return of Christ, and to the establishment of the Lord's universal empire. The Lord's empire will have Jerusalem as its center. Babylon will be gone. God's original purposes will be fulfilled. Until then, all the world empires of scripture held Babylon, all were Babylonian in character, and all trod down the city of Jerusalem.

Daniel dreamed next of *the stormy waves* (7:3). The significant geographical location in Daniel's vision was "the great sea," which in the Bible refers to the Mediterranean. All the world empires of the Bible eventually, if not initially, held territory on the coastline of the Mediterranean. As gentile world power began to move steadily westward, the Mediterranean became increasingly important until, by the time we come to the fourth world empire, "the great sea" was little more, indeed, than a Roman lake.

As the Euphrates was the eastern boundary of the promised land, so the Mediterranean was its western boundary (Numbers 34:6-7; Joshua 1:4). Babylon was five or six hundred miles from this sea, but its conquests brought it to its eastern and southern shores. Persia was even farther away, but it too came to the great sea and hurled its armies and navies against Greece.

One significance of all this lies in the fact that, by the time Rome came to power, Palestine was the geographic center of the prophetic earth. The points of the compass are always given in scripture with reference to Palestine as the center. The prophetic world reached as far north as Armenia, as far south as Ethiopia, as far west as Tarshish, and as far east as China (Sinim, Isaiah 49:12). The lands beyond these boundaries are largely ignored in scripture. The prophetic scriptures contain no hint of any power outside the Middle East and the great sea dominating the area in the days of the ten kings. True, Russia will invade Israel (Ezekiel 38—39) but only to be swept away, leaving the coast clear for the antichrist to extend his power, temporarily at least, over the entire world.

So the expression "the great sea" fixes for us the predominant sphere of interest in this astonishing vision of Daniel. The "four winds of heaven" symbolize four great angel princes (Revelation 7:1-3; 9:14-15), those "principalities" of Satan, who rule over the four nations that were to seize world power. They are the "powers of the air," the forces of the evil one against which we strive today in prayer (Ephesians 6:12). They are subject to Satan (Ephesians 2:2) and through them he holds the nations of the earth in chains. Daniel saw them strive for mastery of the prophetic earth. Each in turn was able to parade his own particular wild-beast kingdom as his prize exhibit, for the prophet saw "four great beasts" come up from the sea, "diverse one from another," as a result of the striving of the four "winds."

The nations represented by the four wild beasts correspond to the nations symbolized by the four metals of the image seen by Nebuchadnezzar in his dream. The sun of the Babylonian empire of Nebuchadnezzar was now beginning to sink toward the horizon. Many years had passed. Daniel, in his teens when he interpreted Nebuchadnezzar's dream, was elderly now. The seventy-year captivity of the Jews was soon to end, though only a few of the liberated Jews would bother to return to their homeland. They had come to enjoy Babylon too much. Daniel had been poring diligently over the prophecies of scripture and was convinced that the prophecy of the seventy-year captivity was due to end. It was time for God to act. It was time, too, for new visions to be given to the aging seer. It was time also for the original revelations of the future to be enlarged, for new details to be added. God's people would need these new prophecies, for heavy seas lay ahead. Chart and compass would be needed. So Daniel dreamed and new visions were given.

2. Information in the Vision (7:4-14)

In his dream of world empire, Daniel saw three similar empires, a subsequent empire, and finally a supernatural empire.

a. *The Similar Empires He Saw* (7:4-6). The first of the similar empires was the one still in power when Daniel dreamed. He saw, first, *the supremacy of the Babylonian empire* (7:4).

The first beast, like the ones that followed, came up from the stormy sea, a symbol of the warring nations of humankind. Each of the four empires rode to power on the crest of a tidal wave of war.

The Babylonian empire had been set before Nebuchadnezzar under the symbol of gold, the richest metal. It was shown to Daniel as a lion, the king of beasts. Both symbols spoke of sovereignty and supremacy. The prophet Jeremiah had already used both symbols to depict Nebuchadnezzar, so they were familiar to Daniel.

Nebuchadnezzar's long reign began with a career of rapid *conquests* (7:4a). He fell heir to a city the roots of which reached back into antiquity. The original founder of Babylon was Nimrod (one of the Old Testament types of the antichrist), who also founded the Assyrian monarchy (Genesis 10). Babylon derived its advantage from a vast spur of tertiary rock projecting from the plain of the Syrian desert into the Mesopotamian basin. This outcropping of rock provided the city with a solid foundation. Also, it stood astride the caravan routes from Persia to the Mediterranean. It was located at the point where the Euphrates ceases to be a vast expanse and becomes a navigable river. The city already had a long history in Daniel's day. It was the fountainhead of idolatry, the home of astronomy and astrology, the "vanity fair" of the ancient world.

Nebuchadnezzar's swift and victorious conquests are depicted under the symbol of a lion with eagle's wings. The battle of Carchemish in 605 B.C., which humbled Egypt before Nebuchadnezzar, opened the way to the west. In a series of swift campaigns, Nebuchadnezzar conquered all of Syria and Palestine, invaded Egypt, and besieged and took ancient Tyre.

But that career of conquest came to an end; the eagle's wings were plucked and we see its *conversion* (7:46). Nebuchadnezzar then turned to domestic affairs. He sent armies westward to punish restless provinces, as he did Judea in 598 and 586, but war had lost its charms. The lion was made to stand on its hind legs. The savage rage of the wild beast was replaced by the heart of a mortal man.

This had all come to pass as far as Nebuchadnezzar, personally, was concerned, as Daniel well knew and had recorded in chapter 4.

The reigning emperor at the time of this vision, Nabonidus, was more interested in peaceful pursuits than in the art of war. Even Belshazzar would sit in the city of Babylon, with the Medes and Persians howling at its gates, secure in the fond illusion that he need not trouble himself. Babylon, after all, was impregnable.

The vision changed. Now the *savagery of the Persian empire* (7:5) was depicted. The second empire had none of the speed of the first one; a bear is relatively slow when compared with a lion. It is *ponderous* (7:5a) in its movements. It achieves its objectives by sheer strength and brute force, seeking to crush its victims in its embrace.

It is *powerful* (7:5b). The three ribs in the bear's mouth accurately describe the initial conquests of the Medo-Persian alliance. The three kingdoms swallowed up by the Medo-Persian empire were Lydia, Babylon, and Egypt. The empire was to devour much flesh, a characteristic of the Medo-Persian method of waging war. It never moved unless it had overwhelming force with which to crush all resistance. It was wasteful of human life.

It is *persistent* (7:5c) in seeking its prey. When Darius marched through Scythia, for instance, he mobilized nearly three quarters of a million men, not counting his fleet of six hundred ships. When Xerxes marched against Greece, he took two-and-a-half million troops with him—the movement of this mass of men looked more like a migration than an army. Even Persia's last and most pacific king brought more than half-a-million men to the battle of Issus and two years after their defeat was able to find another million men for his final battle.

It was the policy of the Persian emperors to fill up the ranks of their armies with hordes of people from conquered lands, territories stretching all the way from India to the Mediterranean. Herodotus counted and described no less than fifty-six nations conscripted by Xerxes for his march against Greece. The feats of organization, the logistics, the provisioning of such enormous hordes stagger the imagination. And these troops were swelled by camp followers of all kinds. We can see what disregard for human life was involved in these wars. "Arise, devour much flesh" was no mere rhetoric but a terrible reality of the Persian Empire.

Once again the scene changed, this time to depict the *swiftness of the Grecian empire* (7:6). The leopard, with its grace and beauty, speed and ferocity, was a fitting symbol of Alexander the Great and the Greek empire. The four wings of the leopard added to the picture, depicting the amazing speed with which the youthful Macedonian subdued the entire world. He virtually leaped across the world. His armies, though small, were strong, brave, well equipped, and brilliantly led. It took Alexander about ten years to avenge Greece on the Persians for the onslaughts of this foe in the past, for the battles of Marathon, Thermopylae, and Salamis, which the Persians had forced on the Greeks. Alexander's astounding victories, although they brought him lasting fame, did not bring him lasting fortune. He died at the height of his success.

The four heads of the leopard symbolize the dividing up of Alexander's empire by his four generals: Cassander, who took Macedon and Greece; Lysimachus, who took Asia Minor and Thrace; Seleucus, who took Syria and Upper Asia, Babylon and the east; and Ptolemy, who seized Egypt, Palestine, and Arabia. Eventually Palestine became a political football, kicked about by the heirs of Seleucus and Ptolemy. These two divisions of the Greek empire, therefore, become the subject of further prophecy (Daniel 8,11).

b. *The Subsequent Empire He Saw (7:7-8)*. The vision now turned to the next empire, one quite different from the others, and marked off in the text by a fresh introductory clause. Daniel was impressed, first, with *the horror of the Roman empire* (7:7a,b). Although never named in Daniel's prophecy, we have no difficulty identifying this empire as the Roman empire, the strongest and most enduring of all the prophetic empires.

In Nebuchadnezzar's dream this empire had been symbolized by legs of iron which took up half the total length of the image. The iron depicted the great strength of the Roman empire, iron being stronger than gold or silver or copper. The long legs revealed that the Roman empire would far outlast the others. The Babylonian empire lasted barely seventy years, the Persian empire about two hundred years, and the Greek empire about one hundred eighty years. The Roman empire lasted some five hundred years, longer than all the others put together. Indeed, in its disunited state it has continued down the centuries to this hour and now awaits its resurrection.

The same idea of iron strength is evident in Daniel's vision; the great monster he saw had iron teeth. Its power to rend and tear was great.

The first phase of this terrible empire has now already passed into history. And what a wild beast it was in its day. By 266 B.C. Rome had subjugated the entire Italian peninsula. In 264 it began its wars with its rival Carthage. Then it brought Spain beneath its sway. The great

Carthaginian general Hannibal was defeated in the battle of Zama in 202 B.C. Greece was absorbed, Macedonia was subdued, and by 1 B.C. the entire Greek peninsula was just another Roman province. The cities of Corinth and Carthage became Roman cities. Then Attalus III willed Pergamum to Rome and the remains of yet another Grecian kingdom became a Roman domain.

The empire began its eastward march. Nicomedes bequeathed Bithynia. Pompey conquered Syria, Palestine, and Jerusalem. Julius Caesar conquered Gaul. Then in 30 B.C. Egypt, the last of the surviving kingdoms of Alexander's empire, was added to the Roman empire. By A.D. 84 Britain was subdued and settled. Trajan added Davia beyond the Danube and subdued Mesopotamia and Parthia. Except for the lands beyond the Euphrates, which became Rome's eastern boundary, all these conquered lands were held by Rome with an iron grip. Magnificent roads were built to bind them to the imperial capital. Disciplined Roman troops put down revolts, and impressed Roman laws and institutions on the vanquished. Along with all this went pagan religious superstition and undeniable savagery.

Daniel caught only glimpses of this in his vision, but what he did see was terrible enough—a monster with great iron teeth and claws of brass, devouring, breaking everything in pieces, stamping what remained beneath its feet. And truly, the history of Rome was more sanguinary than even that of Persia and Greece. Foremost among its many crimes must be counted the crucifixion of the Son of God. Nor was this crime of crimes enough. Ten Caesars from Nero to Diocletian ruthlessly persecuted the church.

At that time in history, when this wild beast was raging against the church, the apostle John was given further details (Revelation 13:1-3). He saw the Roman beast in a new guise, "Like unto a leopard, and his feet as the feet of a bear, and his mouth as the mouth of a lion: and the dragon gave him his power, and his seat, and great authority."

John saw it in its resurrected form, the same but different. He saw that in its final form the Roman beast would absorb the chief feature of all the previous prophetic empires. Like Daniel, John saw the ten horns, but he also saw seven heads—a particularly lucid identification mark. He was expressly told that the seven heads were "seven mountains." In other words, the beast was identified with the city of Rome, which was built on seven hills.

In a still later vision (Revelation 17), further details were added under the symbolism of a scarlet woman. These new details were appropriate once the church age had begun. Since the church was not a subject of Old Testament revelation, these later features were concealed from Daniel.

Daniel saw, first, this beast in all its horror, the part of the vision which has now passed into history. He also saw *the horns of the Roman empire* (7:7c-8). It had *ten horns* (7:7c). The ten horns corresponded with the ten toes of Nebuchadnezzar's image. They likewise identify the beast in Daniel's vision with the beast in John's vision. In both cases the symbolism points to the same thing, the end-time reappearance of the Roman empire in a new form. Horns, in scripture, are used as a symbol of power.

What gripped and mystified Daniel, however, was something new and uncanny: the emergence of a malignant *little horn* (7:8) among the others. This little horn uprooted three of its competitors. But, stranger still (and Daniel drew special attention to it with his arresting word *behold*), this little horn had both eyes and a mouth. He gazed at it in fascinated horror, mystified by it, but he had no time to ponder its significance. The vision continued.

c. *The Supernatural Empire He Saw* (7:9-14). Up to now, the prophet's interest had been taken up with the rise and fall of these empires. Now he was to see all human power, might, and dominion fade into insignificance. His gaze was directed toward heaven. He saw *the throne* (7:9).

The rendering, "I beheld till the thrones were cast down," can be translated, "I beheld till thrones were set." The scene corresponds with the one in Revelation 4 and 5, where we have no less than seventeen references to the throne in two short chapters. Along with these recurring references to the throne of God, mention is made of the four and twenty elders and the "seats" (literally "thrones") on which they sat. The four and twenty elders are celestial beings of might and majesty who form a kind of heavenly hierarchy, a jury of angelic beings whose function it is to observe God's acts in judgment and render him obeisance for his wise and wondrous ways. Daniel saw these thrones being set in preparation for the judgment of the fourth beast and the little horn.

Central to the thrones of the angelic elders was another, on which sat "the Ancient of days" ("the Everlasting One"). His dazzling white garment proclaimed his unsullied holiness. His hair, like pure white wool, advertised his eternal being, his countless years, his experience, his majesty. His throne was like a wheeled chariot. All about him fire played—his throne was bathed in fire. Everything reminds us that "our God is a consuming fire" (Hebrews 12:29).

Adding further details centuries later, Paul said that when the time comes for the destruction of the antichrist and his empire, "the Lord Jesus shall be revealed from heaven with his mighty angels, in flaming fire taking vengeance on them that know not God" (2 Thessalonians 1:7-8).

Daniel's attention was next directed to *the throng* (7:10). A countless host hung on his words and rushed to do his bidding. An even greater multitude stood before him in adoring wonder. Heaven above is interested in the affairs of earth below. This small planet of ours was chosen by God, before its foundation, as the spot in the universe where the age-old mystery of iniquity would be localized. Here the sin question would be settled, once and for all, to God's eternal satisfaction. Our little world has assumed an importance in the universe out of all proportion to its size.

From the throngs now assembled, it is evident that the coming judgment of the fourth world empire and its diabolical prince is something not just of global or galactic interest, but of interest to all the universe. Countless multitudes on high, who tune their songs to sing our great redeemer's praise, are gathered now to watch with breathless interest the actions of God in judgment. The "little horn" was to be judged, and there is more. Along with this monster of iniquity, Satan was to be judged as well (Revelation 19:19-20:10). All heaven desires "to look into" these things.

God's judgment is not arbitrary. Records are kept, not because He needs them, but so that those about to be condemned might face the record of their own actions and words. There is not an incident, however small, however seemingly insignificant, in all the long history of humankind's tenure of this planet, that has escaped the all-seeing eye of God. It is all written down.

Historians often miss significant facts or deliberately or unwittingly distort the facts. God misses nothing. The crimes against humanity and the highhanded sins against God of which all this world's Alexanders and Caesars, Genghis Khans and Napoleons, Hitlers and Stalins, are guilty, are all part of the record. The miscarriage of justice by every unscrupulous magistrate, the untold sufferings caused by crime lords, dope kings, vice peddlers—all are written down. And the books are to be opened. Their records are detailed and complete: the place where, the time when, the manner how, the motives for, the consequences of. The books contain it all. Every thought, word, and deed of every man, woman, boy, and girl—all are written down.

God has a long account to settle with the rulers of this world. The witness for the prosecution will be the omnipotent, omniscient, omnipresent Spirit of God. Justice will be done. "Vengeance is mine; I will repay, saith the Lord" (Romans 12:19). Belshazzar discovered this not long after Daniel had this vision. Out of the sleeve of the night came the hand of God to write with awesome finality on the palace wall: "Weighed in the balances. Found wanting."

Then came *the thrill* (7:11-14). There was first the thrill of seeing *the vanquished one* (7:11-12). The doom of the fourth beast is described. The language embraces both the empire and its head, the antichrist. Modern totalitarian dictatorships have familiarized us with the identification of the state with its titular head. During the Nazi regime in Germany, Hitler was the state; in the Soviet Union, Stalin was Russia.

The fearful blasphemies of the antichrist will bring the undiluted wrath of God. The apocalypse fills in the details. The antichrist, together with his confederate, the false prophet, will be cast alive into the lake of fire (Revelation 19:20).

The antichrist's empire will be destroyed. The disintegration will begin when the eastern part breaks away and mobilizes against him. Its final demise will take place at the battle of Armageddon when Christ will come (the stone of Nebuchadnezzar's dream) and put an end to the entire evil empire.

All this, of course, assumes the resurrection of the Roman empire in the end-time. In its new form it will rule the world (7:23). Signs of that empire's revival abound today.

By the Treaty of Rome (March 25, 1957) half a dozen European nations began a new chapter in history. Instead of fighting one another, France, Belgium, West Germany, Luxembourg, Italy, and the Netherlands pledged themselves to union. Thus was born the European Economic Community (E.E.C.), usually called the Common Market, and the first stirrings toward a revival of the Roman empire. A dozen years later the Common Market had been increased to nine members (adding Great Britain, Denmark, and Ireland). A common agricultural policy was worked out; the member nations abolished all customs duties among themselves and agreed on a common customs tariff for nonmember nations. Free movement of workers between the various E.E.C. countries became law, and the universal rights of workers within the union were established. In June 1979 the E.E.C. countries had their first election and 410 members were chosen to sit in a new European Parliament. In October 1979 preferred trade status was conferred on most of the countries that had been former colonies of E.E.C. members. On January 1, 1981, Greece joined the union, bringing the number of E.E.C. countries to ten. Speculations by would-be prophets were soon squelched when that particular number was exceeded. Spain and Portugal became members, bringing the number of E.E.C. countries to a dozen. In 1979 a new European Monetary System was introduced to bind together Common Market currencies and to protect E.E.C. members against fluctuations in the U.S. dollar and the Japanese yen. A new fund was begun, to which member nations contributed twenty percent of foreign reserves toward the creation of a joint European currency denominated in *ecus* (European Currency Units).

The E.E.C. is already the world's largest trading cartel, accounting for nearly a quarter of the world's trade. The United States alone does an annual $100 billion worth of business with these countries. High level consultations between the E.E.C. and the U.S. administration are held regularly.

We can expect to see a continuing ebb and flow in the affairs of the E.E.C. Its ultimate goal is full political union. More members may join, some may amalgamate, some may drop out. Several of the present nations are difficult to deal with; some are politically unstable.

By the time Daniel's end-time prophecies come finally into focus there will be a ten-nation European union. The "little horn," the personal antichrist, will be an insignificant person to begin with. His rapid rise to power is the subject of other prophecies in Daniel, in 2 Thessalonians, and in the book of Revelation. Once he is in control of this European federation, this "revived Roman empire," as it is often called, the antichrist will steer the empire toward total world domination.

Mention is made in passing of the doom of the former beasts. One by one the empires were swallowed up. The Medo-Persian empire swallowed up the Babylonian empire which fell to it intact. Alexander's empire swallowed up the Persian empire. The Roman empire swallowed up the Greek empire. So, in a sense, the former empires had their lives prolonged "for a season." The revived Roman empire will incorporate the features of all the former empires (Revelation 13:2). Perhaps that is what is meant by the former empires having their lives prolonged "for a time."

But Daniel's greatest thrill was that of seeing *the victorious one* (7:13-14). He saw *the presentation* (7:13). When the Lord Jesus was put under oath by the high priest, "I adjure thee by the living God, that thou tell us whether thou be the Christ, the Son of God" (Matthew 26:63-64), the Lord referred him right back to Daniel 7:13-14. "Jesus saith unto him, Thou hast said: nevertheless I say unto you, Henceforth ye shall see the Son of man sitting on the right hand of power, and coming in the clouds of heaven." Thus Jesus claimed that He himself was the person referred to in these verses of Daniel. The Jewish high priest and the Sanhedrin understood quite well the Lord's claim. No one doubted that the mysterious being seen in Daniel's vision was divine. The unbelieving Jewish high priest immediately declared that Jesus had spoken blasphemy. In fact He had spoken the truth.

Everything about the scene in Daniel's vision speaks of grandeur and solemnity. Who is this, then, who comes with the clouds of heaven in a manner we associate with deity? Who is it thus led by attendant ministers of the supreme court of the universe and presented to the "Ancient of days"? Who, but Jesus! A similar scene is set before us in Revelation 5 where Jesus, as the Lord of creation and the lamb of Calvary, steps into the spotlight of eternity to receive from him who sits on the throne the title deeds of planet Earth.

This is Jesus, arrayed in the clouds of heaven. Clouds are the garments of deity. In Old Testament times, when God marched across the desert sands in the company of his people and sat enthroned among them in the holy of holies, He wrapped himself around with a pillar of cloud by day and a pillar of fire by night (Exodus 13:21). On the mount of Transfiguration, when the Lord's glory was revealed to three of his own and when Peter began to babble nonsense, a cloud overshadowed them and out of it came a voice that spoke of the deity of Christ. When the Lord stepped from the brow of Olivet to begin his journey home, when his days on earth were done, a cloud came and received him out of their sight. When in the apocalypse the Holy Spirit tells us on the very first page how it's all going to end, He says: "Behold, he cometh with clouds." This one, arrayed in the clouds of heaven, is Jesus, as He was, is, and ever will be, God the Son, uncreated, self-existing, over all, blessed for evermore.

Then comes *the proclamation* (7:14): This glorious one, who is unmistakably God, is also man. When God created Adam and placed him in the garden, He said, "Let them have dominion" (Genesis 1:26,28). When Adam fell, that dominion fell into the hands of Satan. The Lord Jesus came as man to reclaim man's lost estates and to wrest them back from the evil one. Redemption is incomplete without a millennial reign on earth when Jesus, as man, will sit on the throne of the world and reign. So runs the eternal counsel.

The world has little use for Jesus. He has been voted out of the counsels of the United Nations, though a statue of Zeus, the pagan thunderer of Olympus, adorns its vestibule. Communist nations, Hindu, Muslim, Buddhist, Shinto, and pagan lands pay no heed to him. The humanist assemblies of the world ignore him. Lip service is paid to him in some arenas but even there the term *God* is used rather than the name of Jesus, lest some be offended. It never seems to occur to anyone that they are offending both him and the God they invoke. But the day is coming when every knee shall bow and every tongue confess that Jesus Christ is Lord, to the glory of God the Father (Philippians 2:10-11). Daniel saw that coming day being celebrated in heaven.

3. Interpretation of the Vision (7:15-28)

The prophet was greatly perplexed by this vision. While some of it marched in step with Nebuchadnezzar's dream, much was new. It was the new parts that particularly disturbed him.

a. *Daniel's Puzzled Request* (7:15-16). He made no pretense about *his distress* (7:15). Daniel already knew that with the accession of Nebuchadnezzar and the downfall of Jerusalem "the times of the Gentiles" had begun. Jewish world empire would now have to wait; the Jews had failed. Theocracy and monarchy alike had ended in apostasy and disaster. He himself was an exile in Babylon and had been there for many years. Once, perhaps, he had hoped that, when the seventy years of captivity foretold by Jeremiah were over, there would be a restoration of the monarchy. Perhaps he hoped that, as a result of the Babylonian exile, there would be national repentance, a wholesale regathering of Hebrew people from all parts of the world to the ancestral homeland, a spiritual awakening, the arrival of the messiah and the establishment of a new theocratic kingdom under Christ, universal in scope and centered in Jerusalem. But Nebuchadnezzar's vision had made it clear that there were to be four gentile empires, not just the Babylonian, before the establishment of the messianic kingdom. Now this new vision seemed to lengthen out the period of the times of the gentiles almost indefinitely. Even as he received the vision the Babylonian empire was still intact.

The fact that Cyrus the Persian was now making international headlines would not have escaped Daniel. The seventy-year period of Jewish captivity must have been coming to a close. The prophet

Isaiah had foretold the coming of Cyrus some 175 years before (Isaiah 44:28—45:4). It seemed probable that the fall of Babylon could not be far distant. Even so, seventy or eighty years was a very short time for the duration of an empire. Could it be hoped that the three empires to come would be equally as brief in their tenure of world power? Probably not. The Assyrian empire had lasted twice as long as that. But even if it could be that the rise and fall of the remaining empires were to be as rapid as that of the Babylonian, it still meant that more than two centuries would have to elapse before the coming of the messiah and his kingdom. Assured as he was by the closing part of his vision (7:11-14), that the messiah's kingdom *would* come, all Daniel could see for now was delay after delay. He was greatly disturbed.

What disturbed him even more than the time element was the wild beast character of the coming kingdoms and what this would mean for the world in general and for God's people in particular. The Babylonian empire had been relatively benign. The symbolism of the lion with the plucked wings and the man's heart aptly portrayed that. But no such humane elements softened the symbolism of the coming beast empires. As for the fourth one, Daniel trembled at the thought of it. No wonder he was grieved in his spirit and plagued with troubled thoughts.

He made no pretense, either, about *his desire* (7:16). Whatever natural shyness Daniel might have had of approaching a celestial being, and confessing his human inability to grasp the significance of the vision, he overcame it at once. The desire to know far outweighed any false modesty or reluctance to admit ignorance that he might have had.

One wonders about this celestial being who was simply standing by. Who was he? How old was he? What did he look like? What kind of expression did he have on his face? What rank did he hold? What was he wearing? What did he do? Where did he live? How did he feel about these things? How much did he know? We can think of a thousand things we would like to have asked this shining one. How did it happen that he stood by? There is something provocative about such a passing statement of scripture.

Evidently one reason he stood by was to answer Daniel's questions. God had made this provision to resolve the bewilderment of his beloved seer.

b. *Daniel's Prophetic Review* (7:17-27). The angelic being took him by the hand, as it were, and guided him through the maze. The first answer of the angel was brief enough. It concerned *the five kingdoms* (7:17-18). There would be four passing kingdoms of men and the fifth permanent kingdom of the messiah. The point that interested the celestial being, and which he seems to have presumed would most interest Daniel, was the fact that eventually "the saints of the most High shall take the kingdom, and possess the kingdom for ever, even for ever and ever." He showed not the slightest interest in the rise and fall of human empires, the wars and ways of human monarchies. He saw the wonders of the great white throne, the splendors of the ancient of days, the might and majesty of the most high God, before whose throne galactic affairs, let alone global affairs, were but the affairs of a moment. Why should he be concerned about "these great beasts, which are four" and which were merely "four kings"?

The whole sad and dreary history of Cyrus the Persian and Alexander the Great and Julius Caesar and all the rest of them was of small significance, as far as this angel was concerned. All were eclipsed by the fact that once the saints of the most high took over, there would dawn at last a kingdom that would never end. He delighted in that.

Elyon, the most high, was God, not so much as the creator of the universe but as the possessor of heaven and earth. The title first occurs in Genesis 14:18. It is *Elyon* who divided the nations their inheritance. The title occurs thirty-six times.

Daniel, however, was not satisfied. For the time being, at least, he was more interested in the four beasts; particularly he was concerned about *the fourth kingdom* (7:19-26). He appealed to the angel. He wanted to know about the ferocity of the fourth beast and about its features, especially about the ten horns and the tiny horn, the horn that could see and speak. He wanted to know how it made war with the saints but could not win and how the ancient of days came and how the saints went marching in to victory.

In answering his questions, the angel told Daniel first about that fourth kingdom. And now we know that during its first phase the Roman empire never did conquer the entire earth. It held sway from the Atlantic to the Euphrates, from the north of England to the reaches of the Nile. But the Romans never did subdue the Scots or the Parthians or the wild German and Scythian tribes. They never crossed the Caucasian mountains, never subdued Armenia or penetrated beyond the Sahara. But another phase of this empire is on the way.

When the empire begins to take shape again, it will be in the form of a confederacy, a union of ten "kings," or heads of state. The shadow of this coming union lies across western Europe today, as we have seen. But the ten kings are still kings, each hanging on to a sphere and measure of sovereignty. That is the inherent weakness of the Common Market countries today. They cannot bring themselves to take the final step, surrender all individual sovereignty, accept total federation, and become one as, for instance, the United States of America. Nor will they until the antichrist, the little horn, comes.

Daniel wanted to know more about him. This "little horn" is known by various names. He is called "the Assyrian" (Isaiah 14:25), "the prince that shall come" (Daniel 9:26), the "man of sin" (2 Thessalonians 2:3), "a king of fierce countenance" (Daniel 8:23), "a vile person" (Daniel 11:21), the willful king (Daniel 11:36), "that Wicked" or "the lawless one" (2 Thessalonians 2:8), "a beast" (Revelation 13:1), "antichrist" (1 John 2:18). We are told much about him in scripture.

We note here how that person deals with the divisions that keep the ten kings from forging an effective European federation. There are three particularly uncooperative members of the Common Market, but which three they are we are not told. The antichrist, rising from obscurity to a position of great authority in the European community, will clearly see that Europe can no longer afford the luxury of simply being a collection of rival or cooperating states. He will act swiftly and decisively. The three obstructionist states will be struck down and their leaders removed. The little horn, the antichrist, will then assume control of all ten states into which the European community will be divided. He will put people of his choice in power in the three countries he humbles. They, and the other "kings," will henceforth take their orders from him.

At this point it seems he will look across the Atlantic. The western hemisphere, in many ways, is an extension of the European world. Its territories were occupied and conquered by Europeans. A majority of its peoples speak the languages of Europe. They have European institutions, customs, and culture. The predominantly Roman Catholic lands will be brought into line by the antichrist through his crafty manipulation of the Vatican (Revelation 17). Probably Canada and the United States will be forced to join a new Atlantic alliance, ruled from Rome. Possibly the antichrist will use his economic power to force cooperation, although possibly the people of North America will be quick to see the advantages of a true and powerful Atlantic alliance, even if it does mean surrendering some aspects of sovereignty. European bankers already have considerable voice in American affairs. Possibly, when he assumes supreme power, the antichrist will pull the economic rug out from under the United States and say, "Join, or else."

He will now be in control of the enormous political, economic, and military might of the west, and will be in a position to make his next move toward total world dominion. He will sign a treaty with the nation of Israel, unconditionally guaranteeing the security of that country, which will win him the applause of humanistic Jews. He will endorse the rebuilding of the Jewish temple in Jerusalem on its ancient site, which will win him the cheers of religious Jews. The Arabs will turn in impotent rage to the Soviet Union, something the antichrist has already anticipated.

What the Soviet Union will be doing while the antichrist is thus consolidating his power in the west is not known. Perhaps the Soviets will be embroiled in a border war with China or in putting down internal disorders. The antichrist will be far too pragmatic to ignore the internal economic and racial tensions of the Soviet Union. Be that as it may, the rise of the antichrist to supreme and dictatorial power in the west will be a matter of great concern to the Soviets. It is one thing for the Soviet Union to play the international bully when faced by a disunited Europe and a divided America. It will be an entirely different world picture when the west is finally united under a determined and brilliant leader who knows exactly where he is going, and who has already mapped out his moves to get there.

Thus it will be that the Soviet Union will risk all on a single throw of the dice. It will summon its satellites, and its sympathizers and will invade Israel—only to meet the disaster long ago foretold by the prophet (Ezekiel 38—39). The overnight collapse of the Soviet Union as a global superpower will leave an enormous geopolitical vacuum in the world. Before the rest of the world can recover from the shock, the armies of the antichrist will have moved. Russia and its former spheres of influence will be taken over by the beast.

The antichrist will now turn his attention to the nations of the Far East: India, China, Japan, and the rest. They will be invited to join the new world empire of the antichrist, on his terms—or else. Employing the language of the apocalypse (Revelation 13:4), they will quickly come to terms and accept membership in the empire. The antichrist will now rule the world or, as Daniel puts it, he will "devour the whole earth."

Daniel is now instructed further about *the final emperor* (7:24b-26). "He shall speak great words against the most High." As we look over the various scriptures that deal with the coming, career, and collapse of the antichrist, we get the distinct impression that his most outstanding feature is his blasphemies.

Down through the ages men have harbored hard thoughts against

God. They have said wicked things about God and his Son. They have blasphemed his Holy Spirit. In our own age, wicked persons are becoming more and more outspoken in their verbal onslaughts against God. Communists and humanists have created a climate for blasphemy. But the antichrist will outdo them all. From the recesses of his evil heart there will well up blasphemies, and like lava from an erupting volcano, they will be spewed forth. Revilings, sarcasms, falsehoods, obscenities, rantings and ravings, all will pour out of his lips. The book of Jude speaks of the apostates of the last days and mentions "all their hard speeches which ungodly sinners have spoken against him" (verse 15). The man who will inspire them will be the antichrist, the little horn with the big mouth.

He "shall wear out the saints of the most High." Millions of people will be saved after the rapture of the church (Revelation 7). They will not be in the church, of course; the church is made up of those who trust Christ between Pentecost and the rapture, people who are baptized by the Holy Spirit into the mystical body of Christ (Acts 1:4-5; 1 Corinthians 12:13). They will, however, be in the kingdom, which is why the post-rapture gospel is called "the gospel of the kingdom" (Matthew 24:14). There will be a second "Pentecost" after the rapture. What happened on the church's day of Pentecost was only a partial fulfillment of Joel's prophecy (Joel 2:28-31; Acts 2:16-21).

After the rapture God will raise up two extraordinary witnesses, armed with miraculous powers (Revelation 11). These will witness primarily to the Jews, of whom 144,000 will be saved, sealed, and sent forth to evangelize those untold millions of humankind who are still untold. They will reach "a great multitude, which no man [can] number, of all nations, and kindreds, and people, and tongues" (Revelation 7:9). It is against these late converts and against the Jewish people that the antichrist will now turn his hate and spite.

The collapse of the Soviet Union and the beast's accession to the throne of the world will mark a turning point in time. He will now have no more use for the Jews and so he will tear up his treaty with Israel, move his armies into their country, seize their temple, set up his image in the holy place, and begin a blood bath of God's people on earth. This coming universal holocaust is known as the great tribulation (Matthew 24:15-22).

He will "think to change times and laws." He will repeal the Judeo-Christian system of laws, religion, and institutions. A divine limit is set, however, on the antichrist's villainous persecution of God's people. "A time and times and the dividing of time" is an unusual formula. The plural *times* can probably be regarded as a dual, so that we could read "a time, two times, and half a time," a "time" being taken as a year. In other words, he will be allowed three-and-a-half years to carry out his evil designs. There may be a reason for the use of this unusual formula (see chart on p. 129).

Once those years have run their course, God's judgment on the antichrist will be swift. The reign of terror will be over. Gentile misrule of the earth will be terminated abruptly and on time by the personal intervention of God and the personal return of Christ.

This remarkable vision, given when Babylon was still a world power, has a fitting climax in *the fifth kingdom* (7:27). The storm clouds roll away and the sun breaks through at last. The drums of war are stilled. The messianic age dawns, an age heralded by the prophets, when men will beat their swords into plowshares, when the deserts will blossom as the rose, when the lion and the lamb will lie down together in peace, when universal peace and prosperity will be the norm, when a man will have but begun his life at the age of a hundred, when the world will be filled with the knowledge of God, as the waters now cover the sea, and when Jesus will reign from Jerusalem to earth's remotest bounds. No wonder Jesus taught us to pray: "Thy kingdom come. Thy will be done in earth, as it is in heaven."

c. *Daniel's Personal Reaction* (7:28). The angelic interpreter had finished. He had dwelt encouragingly on the final outcome. Daniel was to be comforted, but not by an angel, not by a creature of a different order. An angel could answer questions about the future and could dwell on the glorious end of the story, but he could not administer human comfort. For that, one different from an angel was required. Daniel needed, as we do, one "touched with the feelings of our infirmities."

We can picture the celestial being looking with astonishment at Daniel's face. Daniel was troubled, baffled, by the angel's words. It showed on his face. The angel could rejoice at the certain outcome. But it was not him or his people, it was not his flesh and blood, his loved ones, who were to face the stormy centuries ahead. He had no comfort to offer Daniel. His interest was academic; his point of focus was the glorious outcome. Daniel was deeply upset because such terrible tribulation lay in store for his people. He could not shrug that off.

We leave Daniel there for now, moved to the depths of his being by the scenes he had just been shown.

We can be taken up with study of prophecy, with this, that, or the other aspect of prophetic truth. The saint of God, however, feels the iron in his soul. His heart is moved, broken before God. Like Jesus weeping over Jerusalem, he cannot divorce his feelings from the facts of the troubles still to come. Daniel couldn't, nor can we.

B. The Coming of Antiochus (8:1-27)

Divine inspiration is evident in Daniel's prophecies, not only in the remarkable predictions that covered things both near and far with astonishing detail, but also in the language employed by the prophet in writing his book. In chapters 1:1–2:4 and from chapters 8–12 Daniel wrote in Hebrew; these sections deal particularly with the Hebrew people. They are concerned with the fall of Jerusalem, with the beginning of the Babylonian captivity, with the changing fortunes of the Jews down through the centuries, with events concerning Jerusalem and the temple in the onward march of history. They are particularly concerned with the coming of the antichrist, the archenemy of the Hebrew people, and with how he will possess Jerusalem, pollute the temple, and persecute the Jews. From chapters 2:5–7:28 Daniel wrote in Aramaic, a gentile language; these chapters relate specifically to the gentile world empires (see Appendix 8). Thus, beginning with Daniel 8, we have not only a change of language, we have a change of viewpoint and emphasis. From now on in this book everything will be seen from the perspective of the Hebrew people.

Even though the remaining prophecies are Jewish and all of them concern Jerusalem and the temple, there is the closest connection between these prophecies and the gentile prophecies with which Daniel has so far been occupied. He was not standing in the courtyard of the Jewish temple as he wrote, but in the court of a gentile world power. Each of the remaining prophecies, though Jewish, foreshadows the coming of that terrible emperor who will so mercilessly persecute the Jewish people. Daniel's prophecies are preeminently prophecies of the antichrist, in contrast with those of Isaiah, which are preeminently prophecies of the Christ.

As was indicated at the beginning of Part One, in Daniel 7–8 we have set before us two coming dictators, both depicted as a "little horn." As we have seen, the one in Daniel 7 prefigures the coming of the antichrist. The one in Daniel 8 prefigures the coming of Antiochus Epiphanes.

The visions of Daniel 7–8 are not the same. The scenes in Daniel 7 are wide from beginning to end; they have the entire world as a stage. The scenes of Daniel 8 begin with a fairly wide field of vision (the conflict of two world powers, Greece and Persia) but they quickly narrow until the focus is on persecution raging in the tiny land of Judah. The atmosphere of Daniel 7 is cosmopolitan and gentile, that of Daniel 8 theocratic, local, and levitical. Daniel 7 widens out until it ends with a kingdom that will last forever and will embrace all nations on earth. Daniel 8 ends with the cleansing of the temple in Jerusalem. Daniel 7 is concerned with the coming of the antichrist. Daniel 8 is concerned with a petty tyrant who, despite his blusterings and blasphemies, is only a shadow of that one. Daniel 7 is concerned ultimately with the Roman world; Daniel 8 is concerned solely with the Grecian world, particularly the Syrian segment of that world.

1. An Introduction (8:1-2)

a. *When Daniel Received This Vision* (8:1). Two years had passed since Daniel had seen the vision of the four wild beasts, so he had been given plenty of time to digest that information.

It was surely with renewed attention that he reviewed Babylonian history and studied current events both within the Babylonian empire and abroad after he received the vision of chapter 7. To a statesman-prophet of Daniel's stature, it must have been obvious that the Babylonian empire had begun to decline—how could it be otherwise with two kings on the throne? True, they were father and son, but usually a co-regency was designed to teach the son statecraft or to hold the throne in the family because of the father's incapacity to run things because of illness or age. But this co-regency existed because the rightful king was more interested in his hobbies than in his kingdom. As for the son, his youth, insolent pride, and foolish contempt for the growing power of Medo-Persia all told wise old Daniel many things.

Beyond the walls of Babylon, the Medes and Persians were marching to the drumbeat of the future. The vision of chapter 7 had confirmed for him the certain knowledge that the future lay with them.

The Babylonian empire in which he lived had always had a healthy respect for the Medes, growing at times to fear. The Medes and Babylonians had once been allies because the awesome might of Assyria had thrown them together for common defense. But when Cyaxares the Mede put down Assyria, Nabopolassar, king of Babylon, took great care not to interfere in any way with his powerful ally's operations. The same policy of handling the Medes with the greatest diplomatic caution had been followed by his son Nebuchadnezzar.

Nebuchadnezzar, however, had his own dreams of empire. To secure his kingdom he pragmatically built the virtually impregnable fortress of Babylon, and also the "Median Wall" from Sippora on the Euphrates to a site on the Tigris. When Cyrus overthrew the Medes, Nabonidus publicly rejoiced—little knowing that this same Cyrus was God's future minister of vengeance on the Babylonians. But Daniel knew.

Daniel knew, too, that Medo-Persian power was also to be overthrown; the belly and thighs of brass would replace the arms and breast of silver (chapter 2) and the leopard would destroy the bear (chapter 7). But as yet he had no real light on the identity of that leopard kingdom. Hence this vision.

b. *Where Daniel Received This Vision* (8:2). Daniel seems to have been in retirement (see Appendix 12). The dissolute young Belshazzar would have no place in his government for an elderly Jew known mostly for his godliness. It is not certain whether Daniel had retired to the fortress of Shushan or if, as seems more likely, he was carried there in his vision.

Elam was in the mountainous region of western Asia. One of its earliest kings was the famous Chedorlaomer, who invaded Palestine with his allies in the days of Abraham (Genesis 14) and who founded a great empire. It is not sure that Elam was part of the Babylonian empire, although it was certainly part of the Persian empire. Its capital city was Susa (Shushan), named after the goddess Shushinak. In time the city became the winter residence of the Persian kings. Two rivers flowed to the south and east of the city joined by a large man-made canal called the Eulaeus (the Ulai of Daniel's vision).

2. An Intimation (8:3-12)

The vision is in two parts.

a. *The Last Eastern Empire* (8:3-4). The ram was the symbol of Persia (see Appendix 14). The king wore a ram's head of gold, and rams' heads are to be seen on the sculptured pillars of Persepolis.

This ram had two horns, *powerful horns* (8:3), symbolizing the Medo-Persian alliance. The horns were high, depicting the great power of this empire. As we have noted, throughout the Old Testament a horn is a symbol of power. The two horns did not grow evenly. One power came up ahead of the other one, but the second one, in the end, was higher than the first one. Daniel would have had no difficulty in recognizing the original primacy of the Medes. But with the coming of Cyrus, the balance of power tipped decisively and permanently to Persia.

This ram had a *powerful hold* (8:4). Daniel must have been fascinated by all this, since he already knew that the Medo-Persian empire was to succeed the Babylonian empire. That point had been cleared up for him in his previous vision in which the bear had symbolized the next world power. The three ribs he had seen in the bear's mouth obviously corresponded to the threefold direction of the ram's conquests.

The Persians came from beyond the Euphrates and were an eastern power. The river Euphrates is the natural dividing line between east and west, both in scripture and in secular geography. The Persian conquests were in the directions seen by Daniel in his dream. They conquered westward, taking Babylon, Mesopotamia, Syria, and Asia Minor. They conquered northward, subduing Colchis, Armenia, Iberia, and regions around the Caspian Sea. They conquered southward, seizing Palestine, Egypt, Libya, and Ethiopia. In the days of its power no country or combination of countries could stand against the might of the Persian empire. As we have already noted in our consideration of the bear, the Persian empire overwhelmed opposing armies by massing millions of men against them and crushing them by sheer weight of numbers.

b. *The First European Empire* (8:5-12). The revelations concerning the coming Grecian empire had two points of special interest—a large horn and a little horn—and the vision concentrates on these. It must have interested Daniel to learn that the Greeks, a western people, would one day assume the mantle of world power and become God's instrument to overthrow the Medo-Persian empire which then was just coming on stage. In Daniel's day, the mad obsession of Xerxes to conquer Greece was far in the future, and so was the youthful Alexander, with his determination to avenge Greece on the Persians.

The vision begins with *the large horn* (8:5-8), which was *conspicuously big* (8:5-7). Two things about the Grecian conquests that astonish us to this day are the incredible speed with which Alexander the Great overthrew the Persian empire—he "touched not the ground," seeming to bound forward in a series of giant leaps—and the youthfulness of the all-victorious Alexander.

The goat was a symbol of Macedonia. According to tradition, Caremus, the first Macedonian king, was directed by an oracle to take a goat for a guide and build a city. This he did, following a herd of goats to Edessa which he made his capital, changing its name to Egaea (the goat city).

When Alexander was thirteen, his father, Philip of Macedon, decided that the boy needed a first-class teacher, and he chose Aristotle. Aristotle believed slavery to be natural, believed that all barbarians (non-Greeks) were slaves by nature, and believed, consequently, that it was only right that Greeks should rule over barbarians. This was heady stuff for the already ambitious Alexander.

Alexander's first task, after the death of his father, was to thrash the independent Greek city-states into submission—something he did with characteristic speed and thoroughness. Very early he displayed an uncanny trait of always being able to discern the enemy's tactics in advance. His treatment of the recalcitrant city of Thebes warned others of his ruthlessness. When he finally took the city he handed it over to wholesale butchery and debauchery and sold the survivors as slaves. The other Greek states rushed to make their peace with the terrible new king.

In early spring 334 B.C. Alexander set forth from Pella, at the head of an expeditionary force of less than fifty thousand men, to avenge Xerxes' historic invasion of Greece. He crossed the Dardanelles and fulfilled a boyhood dream. Halfway across he sacrificed a bull to Poseidon and made libation with a golden vessel, just as Xerxes had done long ago.

The Persians decided to stop the audacious Greek at the river Granicus, where they thought they had all the advantage. The battle of Granicus, however, turned out to be another victory for Alexander. The Persian king, Darius III Codomannus, could no longer mistake Alexander's intentions or his military genius.

The whole of western Asia Minor now lay open before the conqueror. Miletus fell, Halicarnassus fell, and Alexander marched through Asia Minor to the Cilician gates and on to Tarsus. Up to now, Alexander could still say he was "liberating" the Greeks, but once he was through the Cilician gates he was henceforth a conqueror.

Meanwhile, a tardy Darius had finally mobilized and marched. A decisive battle was fought at Issus, ending in the rout of the Persians. At that point Darius tried diplomacy, but Alexander was after revenge, not a truce. He answered Darius's overtures with an insulting letter to provoke him into further military action.

Alexander's march continued. Byblos and Sidon fell, but then Tyre, an important and immensely strong island-fortress, decided to hold out. Alexander's successful strategy at Tyre was not only a masterpiece of ingenuity and determination, it fulfilled an Old Testament prophecy (Ezekiel 26).

Meanwhile, Darius was building up a new army. He decided, however, to sue for peace a second time and sweetened his appeal with the offer of his daughter Stateira's hand in marriage, along with all the benefits that should accrue to a great king's son-in-law (332 B.C.). But by now Tyre had fallen, and Alexander told the Persian envoys he could take daughter and dowry himself, any time he pleased. His goal was now Persepolis and the eastern provinces.

With Tyre behind him, Alexander marched on south. At once, every coastal city along the direct route to Egypt made its submission, except Gaza, a powerful walled stronghold on the edge of the desert; Alexander took it by direct assault. On he went to Egypt, where he was welcomed as a liberator and where, on November 14, 332 B.C., the young Macedonian was crowned as pharaoh. From then on, in his own mind, Alexander was a god and the son of a god. As Egypt's new pharaoh, he decided to build a new city, Alexandria, which soon became one of the most important cities of the ancient world. Little did Daniel know of all this, or how vital a place this Greek-Egyptian city would be to the Jews of a future day.

Alexander's Egyptian holiday came to an end, and in the summer of 331 B.C. he set out across Syria for Babylon. Darius now hoped to stop his enemy at the Tigris, but first he made a final bid for peace. One of his generals, Parmenio, when acquainted with the generous terms offered, said to the youthful conqueror, "If I were Alexander, I should accept this offer," to which Alexander replied, "So should I, if I were Parmenio."

The battle of Gaugamela followed, the army of Darius was defeated and demoralized, and Alexander marched on Babylon, some three hundred miles to the south. Alexander wanted a bloodless victory and promised to honor the gods of Babylon. The glittering city on the plain opened its gates in mid-October 331 B.C. and Alexander was given a triumphal entry.

Some 375 miles southeast from Babylon was another royal city, Susa, close to the Persian Gulf. This key city capitulated and, in a symbolic act, Alexander seated himself on Darius's throne, beneath its famous golden canopy—an act that meant death for anyone other than its legitimate occupant.

But the conqueror could not stay. In spite of the bitter cold of winter he set forth again. Before him lay the strongly defended Susian Gates, which barred the way to Persepolis, a Persian holy city. The gates were forced and Alexander entered the famous city on January 31, 330 B.C. In spite of the fact that its commander had surrendered the city peacefully, Alexander ordered his troops to sack the place—but not before he himself had plundered its fabulous treasure vaults.

Alexander now headed for Ecbatana. Here he learned that his enemy had retreated and was heading for Bactria and the shores of the Caspian Sea. Wasting no time at Ecbatana, the avenging Alexander set off after Darius, hoping to catch him before he was through the Caspian Gates. But Darius managed to keep ahead. When Alexander arrived back at the Gates, news came that Darius had been deposed and was now a prisoner, and that Bessus, satrap of Bactria, had declared himself king and was calling himself Artaxerxes IV.

The wretched Darius was murdered and his former followers fled in different directions, Bessus heading for his own province of Bactria. Shortly afterward, Alexander and his weary men found the spear-riven corpse of the once all-powerful king. Alexander covered it with his own cloak and sent it back in state to Persepolis to be given a royal burial.

More campaigns followed. Those who formerly conspired with Bessus began to desert to Alexander, who by now was beginning to display an ever-increasing orientalism. To indulge his troops he provided them with luxurious feasts and parties.

Meanwhile the pursuit of Bessus continued. In the spring of 329 B.C. Alexander crossed Hinda Kush by way of the Khawak Pass. After a short rest at Drapsaca, Alexander occupied Aornus and Zariaspa, capital of Bactria, the birthplace of Zoroaster. He marched on, in spite of the growing restlessness and mutiny of his men, to the river Oxus, a formidable obstacle. Alexander eventually made his crossing at a point that was not only almost a mile wide, but also deep. There Bessus was betrayed and handed over to Alexander, who carried him back to Ecbatana, to be mutilated and publicly executed as a warning to other Median and Persian nobles.

In 327 B.C. Alexander married Roxane the daughter of Oxyartes, one of the great feudal barons who had been allied to the ambitious Bessus. After being defeated by Alexander at the famous mountain stronghold known as the Soghdian Rock, Oxyartes sided with his former foe and helped him subjugate the rest of Soghdiana.

Alexander's thirst for conquest, however, was by no means quenched by his overthrow of Persia. In the early summer of 327 B.C. he set out to conquer India. His ideas were sketchy about India, which he envisioned as a small peninsula. He knew nothing of the vast Indian subcontinent or of the vast reaches of Asia beyond, or of China beyond that. It was chiefly curiosity that drove Alexander to invade this fabled region. His ruthlessness grew. When walled towns put up resistance, he retaliated by butchering the inhabitants. One by one the cities fell—Massaga, Nysa, Aornus. The army crossed the Indus and came to Taxila, a former Persian satrapy, and the greatest city between the Indus and the Thelium. Taxila surrendered. And so it went on. Then a vision of the Ganges and the Indian ocean beckoned the conqueror.

But Alexander's troops were tired of it. Coenus, one of his faithful officers, now old and ill, tried to get through to the infatuated Alexander, saying to him: "Sir, if there is one thing a successful man should know, it is when to stop." Alexander was furious. He tried persuasion and bluff, but it was no use. It was the end. Enraged, Alexander turned back. It was the fall of 326 B.C. There were other battles. Alexander was seriously wounded by an arrow. His men could not imagine another leader and as the great conqueror hung between life and death they wondered how they would ever get back home. Alexander recovered and the long return march continued with more battles, more victories.

Alexander's character had begun to deteriorate. It has been well said that power corrupts, and absolute power corrupts absolutely. Alexander had known a long series of unbroken victories and this, combined with wealth and power and stress and a growing dependence on alcohol, was beginning to take its toll.

In 324 B.C. Alexander arrived back at Susa, where he proceeded with a plan he had been nurturing for some time: the orientalization of his empire. Alexander had long since outgrown Pella and Greece; Babylon was now the center in his thinking. Greece was only a province on the remote perimeter of his empire. His efforts to enforce integration at the upper levels of his administration resulted in the Susa mass-marriages, when nearly a hundred of his senior Macedonian officers took Persian and Median brides. Alexander himself took two.

Such is the story of the "he-goat" with the "notable" horn between its eyes. So ran the prophecy and so it was. Alexander crossed the Hellespont (the Dardanelles) in March or April of the year 334 B.C. Darius III Codomannus was left for dead after retreat upon retreat in July 330. In a bare four years the Persian ram was no more (see Appendix 15).

The notable horn was not only conspicuously big, it was *completely*

broken (8:8). With a few short words, the death of the still youthful
Alexander is chronicled. The story has often been told. It was toward
the end of May 323 B.C. Alexander was back in Babylon, preparing
to invade Arabia, but that country was spared. Death had come on
stage.

On the evening of May 29, Alexander attended a function held
in honor of his admiral, Nearchus. There was heavy drinking. After
dinner Alexander decided to go to bed but was persuaded by his
friend Medius to attend another party instead. After further drinking, someone handed Alexander a large cup of undiluted wine. He
drained it off at a draught. Then he cried out as though smitten. He
was carried off to bed and awoke the next morning with a high fever,
which he chose to ignore. He got up and later in the day ate and
drank with his friend Medius. That night his fever rose. He spent the
night in the bathhouse trying to keep cool. The next day he was
back in his bedroom playing dice.

He made a valiant effort to conduct business, discussing the
planned invasion of Arabia with his admiral and other senior officers. But it was no use. The evening of June 3 found him very ill. On
June 5 he retired to his bedroom. On June 6 he handed his ring to
Perdiccas, his senior officer, so that the everyday administration
could continue functioning smoothly. He was still lingering that
night when his Macedonian troops, crowding around his palace,
demanded to be allowed to see him. They filed past his bed endless-
ly, taking leave of the man who had led them so far. Early in the
morning of June 10, 323 B.C., he died, cut off in his youth and at the
pinnacle of success. The great horn was broken.

Few mourned his passing. He had led his troops over twenty thousand miles of war and bloodshed, leaving behind a long trail of
burned and ravaged cities, mountains of dead men, rivers of tears.
He savagely subdued cities and kingdoms, but as soon as he was safely on his way, insurrection broke out behind him. When he died, his
empire descended at once into anarchy. His wife Roxane and his
thirteen-year-old son were murdered in 310 B.C., so that no direct
descendent remained.

Rumor persisted that Alexander had been poisoned, that his old
tutor, Aristotle, had prepared the brew, that Cassander brought it
to Babylon, and that it was administered by Iolaus, the king's cup-
bearer. It may have been so. It may have been that he died from
malaria, aggravated by his drunkenness. It may have been that he
never fully recovered from the terrible wound he had received in
India. In any case, the tyrant was dead.

So what would happen to his vast empire? On the night of his death, a group of his friends asked him who should have his kingdom. Alexander was beyond caring. "The strongest," he whispered. His last words are said to have been these: "I foresee a great funeral contest over me." So, indeed, there was.

The rest of the prophecy came true too. The notable horn was replaced by four notable horns. With the death of Alexander, the central power was broken and there followed a period of chaos. His empire lasted for only a few years as the Diadochi, "his successors," fought each other for power. The long wars of succession resulted in the division of the empire into four parts by his leading generals. Cassander took Macedon, Thessaly, and Greece. Lysimachus took Thrace, Western Bithynia, Lesser Phrygia, Mysia, and Lydia, the Meander being the boundary. These two pass off the sacred page, the prophetic focus being Palestine and its neighbors. Ptolemy took Egypt, Cyrene, and Cyprus. Seleucus took Syria, Babylonia, and Media. These two, Ptolemy and Seleucus, became the king of the south and the king of the north respectively in the prophecies of Daniel 11.

The prophecy of the ram and the he-goat turns now to *the little horn* (8:9-12). The prophecy ignores the intervening years from Seleucus I Nicator (311 B.C.) to the coming of Antiochus IV Epiphanes (178 B.C.) and concentrates on him. Much that happened in the intervening period of over a century is covered in Daniel 11. Antiochus Epiphanes is one of the supreme types of the coming antichrist in scripture and in history. That is why so much space is given to him in the prophecies of Daniel and why here, in Daniel 8, the verses describing Antiochus not only describe him but leap the centuries and also describe the age and wiles of the antichrist (see Appendix 13).

The "little horn," then, primarily is Antiochus IV Epiphanes who ruled Syria from 178 B.C. to 164 B.C. and whose despicable career is of interest because of what he did to the land and people of Israel.

We note first, his *battles* (8:9). The first thing to impress us about this coming dictator (this was all far in the future when Daniel wrote) is his littleness.

Here we have one of those remarkable evidences of scripture that each word in the sacred original text was "God breathed," for the words for "little horn" in chapters 7 and 8 are not equivalents. This careful choice of words is designed to underline the fact that the two little horns are not the same. The coming world dictator depicted in chapter 7 is described by an aramaic word that can be translated "a horn, a little one" (7:8). The vile dictator depicted in chapter 8 is described by a Hebrew word that can mean "a horn less than little" or "a horn from littleness" (arising from a small beginning), pointing to his development from insignificant beginnings.

The "little horn" in chapter 7 (the antichrist) will arise out of the Roman world. Let us pause, for a moment, to outline the differences between the Roman world and the Greek world. The Roman world was a world of martial might and rigidly imposed universal law. Rome bent everything to its will. Rome borrowed from others but crushed all that stood in its way. The heroes of the Roman world were its engineers, statesmen, conquerors. Rome ruled the world with a rod of iron, glorying in its ability to subdue. Yet all this was married to a savage temper. It crucified men without mercy. It gathered for its holidays to witness scenes of carnage and cruelty in its Colosseum. The more gory the scene, the greater the glee.

The Greek world was a world of intellectual splendor. The names that made Greek history were those of men like Aesop and his fables; of Pythagoras, who formulated the multiplication table and the theorem about right-angle triangles; of Pericles, who ushered in the golden age of Greek learning; of Herodotus, the "father of history"; of the playwrights Euripides, Sophocles, Aristophanes; of Hippocrates, the "father of medicine"; of Plato, whose philosophies have been resurrected in our own day; of Aristotle, the tutor of Alexander; of Zeno, the Stoic; of Euclid, the mathematician; of Aristarchus, who declared that the earth moves around the sun; of Eratosthenes, who calculated the earth's circumference; of Archimedes, the old-world physicist; and of Hipparchus, who invented trigonometry and calculated the earth's circumference; of Archimedes, the old-world physicist; and of Hipparchus, who invented trigonometry and calculated the lunar month. These were the immortal names of Greece. But all this intellectual prowess was married to perfidy in contract, to gross immorality, and to abject superstition—witness the gods of Mount Olympus, who delighted in lust, lawlessness, and every kind of decadence and depravity.

No, we must not make the mistake of equating the two little horns as though they were one and the same person, when the Holy Spirit uses different words to distinguish between them. Historically, the little horn of chapter 8, representing Antiochus, comes first. It rises out of the Greek world, a world characterized by craftiness, religious superstition, and moral turpitude. The little horn of Greece is made dangerous by his lust for power and the opportunity to do great harm.

Antichrist comes last, rising at the endtimes, out of the Roman world. He will be characterized by Greek brilliance of mind and moral turpitude, but also by Roman determination and savagery.

No, the two are not the same, but the one is a type or picture of the other. The character and career of Antiochus Epiphanes illustrate the character and career of the antichrist. We must recognize that fact. It explains why parts of the text of Daniel 8, which describe the little horn of Greece (Antiochus), can often be carried over to describe the Roman antichrist as well.

The horn out of which the little horn sprouted was the Syrian kingdom of Seleucus. We now know that the "little horn" is Antiochus Epiphanes ("God manifest," or "the illustrious one"). He was the younger son of Antiochus III (the Great) whose story is prophetically told in Daniel 11. The Romans, who had curbed the ambitions of the elder Antiochus at the battle of Magnesia, carried off the younger Antiochus to Rome as a hostage for his father's good behavior. He remained in exile at Rome for fourteen years. When Antiochus III was murdered, his oldest son, Seleucus Philopator, took the Syrian throne. The new king decided to send his own son Demetrius to Rome in exchange for his brother Antiochus. While Antiochus was on his way to Damascus, however, Seleucus was murdered by Heliodorus, the Syrian treasurer, who seized the throne for himself. Antiochus was undaunted. He persuaded Eumenes, king of Pergamum, to help him, overthrew the usurper, and finally seated himself on the throne.

Thus the prophecy was fulfilled. Who would have thought that Antiochus Epiphanes, a younger brother, exiled far from home, in spite of court intrigues and a palace coup, would have become king?

Daniel said that he "waxed exceeding great, toward the south, and toward the east, and toward the pleasant land." And so he did. His conquests were southward to Egypt and eastward toward Babylonia and Persia but especially toward Palestine, described here as "the pleasant land." This phrase conveys God's own thought about the country of Israel. The expression can be rendered "the glory of gems." Only Daniel and Ezekiel (20:6,15), both of whom were exiles, used this term to depict the Holy Land. The term tells us how precious that land is to God and how serious a matter it is for other peoples to seize it or despoil it.

The vision turns next to "the little horn's" *blasphemies* (8:10-12). First, the little horn attacks *the saints* (8:10). The "host of heaven" is a poetical description of God's chosen people; "the stars" are prominent individuals among them. The obsession of Antiochus

Epiphanes to force all people throughout his empire to worship the Olympian Zeus is now a fact of history. Here, remember, it was a detail of prophecy. Antiochus was such a monomaniac about this that his subjects called him Antiochus Epimanes ("the mad") behind his back. His pagan subjects would have no great problem in worshiping Zeus, but not so the majority of the Jews. They had returned from Babylon forever cured of idolatry, and they fiercely resisted the attempts of Antiochus Epiphanes to force his pagan religion on them. The more they resisted, the more determined he became to break their resistance. He persecuted the Jews unmercifully—but more will be said about that when we come to Daniel 11 where this vile person's career is given in greater detail.

He attacks also *the sanctuary* (8:11-12a). Antiochus Epiphanes was not content with attacking the people of God. He assailed the creator of the universe himself ("the prince of the host").

This passage (8:11-12a) is probably a parenthesis. More details are given about the desecration of the temple by Antiochus Epiphanes in chapter 11. Here we are told that the outrages performed by the mad Syrian king were allowed "because of transgression." A portion of the Jews was already apostate. They were rationalizing the Jewish religion, embracing Hellenism and adopting Greek ways and patterns of thought. These Jews admired Antiochus.

After his Egyptian campaign, Antiochus plundered the temple in Jerusalem and with great ferocity massacred Jews who resisted him. This initial persecution, however, was but a passing storm. He came back later, defiled the temple, and committed terrible sacrileges that made his name a byword among the Jews. The evil high priest Jason, who wanted to snatch the high priesthood away from his brother Oniaswas, was party to much of this. To gain his ends he treacherously opened the gates of Jerusalem to Antiochus and then participated in the slaughter of those loyal to his brother (see Appendix 13).

Moreover, Antiochus attacked *the scriptures* (8:12b). The Jews who had returned from Babylon, whatever other faults they had, treasured their scriptures. They preserved them, copied them with care, expounded them, wrote commentaries on them. Antiochus recognized at once that the source from which the Jews derived their strength was their scriptures and the religion based on those scriptures. He sought to uproot both, and he prospered.

It seemed that nothing could stop him. Antiochus Epiphanes made many martyrs. His cruelties were terrible. God allowed him to go from one atrocity to another.

God's permissive will is a source of mystery, especially when evil seems to ride triumphant and roughshod over God's people. We wonder why God remains silent. It is all part of that dark "mystery of iniquity" which, in the inscrutable wisdom of God, is being brought to a head on this planet. Nor is it over yet. All these factors, in the equation of sin, must be brought down to the bottom line in that balance sheet of wickedness yet to be drawn up by antichrist himself.

3. An Interruption (8:13-19)

Much of this was new to Daniel. He knew from the dream of Nebuchadnezzar about the four world empires to come, but that dream had focused chiefly on the first empire, Babylon ("Thou art this head of gold") and the final empire, unnamed and unknown. His own vision of the four wild beasts had confirmed the dream of Nebuchadnezzar. Doubtless he was able to identify the Medo-Persian bear. It must have been obvious to a statesman of Daniel's stature that Babylon's successor was to be Persia. But his vision of the four beasts had concentrated on the still distant Roman empire. The vision of the ram and he-goat clarified things about the two middle empires. It must have been a surprise to learn that the Persian empire was eventually to have such a fall at the hands of a western power.

Any informed student of world affairs in Nebuchadnezzar's court, or in the Persian world, knew about the Greeks. No merely human political acumen, however, could have led an observer in Daniel's day to conclude that the Greek peninsula and islands would spawn a world empire. The Greek world was a fiercely independent world. Its peoples were seafarers and traders rivaling the Phoenicians, but the country itself was no more than a collection of mutually suspicious city-states.

As for "the little horn," one cannot be surprised if Daniel was confused by that. Was it the same as the little horn of his previous vision? If so, how could it arise from the third empire *and* the fourth empire? And why did the inspiring Spirit of God use different words to describe them? If *we* need help unraveling the mysteries of these visions, with all history and a completed canon of scripture to help us, how much more did Daniel. So we have an interruption in which Daniel is partially enlightened.

a. *What Was Overheard by Daniel* (8:13-14). Angels, too, have questions about the mystery of iniquity. It was one of the heavenly hierarchy,

Lucifer, who introduced sin into the universe. Sin did not begin on earth; it began in heaven. Although the planet Earth has become the chief theater of operations, sin has cosmic significance. Angels are involved. An untold number of them help Satan rule behind the scenes and keep this world in thrall.

A certain saint (literally, "a certain unnamed one"), an angelic being, as we infer from 8:16, was seen by Daniel talking to another angel, and in his vision the prophet overheard the conversation. The questioner was not surprised that Jerusalem and the temple should be trodden underfoot and defiled. Sin and apostasy, running rampant among the Jews, would account for God's permitting his displeasure thus to be shown. But if that did not surprise the angels, it must have surprised and horrified Daniel. The Jews were even then, at the time of this vision, being punished by God for their sins by a seventy-year captivity in Babylon. That captivity had not yet ended. Was the entire cycle to be repeated all over again? Would the Jews learn nothing from the destruction of Jerusalem and the temple and from their exile from the promised land? We can imagine with what eager attention Daniel listened to this conversation. He, too, was keenly interested in that question, "How long?"

The expression "that certain saint" may be retained, perhaps, as a proper name meaning "the wonderful one" or "the wonderful numberer" (See Judges 13:17-18. The word *secret* means "wonderful." Cp. Psalm 139:6,17-18.) "That certain saint" or "that unnamed one" or "the wonderful numberer" (as the case may be) was keenly interested in the number of days involved in all this. "How long?" he said.

The answer came at once. A time limit was set. Beyond that, the evil tormentor of the Jewish people would not be permitted to go. Long before that one was born, God had drawn the line. All kinds of suggestions have been made to explain this period of 2,300 days. One is that it began when Menelaus bribed Antiochus Epiphanes to appoint him high priest in 171 B.C. and that it expired when Judas Maccabeus cleansed the temple in 165 B.C. Doubtless the exact period had its significance to those living in the land in those terrible times. Since the vision of the little horn carries forward to the antichrist, it might well be that the 2,300 days has ultimate reference to the antichrist.

The various time periods mentioned in Daniel present us with one of the difficult features of the book. Let us tabulate the various overlapping visions of the book and then look more closely at the time periods involved.

DANIEL 7	DANIEL 8	DANIEL 9	DANIEL 11	DANIEL 12
A little horn (vv. 8, 20-21, 24-26)	The little horn (vv. 9-12, 23-25)		A vile person (vv. 21-30)	
	The daily sacrifice taken away (vv. 11-13)	The daily sacrifice taken away (v. 27)	The daily sacrifice taken away (v. 31)	The daily sacrifice taken away (v. 11)
	Abomination of desolation set up (v. 13)	Abomination of desolation set up (v. 27)	Abomination of desolation set up (v. 31)	Abomination of desolation set up (v. 11)
The midst of the week (1,260 days) (v. 25)	The 2,300 days (v. 14)	The midst of the week (1,260 days) (v. 27)		The midst of the week (1,260 days 1,290 days 1,335 days) (vv. 7, 11-12)
	The sanctuary cleansed (v. 14)	The anointing of the holy of holies (v. 24)		
The end (v. 26)	The time of the end (vv. 17, 19)	The end (v. 25)	The time of the end (v. 40)	The time of the end (vv. 4, 9, 13)

It will be observed that there are repeated references to the little horn, to the daily sacrifice, to the abomination of desolation, to various time periods, to the sanctuary, and to the time of the end. References in Daniel to the coming reign of antichrist are many and varied. No period of prophecy is more significant.

As for the time periods, it will be helpful, when they occur, to refer to the following chart. In summary, we observe that the main time period is the seven-year treaty which the antichrist will sign with the nation of Israel, the seventieth "week" of Daniel 9:25. If we translate this "week" into actual days it is 2,520 days (360 x 7 = 2,520). (The Jews used a lunar calendar in which a month was thirty days and a year was 360 days. This is the calendar used in Bible datings.) The antichrist will break this treaty "in the midst of the week." This breaks the period into two equal periods of 1,260 days (360 x 3 ½). During the first half of this "week" the antichrist will consolidate his power and extend his rule over the entire earth. The second half of the "week" (variously denominated as "a time and times and the dividing of time," 1,260 days and 42 months) is of supreme prophetic interest. In Daniel 12, two other time periods are mentioned, both extending beyond the termination of the main 1,260-day period, which brings to an end the antichrist's rule.

The period of interest to us in Daniel 8 is that of 2,300 days as it relates to the antichrist. A glance at the chart shows that it is 220 days short of the entire seven-year, final-week, 2,520-day period. The question is, why is the 220-day period important? What happens 220 days after the antichrist signs his treaty with Israel? About seven months and some days after the signing of the treaty with Israel something happens to the antichrist of such significance that this period of 2,300 days is dated from it.

We learn elsewhere that two events of the first magnitude happen during the antichrist's reign. Russia will make its disastrous invasion of the state of Israel, which will result in the catastrophic demise of the Soviet empire and the opening of the path to world dominion for the antichrist. It is likely, however, that this event will take place more toward the end of the first three-and-a-half- year period.

The other event is the assassination of the antichrist and his return from the dead (Revelation 17:8). No clue is given as to when this dramatic event takes place. But it could, perhaps, be the starting point of this mysterious period of 2,300 days.

At the end of the period the sanctuary will be cleansed. The Lord will come from heaven and will personally superintend the building of Ezekiel's new temple.

◄——— THE ANTICHRIST'S SEVEN-YEAR TREATY WITH ISRAEL ———►

3½ YEARS 1,260 DAYS "TIME, TIMES, AND AN HALF" 42 MONTHS	3½ YEARS 1,260 DAYS
THE GREAT TRIBULATION	THE TREATY BROKEN

1. ◄—— "TIME, TIMES, AND AN HALF" ——►
        (7:25)

2. ◄———————— 2,300 DAYS ————————►
              (8:14)

3. ◄———————— 2,520 DAYS ————————►
              (9:24)

4. ◄—— "TIME, TIMES, AND AN HALF" ——
        (12:7)

5. ◄———— 1,290 DAYS ————
          (12:11)

6. ◄———— 1,335 DAYS ————
          (12:12)

At the end of the period the sanctuary will be cleansed. The Lord will come from heaven and will personally superintend the building of Ezekiel's new temple.

b. *What Was Overwhelming to Daniel* (8:15-19). First, there was *the man* (8:15-16). The word for "man" here signifies a mighty man. The "man" is Gabriel, the herald angel, who has assumed human form for the occasion. Gabriel is the first of two angels to be actually named in scripture (Daniel 9:21; Luke 1:19,26). The other is Michael (Daniel 10:13,21; 12:1; Jude 9; Revelation 12:7).

Then there was *the messenger* (8:17-19). The near approach of the angelic messenger, the mighty Gabriel himself, struck terror into Daniel's heart. Holy man of God that he was, beloved of God as he was, he trembled when that shining one, though to all appearance a man, drew near to him. Perhaps he was all of a sudden aware of the vast distance between relative holiness and complete holiness. Or perhaps this close contact with a creature of another, higher kind overwhelmed him. The gulf between an unsullied angel, who stood in the immediate presence of God, and a mortal man, tainted by sin, caused Daniel to fall on his face.

After the day of Pentecost, fear of angels seems to have been banished from the hearts of God's redeemed. John could walk in scenes of splendor, approach angels with calm and poise, talk to them without embarrassment or reserve in the apocalypse. Those now in Christ are seated with him on high, "far above principalities and powers."

The angel Gabriel had not come to terrorize but to teach. The vision assuredly concerned Greece and Persia and Antiochus Epiphanes, but the ultimate focus of it all was the endtime.

Daniel, however, was still overcome with terror. He was "in a deep sleep," and the angel's instruction was being wasted. An unconscious man cannot take anything in. The angel touched him, took hold of him, and stood him on his feet—the proper posture for a man. He repeated, "Behold, I will make thee know what shall be in the last end of the indignation: for at the time appointed it shall be."

"The indignation" is another expression for God's wrath. We learn from the apocalypse that God's wrath will be poured out from bowls (vials) at the end of the judgment age when the antichrist will be at the zenith of his power. The bowls of wrath will break his stranglehold on the earth, the earlier bowls being directed against the seat of his power and the later ones designed to prepare the way for Armageddon (Revelation 16). This is another indication that Antiochus Epiphanes does not, in himself, exhaust the vision of the chapter.

4. An Interpretation (8:20-26)

a. *The Commencement* (8:20-22). Daniel was now plainly told that the ram symbolized the Medo-Persian empire, something he probably already suspected, and that the he-goat represented the Greek empire. The great horn, he was told, "is the first king," the man we now know as Alexander the Great. The breaking of the great horn would result in a fourfold division of the empire, but none of those who seized power would wield the authority of the king who founded the empire. This was all preliminary. Doubtless it was of considerable interest to Daniel as it is to us.

b. *The Consummation* (8:23-25). There is no doubt that the initial interpretation points to Antiochus Epiphanes. He was a king of "fierce" (bold) countenance—the expression is that used of a harlot (Proverbs 7:13) who is brazen and shameless. He was a master of deception. He did not come to power until the end of the Syrian period. He did perform the kinds of things the angel says. So, although we can apply these verses to Antiochus Epiphanes in a general way, the more specific application is to the antichrist.

The angel drew attention to *the coming of a diabolical prince* (8:23-25a). We note first that the antichrist will be a *deceiver* (8:23). As a politician, the antichrist will be the ultimate master of deceit, "full of all deceivableness," the idiom of whose language will be the lie. He will be full of Machiavellian cunning, willing to use every trick to persuade a gullible world that he is the answer to its needs.

But there is more to it than that. He will be an initiate into the deep things of Satan. The Hebrew noun for "dark sentences" is used of Samson's riddle (Judges 14:12) and of the "hard questions" put to Solomon by the Queen of Sheba. The antichrist will have access to forbidden secrets, to the lore of occultists and initiates of eastern religions. One of the reasons why the world will be dazzled by this coming antichrist will be his mastery of satanic mysteries. As in Christ are to be found "all the treasures of wisdom and knowledge" (Colossians 2:3), so in antichrist men will find a "revealer of secrets." He will have Satan's knowledge at his disposal. He will teach men how to exploit unsuspected powers, untapped secrets of nature, the depths of evil potential within the human soul. He will show them marvelous new ways to do things—at a price. But woe betide those who trust him, who follow where he leads. He will lead people into the dark coils of Satan, his lord and his god.

He will be a *destroyer* (8:24). His power will be derived from Satan. When Satan tempted Christ he offered him the kingdoms, the power (delegated authority, power subject to another power), and the glory (Luke 4:5-8) if He would fall down and worship him. What the Lord Jesus instantly refused, the antichrist will promptly accept. Satan will be his mentor, the source of his diabolical cleverness and cunning, the one who gives him the power to work miracles and the authority to rule the world.

He "shall prosper." At first everything he does will succeed. The Holy Spirit will no longer be restraining, so he will have a clear field before him. People will adulate him. He will seem to have the answers to all this world's ills. Nations will put their sovereignty into his hands, and those who resist will be swept into oblivion. He will "destroy wonderfully," until at last, seeing the wreckage and carnage he brings on his foes, the remaining nations will cry, "Who is like unto the beast? who is able to make war with him?" (Revelation 13:4).

But the secret goal in all this will be the destruction of the nation of Israel, the Jewish people, and those who, through the ministry of the two witnesses and the 144,000 witnesses, will have accepted Christ as Savior and king and who will be eagerly anticipating his coming kingdom. As with Antiochus, so with antichrist. Satan hates the people of God. He has had his dupes down through the centuries who have created havoc and unleashed the dogs of war against Jew and Christian alike. The antichrist will surpass them all. He will be Satan's ultimate tool to attempt the total extermination of the Jews and of those gentiles who profess faith in God.

The Jews will seem a feeble folk to the citizens of this last world empire, an easy target for their hate. This world has always detested Jews; antisemitism is present in all gentile societies. This world has always hated true believers in the Lord Jesus Christ. Satan sees to that, and this world has persecuted them as well through the ages.

This last outbreak of terror, inspired by Satan, instigated by the false prophet, and instituted by the antichrist, will be a blood bath surpassing all those of history. The victims will have the world against them. They will be "tortured, not accepting deliverance," they will have a "trial of cruel mockings and scourgings, yea, moreover, of bonds and imprisonment." They will be stoned and sawn asunder, tempted and slain with the sword. They will wander about "in sheep-skins and goatskins; being destitute, afflicted, tormented; (Of whom the world was not worthy)." They will wander "in deserts, and in mountains, and in dens and caves of the earth" (Hebrews 11:35-38). They will seem defenseless before their tormentors.

But God calls them "the mighty and the holy people" (8:24). Literally, they are "the mighty ones." They are "the saints of the most High" (7:18). In them Satan will see his failure and his doom.

All this will happen "when the transgressors are come to the full" (8:23). They have not come to the full yet. God will not allow Satan to have his way yet. The God who could wait four hundred years in the days of Abraham, because "the iniquity of the Amorites is not yet full" (Genesis 15:13-16), can wait a little longer now. Already the signs are multiplying in our own day that wickedness and lawlessness are on the rise. In the past, God has sent revival to stem the tide. This time it seems he will send rapture to remove the saints. The salt will be gone and the total corruption of the world will be rapid.

He will be a *defamer* (8:25a). Then Satan's man will come. His successes will go to his head. His blasphemies against God and his defilement of the rebuilt temple will already be a matter of record when the stage is set for the battle of Armageddon (Revelation 13:11-15; 16:12-21; 2 Thessalonians 2:3-4). The battle of Armageddon appears to begin as a confrontation between east and west; it concludes as a confrontation between earth and heaven. The antichrist himself will now be deceived by Satan and will actually think he can successfully oppose the second person of the godhead. He will be Satan's supreme dupe.

In a brief statement, Gabriel described *the collapse of this diabolical prince* (8:25b). More details about the swift doom of the antichrist are given in Isaiah 11:4; 2 Thessalonians 2:8; and Revelation 19:19-20. As far as Antiochus Epiphanes was concerned, his death was fairly sudden. He died from complications of ulcers and worms.

c. *The Commandment* (8:26). Gabriel added his certification to the truth of this vision. Then Daniel was told to seal up the vision because there was no way its full import could have been understood by people in his day. It became clearer in the days of Antiochus Epiphanes. It is clearer still today. It will be fully understood in the days of antichrist. In the meantime, it is true.

5. An Introspection (8:27)

Daniel, exhausted and overcome by the ordeal of all this, was ill for some days. The strain left its mark on the old prophet. More than that, the new revelations concerning the future sufferings of his beloved people upset him.

Daniel, however, was not the kind of man to let spiritual things interfere with secular responsibilities. He recovered from his illness and gave his mind to business. We do not know what position Daniel held in the government at that time. Whatever it was, he undoubtedly gave it his diligent attention, keeping his spiritual problems to himself.

As the angel warned, nobody understood the vision. Daniel himself was astonished at it. At a later date God added further details to this vision (chapter 11) but, until then, Daniel got on with his work and pondered these things in his heart.

II. Two Critical Delays (9:1–10:21)

The aged prophet had received two disturbing visions. The first had left him troubled in mind; the second had left him physically ill. The first was concerned with the course of gentile history, climaxing in the revival of the Roman empire and in the coming of a royal tyrant we recognize as antichrist. The second was closer at hand and concerned the course of Greek history, climaxing in the rise of Syrian power and in the coming of a royal terrorist we recognize as Antiochus. When Daniel received the first vision, the empire of Babylon was still intact. Belshazzar, its last king, was installed in the capital city. It was his first year. The empire had ten more years to go. When Daniel received the second vision, it was Belshazzar's third year. He had seven more years to reign. The fall of Babylon was still a future event.

During this week of years, Daniel seems to have been living a contemplative life. His visions required time for Bible study, meditation, and prayer in order to be assimilated. Remember, Daniel did not have the help of history to enlighten him. We can look back today and see how much of the prophetic truth in the book of Daniel has already come to pass. We have the wisdom of hindsight, but Daniel did not have that. Nor could he go to his library and pull down a dozen books to help him in his prophetic studies. It all took time—long hours, days, weeks, of waiting on God. Then, in the first year of Darius, light dawned.

A. The Seventy Weeks (9:1-27)

In Daniel 9–10 we have two critical delays. In chapter 9 we have a delay centering around the seventy weeks. In chapter 10 the delay centers around the secret war.

Chapter 9 revolves around two focal points. First, Daniel believed an old prophecy. Then Daniel received a new prophecy. In between, the aged seer poured out his heart in prayer.

1. Daniel Believed an Old Prophecy (9:1-19)

a. *A Word of Prophecy* (9:1-2). We begin with that old prophecy, the prophecy of the seventy years.

The prophecy concerned a *time* (9:1). It was the year 538 B.C. Daniel had been carried into captivity at the time of the first Babylonian invasion of Judah in the year 605 B.C. He had been in Babylon for almost as long as the empire itself had lasted. Cyrus the Persian had taken Babylon just the year before the events recorded in this chapter. Darius the Median, in control of the capital, was the vice-regent of the victorious emperor.

The prophecy was also concerned with a *text* (9:2). The "books" were the Old Testament scriptures, especially the writings of the prophet Jeremiah.

Years before the Babylonian invasion, Jeremiah had warned the Jews: "And this whole land shall be a desolation, and an astonishment; and these nations [i.e., Judah and its neighbors] shall serve the king of Babylon seventy years" (Jeremiah 25:11). The false prophets, who abounded in the land in those days, laughed at Jeremiah. Their lying prophecies encouraged people to believe that the captivity would not last long at all. In response, Jeremiah wrote to those already in exile in Babylon, telling them they might as well settle down there. It would be a long time before they would be free to leave.

> Thus saith the Lord of hosts, the God of Israel . . . Build ye houses, and dwell in them; and plant gardens, and eat the fruit of them; take ye wives, and beget sons and daughters; and take wives for your sons, and give your daughters to husbands, that they may bear sons and daughters; that ye may be increased there, and not diminished. And seek the peace of the city whither I have caused you to be carried away captives, and pray unto the Lord for it; for in the peace thereof shall ye have peace . . . For thus saith the Lord, that after seventy years be accomplished at Babylon I will visit you, and perform my good word toward you, in causing you to return to this place [Jerusalem] (Jeremiah 29:4-10).

Daniel knew it by heart. The pledged word of the living God, a God who could not lie, a word given through the Old Testament "man of sorrows," a word poured out of the lips of a brokenhearted prophet who had paid a high price in suffering for saying such things—Daniel was willing to stake his all on the inspired, inerrant, infallible word of God.

But there was another prophecy, one that marched in step with Jeremiah's, one given more than a century before. In a remarkable statement, the prophet Isaiah had given the name of the pagan king who would be anointed by God to serve him in setting the captives free:

> Thus saith the Lord, thy redeemer, . . . I am the Lord that . . . saith to Jerusalem, Thou shalt be inhabited; and to the cities of Judah, Ye shall be built, and I will raise up the decayed places thereof: . . . That saith of Cyrus, He is my shepherd, and shall perform all my pleasure: even saying to Jerusalem, Thou shalt be built; and to the temple, Thy foundation shall be laid. Thus saith the Lord to his anointed, to Cyrus, whose right hand I have holden, to subdue nations before him, and I will loose the loins of kings, to open before him the two leaved gates; and the gates shall not be shut; I will go before thee, and make the crooked places straight: I will break in pieces the gates of brass, and cut in sunder the bars of iron: And I will give thee the treasures of darkness, and hidden riches of secret places, that thou mayest know that I, the Lord, which call thee by thy name, am the God of Israel. For Jacob my servant's sake, and Israel mine elect, I have even called thee by thy name: I have surnamed thee, though thou hast not known me (Isaiah 44:24–45:4).

When Isaiah wrote that, Assyria was still a superpower and Babylon had not yet donned the mantle of world empire. Persia was not even on the prophetic horizon. Jerusalem and the temple were still flourishing and there was no visible indication that destruction and deportation lay ahead for Judah and Jerusalem at the hands of the Babylonians.

When Daniel pondered the words afresh, this very Cyrus held the world in his grasp. Herodotus, who visited Babylon openly some eighty years after its capture, told how Cyrus approached Babylon in the spring of the year, fought and defeated the Babylonians outside the city walls, whereupon the Babylonians retreated inside the city, shut themselves up, and ignored the invader. Their city was stocked with provisions, the Euphrates flowing through its heart guaranteed limitless supplies of water, and the towering walls were impregnable. The Babylonians supposed that Cyrus would get tired and go away. They reckoned without God and without the resourcefulness of his "shepherd." Cyrus and his generals, as we have noted elsewhere, actually diverted the flow of the Euphrates so that the Persian troops could march down the riverbed into the city. Xenophon told how the invaders entered the doomed city of Babylon and made straight for the palace, raising shouts along the way as though they, too, were joining in the general revelry of the city.

As Daniel sat and pondered "the books," he was gripped by the minute fulfillment of every detail in the prophecy of Isaiah. Cyrus had come, just as Isaiah had said he would. So why should there not be an equally accurate fulfillment of Jeremiah's prophecies? Of course there would be. Daniel had no doubt about it at all, but the trouble was, there did not seem to be any prospect of the prophecy's being fulfilled. The new emperor had made no move as yet to release the exiles. And why should he? As for the Jews themselves, there was no remorse, no regret, no repentance. They had taken Jeremiah's advice too literally. They had not only settled down in Babylon, they had prospered in Babylon. They had settled down to stay. Indeed, by now many of them had been born in Babylon. Some were the third generation since the captivity had begun, the second generation to be born in Babylon. Babylon was the only home they had known. Daniel was afraid that, even if Cyrus issued the emancipating decree, few, if any, Jews would respond. A word of prophecy? Yes, indeed.

b. A Word of Prayer (9:3-19). Prayer was the answer. Thus we see the practical value of studying prophecy. It stimulates the spiritual life of the exercised believer. We note, first, *the prophet's preparation* (9:3). If Daniel's people had learned nothing by their exile, then Daniel would pray for them. If they would not confess the sins that had brought God's judgment on the nation, then Daniel would confess them. He was a Jew and was one of them. He would identify himself with the sins of the people and confess their sins as though they were his own. He would pray. He would fast. Rich and powerful, clothed in fine raiment, man of God that he was, he would don sackcloth and bathe in ashes. He would assume the garb and guise of a penitent. He would show God how deeply he, at least, felt about these things.

Now comes *the prophet's petition* (9:4-19). Daniel approached God along four lines. He talked to God about his character, commandments, covenant, and compassion. This is one of the great model prayers of scripture.

Since most us us are very poor pray-ers and need all the help we can get, the Holy Spirit, the "one called alongside to help" (as the Lord described him), has put these helpful prayers in the Bible. If in our study of the sacred page we are so eager to get on with exploring prophecies that we neglect such passages as this, then we are in no spiritual condition to study prophecy at all. Prophecy is not in the Bible just to satisfy our curiosity about the future, but to help develop our spiritual capacity.

What could be more exciting than the fact that the eternal God of the universe is willing to listen to our prayers? And not only so, but our prayers actually count. In some mysterious way, God takes our prayers into consideration as one of the factors in the equation of his eternal purpose. How kind, then, of the Holy Spirit to set before us such a prayer masterpiece.

Daniel's prayer began with *God and his character* (9:4-9). At once, four characteristics of God came to the prophet's mind. He thought for a moment about *God's person* (9:4). Daniel's thoughts dwelled for a moment on God's might. He called him "Jehovah, my *Elohim*." The God of covenant was the God of creation, and the God of covenant and creation was his God. Daniel took comfort in that. He had lived all his adult life in Babylon, the heartland of idolatry. The false gods of Babylon were legion. There were Bel, Merodach, and Nebo, along with a host of others. On his arrival in Babylon as a young man, his own name had been changed to Belteshazzar in the hope that he would become a convert to pagan idolatry. And what was more reasonable from the pagan point of view? Hadn't mighty Merodach led the Babylonians to victory over the Jews? Didn't that prove that Merodach was a greater god than the Jewish tribal deity?

But Daniel knew better than that. His God was the creator of the universe who, nevertheless, entered into covenant relationship with his chosen people.

Daniel's thoughts dwelled, too, on God's majesty. True, God entered into covenant with human beings, but let none presume. He was "the great and dreadful God." This time, Daniel used the name *El*, one that described God as the almighty —God in all his strength and power. *El* is the God the omnipotent one, the one in whom all the divine attributes are concentrated. God, in this character, was awesome and terrible.

Daniel thought, too, of God's mercy. He was a God who showed mercy to his people, a God who wrote clauses to that end into his covenants. Those who loved him and sought to obey him could be assured of his mercy. Daniel's long life was a testimony to that.

Thus in his prayer Daniel dwelled on the person of God. Thoughts of God's mercy turned Daniel's mind to thoughts of *God's patience* (9:5-6). He scoured the Hebrew language for words to describe how wickedly the Jews had behaved. "We have sinned," he said. The word means "to miss the mark, to stumble and fall, to come short, to be blameworthy." The word has to do with what we think, say, and do, rather than with what we are.

"We have committed iniquity," Daniel said. The word means "perversity." It comes from a root meaning "to be bent" or "crooked." It means to be wrong.

"We have done wickedly," Daniel continued. This word in scripture describes the restless activity of fallen human nature. It is used to describe the behavior of the impious and ungodly, the lawlessness of such people.

"We have rebelled," Daniel went on. This word is usually used for revolt against God or against royalty. This revolt had expressed itself among the Jews in their departure from God's precepts and judgments (9:5) and in their persistent refusal to listen to that long succession of prophets sent by God to warn and to woo them. Daniel confessed that the kings, the princes, the fathers, and all the people of the land were involved (9:6). Even a cursory reading of the books of Kings and Chronicles substantiates that. Yet God was patient. He kept on sending more messengers over a period of a couple of hundred years as proof of his patience.

Daniel's thoughts proceeded to *God's punishment* (9:7-8). How long could even the patience of God go on postponing the inevitable consequences of wickedness and defiance? Daniel acknowledged God's righteousness. His thoughts dwelled on the confusion that had overtaken the Jewish people. First the ten tribes had been uprooted and marched away into oblivion by the Assyrians. Had Judah learned anything from that? Nothing. He thought of all the countries into which the Hebrew people had been driven "because of their trespass." Here he used another word for sin, a word associated with treachery, unfaithfulness, and breach of trust. It is the word used for the sin of Achan (Joshua 7:1; 22:31).

Daniel thought, too, of *God's pity* (9:9). It had to be so; otherwise there would be no point in praying. The exiled nation was reaping the due reward for its deeds. It had no claims on God's justice, so the thing to do was plead guilty and sue for mercy and forgiveness. Daniel thanked God that those qualities of character indeed were his. The God to whom he was praying was not some pagan thunderer, some implacable deity, some relentless tyrant, who took pleasure in pain and insisted on his pound of flesh. Such were the gods of the pagans. The true and living God was not like that at all. To God belong, not just mercy, but "mercies." He is a God of all grace, of infinite mercy. He is the God of whom Jonah wrote. "I knew," he said, "that thou art a gracious God, and merciful, slow to anger, and of great kindness" (Jonah 4:2).

Daniel's prayer continued with *God and his commandments* (9:10-14). Daniel reviewed in God's presence *the demands of the law* (9:10). "The Lord our God." Those words echoed the decalogue (Exodus 20:1-10). The ten commandments, graven on stone by the finger of God, were divided into five commandments proclaiming man's duty to God (tied together by the expression "the Lord thy God") and five commandments proclaiming man's duty to his fellow man (tied together with the words "thou shalt not"). Daniel was overwhelmed by Israel's failure to keep the Godward commandments: to have no other gods, to make no graven image, to revere God's name, to sanctify his sabbath, to venerate parents (as those who stand in the place of God to the child). He thought of Israel's shocking idolatries, of a nation so obsessed with the adoration of graven images that God at last had seen fit to send the nation to Babylon, the capital city of idolatry, to have idolatry burned out of that nation's soul.

Daniel reviewed the *doom of the law* (9:11-14), its punishments. He thought of the curse of the law and how that *curse was conveyed* (9:11). He used yet another word for sin: *transgressed,* meaning "to go beyond." God, it seems, will let us go so far but when we go beyond the line He has drawn, we can expect judgment to fall. Over and over God had warned Israel against stepping over that line (Leviticus 26:14; Deuteronomy 27:14-26; 28:15-68; 29:20-28; 30:17-19; 31:16-18; 32:15-29). Doubtless Daniel knew those warning passages by heart. Israel was without excuse.

Moreover, the *curse was confirmed* (9:12). Long after Moses was dead, God sent other prophets to warn the nation against sin and of judgment certain to come. Isaiah had preached with eloquence; Amos had spelled it out in cold logic; Hosea had broken his heart; Habakkuk had wrestled with the problem; Jeremiah had wept his heart out over the nation's sins; Ezekiel had resorted to signs. Yet the people remained deaf to what the prophets proclaimed.

Then, too, the *curse was continued* (9:13-14). The foretold evils came. Jerusalem had been reduced to rubble, the temple to a charred heap of stones, and the people were deported to lands of exile. Was there repentance when the Assyrians carried away the entire northern kingdom and ravaged Judah right down to

Jerusalem itself? Only until the death of godly King Hezekiah—then Judah followed Manasseh into worse wickedness than before. Was there repentance when Josiah found a copy of the law in the temple after God's word had been so completely forgotten that he read it with astonishment and resolve? Only until his death. Was there repentance when the Babylonians first appeared and encamped in battle array around Jerusalem? None. Was there repentance when Jerusalem fell in 605 B.C. and the cream of the Judean aristocracy was taken away to Babylon? No. Was there repentance when the second Babylonian expedition appeared before Jerusalem and Jehoiachin was deposed and Zedekiah installed as a puppet king in his place in 597 B.C.? None. Was there repentance when in 594 B.C. Zedekiah was summoned to Babylon? No. Was there repentance when in 587 B.C. the Babylonians appeared in force before Jerusalem for the final siege? None whatsoever. Was there repentance when Jerusalem fell at last and was sacked in 586 B.C.? No. Was there repentance in Babylon? No.

Daniel proceeded with his prayer, concentrating now on *God and his covenant* (9:15-17). Daniel's thoughts went back to *the exodus* (9:15), where God's hand was displayed. Throughout the Old Testament, the exodus from Egypt is heralded as the great exhibition of God's might. His mighty hand had humbled Egypt, that great world superpower, and the fear of God had fallen on the nations of Canaan. Daniel had no doubt that the God who could enforce his demand on pharaoh could enforce his will on Persia.

Daniel's thoughts now turned to *the exile* (9:16-17), where God's holiness was being displayed. There was the *plight of the people* (9:16). The "holy mountain" was Mount Moriah. There the temple had stood; there the holy place and the holy of holies had been. There a thrice holy God had once chosen to take up his residence among his people. What manner of people they should have been (as Peter would have put it), "in all holy conversation and godliness" (2 Peter 3:11).

But what did Israel do, from the days of Solomon to the days of Zedekiah? They provoked God to anger with idolatry and apostasy. They projected to the pagan world around them the image of a people addicted to religious apostasy, moral depravity, and political insanity. God's answer was Babylon. He allowed the temple to be destroyed, Jerusalem to be reduced to rubble, and the people to become captives in an idolatrous city. If the Jews would not manifest God's holiness, Jehovah would take care of his own honor.

Now comes the *plea of the prophet* (9:17). At the beginning of his prayer, Daniel had addressed God as "the Lord my God" (9:4). Confession having been made by Daniel, identifying himself with the sins of the people, the way was clear for the people, in the person of their great intercessor, to address God as "our God." The ground of the plea is not to be found in the prophet or in the people but in the Lord himself. If Daniel's heart was broken over the desolation of the temple, how much more the heart of God, whose home it was. If Daniel was concerned about the negative testimony in a pagan world of God's house in ruins, how much more must God have been concerned. So the answer to the desolation lay in God himself. It was for his sake that He should act.

If we are to be persuasive in prayer we must always find our way to that place. God does what He does because He is what He is. God is holy, wise, loving. God is too wise to make any mistakes; too loving to be unkind; too powerful to be thwarted. If something has overtaken us, God has allowed it. If anything is to be done about it, we must find the answer in God himself. What is his interest in this matter? How can his purposes best be served? What will best minister to his glory? Such supplication lifts prayer from the selfish plane on which we live to the sublime plane on which He lives. To bring God's greatness and glory into our prayers is to set them free from the encumbrances of our humanity.

The prophet's prayer is nearly over. He turned finally to *God and his compassion* (9:18-19). Daniel had two last pleas. He had a plea based on *God's gracious nature* (9:18), on his mercy. The desolation of Jerusalem was terrible. The Babylonian troops had done a thorough job. They had attacked the city three times. The last time, they made sure they would never have to besiege it again. We have Nehemiah's testimony to the destruction (Nehemiah 2:13-14). When the work of reconstruction was well underway, the builders were still discouraged. "There is much rubbish; so that we are not able to build the wall," they complained (Nehemiah 4:10).

The condition of a man's house is a reflection on the man. We remember the dismay with which David Balfour surveyed the ruins of the house of Shaws in which his miserly Uncle Ebenezer was content to live. The neglected condition of the property was an eloquent advertisement of the miserliness of the laird.

Daniel ventured to make an almost daring appeal to God. "Listen!" he said in effect, "Listen to what the heathen are saying about you. Look at the ruins which were once the temple and at the shambles which once were the city associated with your name." Daniel knew, of course, that the ruin was not a reflection on God but on the sinfulness of the Jews. But the pagans did not know that.

So God must act. There was no way Daniel could appeal on the grounds of any goodness in God's people. They deserved a continuation of his wrath. Times without number, in the recorded history of God's people, God has acted in mercy. Let him act in mercy once more.

Daniel's last plea, based on *God's great name* (9:19), is a series of exclamations of emotion and distress. He flung himself on God (9:19).

Behind the multitude, led by Ezra and Zerubbabel, which shortly afterward set forth bravely to reclaim and resettle the promised land, we see the bent figure of aged Daniel bowed in prayer before the throne of God. As we think of the sins of our own land, where the light of the gospel has shone so long, as we think of judgment on the horizon, surely we should take Daniel's prayer and make it our own.

2. Daniel Received a New Prophecy (9:20-27)

This astonishing prophecy was God's immediate answer to Daniel's prayer. The burden of that prayer was Israel's sin. This answer shows God's plan to deal not only with Israel's sin, both in Daniel's day and in a future day, but also with the sin question of the entire world. Having believed an old prophecy, the prophecy of the seventy years recorded by the prophet Jeremiah and about to terminate, Daniel received a new prophecy. One thing that had been perplexing him was the seemingly long time spans needed if all the future world empires of which God had spoken were to have their day. This prophecy of the seventy weeks (weeks of years) sheds light on that.

a. *The Coming of the Messenger* (9:20-23). The angelic beings who surround the throne of God are "ministering spirits, sent forth to minister for them who shall be heirs of salvation" (Hebrews 1:14). In view of the opposition of Satan's fallen angelic beings (Ephesians 6:11-12) we need the ministry of God's holy angels, whom He often uses to effect answers to our prayers. Although angels are normally invisible, that does not make their ministry less real. When Cornelius prayed, God let him see the angel who was sent with the answer (Acts 10:1-7). When the church prayed for Peter, an angel came to unlock his prison doors (Acts 12:5-10). So Daniel prayed and an angel came. We note *when he came* (9:20-21). Daniel's prayer was interrupted. He had said enough. God had heard and answered. He need pray no more. The herald angel was Gabriel, whom Daniel had met before

(8:16). Daniel recorded the time of this visitation as being "about the time of the evening oblation."

The law of Moses provided for an unblemished yearling lamb to be offered morning and evening along with a meal offering and a drink offering (Numbers 28:3-8). The time of the evening oblation was three in the afternoon (the time Christ died on the cross). The ritual of the evening sacrifice was significant. The lamb spoke of Christ being offered as a spotless burnt offering to God. The fine flour depicted his flawless life. The oil depicted the Holy Spirit, who filled and anointed him. The frankincense spoke of the fragrance of his life; the salt, its freedom from corruption; the outpoured wine, the joy that was set before him as He endured the cross, despising the shame.

The words of Gabriel, then, were intended by their ritual timing to take Daniel to the cross. It was no accident he arrived when he did. Although the temple was destroyed and the evening oblation could no longer be offered on its altar, Daniel still observed the set times of the temple services, as he had been taught in childhood (6:10). His actions were not in vain, for the temple would rise again from the rubble and "the time of the evening oblation" would come again.

We note also *why he came* (9:22-23). He had come because of *Daniel's perplexity* (9:22). What Daniel was now about to learn was not something he could acquire by patient and diligent study. It was something that had to be revealed. Yet, once revealed, it required something God alone could give: skill and understanding. What was set before him by the angel was not a vision requiring interpretation so much as a plain statement of coming events. This was a direct prophecy, given in everyday language by the angel who had been sent by God to make everything clear and plain. The angel demanded of Daniel that he employ the skill and understanding God now gave him, that he put his mind to work to grasp the significance of the revelation.

He had come also because of *Daniel's prayer* (9:23a). The moment Daniel began to pray, the herald angel was on his way. How little we understand the cosmic significance of our prayers.

But Gabriel had come for yet another reason; he had come because of *Daniel's person* (9:23b). Like David, Daniel was a man after God's own heart. Like John, he was a beloved disciple. Like Joseph, the Holy Spirit records only good of him. Like Jesus, he had become identified with the erring people of God and had placed himself before God as an intercessor. He was a man "greatly beloved," a man "very precious," as some have rendered the phrase. Think of it—Gabriel the herald angel, who stands in the presence of God (Luke 1:19), was commissioned to leave the heights of heaven in order to tell this man that he was precious to God. To the outward eye he was just an old man, dressed in sackcloth, his body anointed with ashes, worn out with the intensity of his prayer. But to God he was precious. And because he was beloved, no trouble would be spared.

"Understand the matter," the angel said, "and consider the vision." It is folly to receive voices and visions from the unseen world, tongues and prophecies, utterances and revelations, and not to test them. The prophet received a sudden illumination, and he was told to put it to the test of his reasoning faculty. He was given special enlightenment, but he was to "consider" it, to think about it. The people of Berea were commended by the Holy Spirit because they tested the truth of apostolic teaching by the scriptures (Acts 17:11). Paul challenged the Corinthians: "I speak as to wise men; judge ye what I say" (1 Corinthians 10:15). In the early church the prophets were to speak and the interpreters were to judge what they said (1 Corinthians 14:29). We are to "test the spirits" (1 John 4:1-3). With the admonition to ponder the forthcoming message, Daniel was ready to receive one of the most remarkable prophecies now found in our Bible.

b. *The Content of the Message* (9:24-27). The seventy years foretold by Jeremiah had all but expired. But far from the exile's end being the preliminary step to the setting up of the messianic kingdom, a further seventy sevens of years had been determined. We note how the *seventy weeks are decreed* (9:24). Gabriel made the abrupt announcement. The word *determined* signifies "cut off," that is, divided off from all other years, from the period of the "times of the Gentiles," the time when world power is in gentile hands.

The word *weeks* is literally "sevens," and sevens of years are undoubtedly intended. Daniel had been thinking of the seventy years of Jeremiah's prophecy. The idea of sabbatical years made the idea of a seven of years familiar to Jews.

The *focus of the period* (9:24) is significant. The reference here is to Daniel's people, the Jews, and to the "holy city," Jerusalem. This prophecy has nothing to do with the church, an entity in God's future purposes about which neither Daniel nor any other Old Testament prophet had any information. Nor does the prophecy have primary reference to the world in general. In others words, the entire course of the seventy sevens (70 x 7 = 490 years) has to do with the Jewish people in their own country. So then, this period of 490 years was to be marked off from whatever protracted length of time was involved in the "times of the Gentiles," and during this 490-year period God would have special dealings with the Jews while in their own land—this quite apart from any disciplinary dealings with the Jews while dispersed in gentile lands.

Now we can look at the *features of the period* (9:24). Certain things were to be accomplished. In the first place, God would *cancel all sin* (9:24). This is covered in three clauses: "To finish the transgression, and to make an end of sins, and to make reconciliation for iniquity." Daniel had just been using some of these same words.

The three words used by the angel sum up human sin. The word for "transgression" has to do with revolt or rebellion. It is sin against lawful authority. It suggests the defiance of sin. The word sums up the general history of the nation of Israel, almost from the start: their murmurings against Moses in the wilderness; the rebellion of Korah against the authority of Moses and Aaron; at Kadesh-Barnea the people's rebellion against going on into Canaan.

When God pronounced sentence and condemned that generation to death in the wilderness, they rebelled again and attempted to go on toward Canaan in their own strength, only to meet prompt punishment. Under Joshua they took the land but revolted against God's commandment decreeing the total extermination of their enemies. The long centuries of the judges were marked mostly by rebellion. Both Israel's and Judah's history under the kings was so rebellious that both kingdoms had to be deported under the sharp displeasure of God.

The word for *sins* here again is a word meaning "missing the mark." It brings to mind the deficiency of sin. The nation of Israel came woefully short of the glory of God. The nation had been chosen and set apart by God to be a testimony to him. The living God had taken up residence among his people, enthroned in the temple in Jerusalem. God intended that all nations might come to know him through the godly testimony of the Hebrew people. The nation missed the mark. Solomon in his early days came closest to the divine ideal. The Queen of Sheba's testimony should have been the confession of all nations. After she had made the long journey to Jerusalem and had seen and heard for herself, she was overwhelmed. She eulogized God, his people, and their illustrious prince. "The half was never told me," she said. But it did not last long. Solomon turned to other gods and paved the way for centuries of national idolatry and apostasy. It was a terrible missing of the mark.

The third word, *iniquity,* we have also met before in Daniel's confession. It signifies the crookedness and bentness of human nature.
It suggests the distortion of sin. The image of God had been distort-
ed by his people; many of them had acceded to idolatrous practices.
Then, when they returned from Babylon, they became proud and
disdainful of the gentiles, arrogant in their exclusiveness, hypocritical in their Pharisaism, blind leaders of the blind in their rabbinical
traditions.

God proposed to deal with all this. The sin of the world, of course,
was dealt with at Calvary. The angel here, however, was speaking of
Israel's national sins and how God intended to deal with them. As
there was a threefold indictment, so there is a threefold progression
in God's plan for dealing with Jewish national sin. First, sin would
be held back; then it would be bound and confined; finally it would
be done away with completely.

Today God is holding back and confining that sin as part of the
general work of the Holy Spirit in hindering the full development
of the mystery of iniquity (2 Thessalonians 2:6-7). After the rapture
of the church, when God again takes up where He left off with the
nation of Israel, that restraint will be removed. Israel and the Jewish
people will be deeply involved in the terrible events surrounding the
coming of the antichrist, something they will pay for dearly in the
great tribulation.

At the return of Christ to set up his millennial kingdom, sin will
be bound and confined. The beast and the false prophet will be con-
signed to the lake of fire. Satan will be incarcerated in the abyss. The
nation of Israel will belatedly recognize Jesus as messiah. The Jewish
people and the nation of Israel will be cleansed and recommissioned
to be the universal testimony to the nations God always intended
them to be. The Lord will reign with "a rod of iron" (Psalm 2:7-9).
Swift and certain punishment will be meted out to transgressors.
Even the curse itself, the direct result of the fall, will be put under
restraint so that Edenic conditions might appear again on earth.

At the end of the millennial reign, however, Satan will again be
released. He will inspire one last rebellion. Then sin will be done
away with completely. This sin-cursed earth will be renovated by fire
(2 Peter 3:10). Then will come a new earth, and all its inhabitants
will be forever reconciled with God.

But God intends to do more than cancel sin. He will *complete our
salvation* (9:24) "to bring in everlasting righteousness." This has
already been effected at the cross, and is being made good in the

lives of believers today. The emphasis here, however, is on the nation of Israel. As far as the nation of Israel is concerned, fulfillment of this divine goal awaits the national conversion of the Jewish people to Christ at his second coming. Then the Jewish nation, as a nation, will come into the good of the new covenant (Jeremiah 31:33-40).

The church has already come into the good of the soteriological clauses of that covenant (Matthew 26:28). Individual Jews today who accept Christ come into the good of those clauses immediately. But as a nation the Jews remain obdurate in unbelief. When Christ comes back and they recognize their age-long folly, the nation will be "born in a day" (Isaiah 66:8). Then both the eschatological and soteriological clauses of the new covenant will come into effect. God will write his laws on the hearts of the Jewish people, instead of on tables of stone, and then they will love him and keep his commandments.

God will *confirm the scriptures* (9:24), "to seal up the vision and prophecy." All that the prophets have foretold, of both comings of Christ, will be fulfilled to the letter. Not even the most obscure prophetic scripture will be overlooked. The prophetic scriptures will be fully accredited. History will put its seal on the entire prophetic page. Unbelief will be silenced forever. God's word will be universally acclaimed.

God will *consecrate the sanctuary* (9:24). The "most Holy" is the holy of holies. When the tabernacle built by Moses was finished, it was anointed. No such anointing is spoken of in connection with either Solomon's temple or Zerubbabel's. They are viewed as an extension of the tabernacle. But now that the Lord's sacrifice for sins has been made at Calvary, when Ezekiel's temple is built as the center of worship during the millennium, the holy of holies will be anointed as here proclaimed by Gabriel.

Calvary calls for significant changes. The ark of the covenant, which featured so prominently in the holy of holies in both the tabernacle and the Old Testament temples, will be no more (Jeremiah 3:16). Instead of the sacred ark, the throne of the messiah will be set up in the sanctuary (Jeremiah 3:17; Zechariah 6:13). Christ will sit enthroned there as a royal priest. These changes will call for a fresh anointing of the holy of holies.

All these features are millennial in focus. The final close of the seventy weeks will coincide with the end of "the times of the Gentile," and with the inauguration of the millennial reign of Christ.

Thus the seventy weeks were decreed. Their terminus is not Calvary but the second coming of Christ to reign. We now learn that the *seventy weeks are divided* (9:25-27). God has made a threefold division of those weeks: seven weeks, sixty-two weeks, and one week—49 years plus 434 years (equals 483 years) plus 7 years (making a total of 490 years).

We begin with the *first period* (9:25). They key to understanding this countdown to Christ is to determine its exact starting point. The divine clock would begin to tick with a decree authorizing the restoration and building of Jerusalem—not the temple, of which no mention is made, but the city, street, and wall. The work was to be carried out "in troublous times."

Four decrees have been proposed by various authors as being the starting date for the prophecy.

The first decree is that of Cyrus in 538 B.C. We have the biblical record of it in Ezra 1:1-4. Cyrus's proclamation was not a mandate to rebuild the walls of Jerusalem but to build the temple. Considering how strong a position Jerusalem occupied and how practically impregnable it was when properly provisioned and defended, it is no wonder that Cyrus, seeking to consolidate his empire, issued no decree to refortify Jerusalem. The Chaldeans were able to take the city only after it had been reduced by starvation. The same was true of the Roman siege in A.D. 70. In that war the Jews were their own worst enemies. In-fighting between rival gangs and factions was debilitating, but famine brought the overthrow in the end.

As a result of this decree some fifty thousand captives pulled up stakes and returned to Jerusalem (Ezra 2:64-65), only a tithe, so to speak, of the Jewish multitudes now in voluntary exile. The repatriated Jews laid the foundation of the temple in April or May, 536 B.C., aided by a grant from Cyrus. When the Samaritans asked to help, they were refused by the Jews, who were determined now at last to maintain the purity of their faith. The scorned Samaritans then became the determined enemies of those repatriated Jews. They harassed them and hired lawyers to misrepresent the Jews at the Persian court. The work came to a stop.

No further progress was made during the reigns of Cyrus, Cambyses, and Smerdis. Sixteen years went by. Then on August 29, 520 B.C., Haggai began to exhort the Jews to get on with the task of rebuilding the temple. Work was recommenced in September of the same year. In October or November, Zechariah began to prophesy. Tettenai, a Persian governor, wrote to Darius I Hystaspes challenging the rebuilding of the temple.

The second decree, sometimes suggested as the one meant in the prophecy of Daniel 9, was the decree of Darius Hystaspes in 519 B.C.

Ezra recorded how this Darius ordered a search to be made in the house of rolls, where the treasures were laid up in Babylon (Ezra 6:1-12). A record was found of the original decree of Cyrus. Now the inflexibility of Medo-Persian law (Daniel 6:15) worked in favor of the Jews. Darius Hystaspes issued a decree in which he ordered Tettenai the governor to desist from hindering the Jews, but instead to give them help and protection. This decree evidently had nothing to do with rebuilding the walls of Jerusalem.

The third decree was that of Artaxerxes. The temple was completed in February or March, 516 B.C., and was dedicated with pomp and rejoicing. Fifty-eight years went by. Darius Hystaspes died in 486 B.C. He was followed on the throne of Persia by Xerxes (who married the biblical Esther in 478 B.C.) and by Artaxerxes, who came to the throne in 464 B.C. In 458 B.C. Ezra received a commission from Artaxerxes to go to Jerusalem and enact civil reforms. Called "a ready scribe in the law of Moses," Ezra's goal was to bring about a spiritual renewal of the repatriated Jews. "Ezra had prepared his heart to seek the law of the Lord, and to do it, and to teach in Israel statutes and judgments" (Ezra 7:10). The text of the decree of Artaxerxes is recorded in Ezra 7:11-26. Again, this decree was more religious in character than anything else. It certainly did not contain the kind of mandate required by Daniel 9.

The fourth decree was that of Artaxerxes Longimanus. Thirteen years after Ezra's arrival in Jerusalem, news filtered back to Shushan in Persia about the deplorable state of Jerusalem. Nehemiah, a Jewish high court official, was deeply distressed. Under questioning from Artaxerxes, Nehemiah confessed his unhappiness at the continuing desolation of Jerusalem. The king then issued his famous decree commissioning Nehemiah to go to Jerusalem and take whatever steps were necessary to renovate the city (Nehemiah 2:5-9).

This is evidently a decree of quite a different sort. Behind it was a court Jew, a man of courage, determination, and resourcefulness. Here was a decree to rebuild the city and the wall. It was given in the twentieth year of the reign of Artaxerxes and in the month Nisan (Nehemiah 2:1). The year was 445 B.C.

The angel told Daniel about this in the first year of Darius Cambyses (the Mede) in 538 B.C., almost a century before the time came: "The street shall be built again, and the wall, even in troublous times." The expression points to the completeness of the restoration. How troubled the times were can be seen in the books of Ezra and Nehemiah.

Nehemiah arrived in Jerusalem in 444 B.C. He took in the enormity of the task and, in a fury of zeal and organization, accomplished it in fifty-two days. Nehemiah stayed on as governor of Jerusalem for twelve years, returning to Persia in 433 or 432 B.C. Some time later he came back to Jerusalem, where he seems to have remained for the rest of his life.

It is possible that reconstruction work went on long after the walls were rebuilt. The first period of seven weeks (forty-nine years) takes us to 396 B.C. It is likely that Malachi prophesied about this time. If so, then the first seven weeks comes to an end with the closing of the Old Testament canon.

Now comes *the further period* (9:26). Two important events are here connected with the expiration of this second period. The first of these is the *death of Jesus* (9:26a): "Messiah shall be cut off." The word for *cut off* is important. Edward B. Pusey wrote: "The word . . . never means anything but excision; death directly inflicted by God, or violent death at the hands of man. It is never used of mere death, nor to express sudden but natural death" (p. 198). He cited the use of the word in connection with God's covenant (Genesis 17:14; Exodus 30:33, 38; and especially Isaiah 53:8). From the signing of the decree to the cutting off of messiah the prince was to be a period of 483 years (7 + 62 weeks; 69 x 7 = 483 years).

Probably the most convincing attempt to calculate the countdown from the signing of the decree to the death of Christ is that of Sir Robert Anderson (*Daniel in the Critic's Den*, London: James Nisbet and Co., Ltd., 1902). He put the edict for the rebuilding of the city as the first of Nisan, 445 B.C. From that date to messiah the prince was to be 69 x 7 of years = 483 years. The Hebrews used a 360-day calendar, so 483 years x 360 days = 173,880 days. Sir Robert's calculations show that from the first of Nisan 445 B.C. to the end of the 173,880 days brings us to the tenth of Nisan in the eighteenth year of Tiberius, the day when the Lord made his public, triumphant entry into Jerusalem, and presented himself to the nation as "Messiah the Prince." (This use of the title "Messiah the Prince" is used by Gabriel as a proper name or title of Christ.) So, the Lord showed himself to the Jewish people as their messiah and within a few short days He was "cut off" by crucifixion and banished from the world. All He left behind him were the clothes on his back, and the Roman soldiers wasted no time falling upon those.

The greatest calamity that could overtake a man in this life, from the point of view of a Jew living in Bible times, was to die before he could be married and have children to carry on his name. Jesus was "cut off" from life and left no family or human successor, no name to carry on his line. From the human standpoint that is what happened, as was foretold (the clause "not of himself" is rendered alternatively as "and shall have nothing"). Death put an end to everything—or so the Lord's enemies imagined. He needed no successor, however, to carry on his name. He rose from the dead three days later to carry on God's messianic purposes.

The death of Jesus, however, by no means concluded the tragedy associated with the termination of the sixty-nine weeks. There was to follow the *destruction of Jerusalem* (9:26b). The Lord's crucifixion took place just four days after He was hailed by the common people as messiah, but repudiated by the nation's leaders. The masses who hailed him as messiah one day, however, were just as ready to shout for his murder the next. The nation, first its leaders and then its people, rejected Christ and gave him a cross instead of a crown.

That critical tenth of Nisan marked a turning point in the fortunes of the Jewish people. They rejected Christ. God rejected them. There began a long interval during which God has stopped the prophetic clock. Between the sixty-ninth week and the seventieth week of this prophecy is inserted the long parenthesis of the church age. We can express this thus: $7 + 62 = 69(+) \ldots$ (church age) $\ldots + 1 = 70$ (millennial age).

As has been said, neither Daniel nor any other Old Testament prophet foresaw the church age. The seventieth week is evidently severed from the other sixty-nine but the commentary proceeds without a break. The repeated "and, and, and" of the text marches us on.

Thus it is not altogether clear whether the remarks about the destruction of the city have to do with the fate that overtook both Jerusalem and the temple in A.D. 70, or if the comments of the angel belong to the seventieth week and a coming destruction in the days of the antichrist. Commentators differ. In all probability the words refer to both. A well-known feature of Bible prophecy is the fact that many prophecies have both a near and far fulfillment. They have an immediate, initial, and partial fulfillment, which serves as an illustration for a more distant, final, and complete fulfillment.

There can be little doubt that the destruction of Jerusalem by the Romans was one of the most terrible events in recorded history. The fanaticism of the Jews was matched only by the fury of the Romans. When the city finally fell, the temple was destroyed along with the city, in spite of the efforts of Titus to save it. Herod had made it one of the unsung wonders of the world.

The Romans fell on the survivors with savage rage. Jews were crucified by the hundreds. The death roll came to over a million. Multitudes more were marched away to slavery and to the arena. "The end thereof" was indeed "with a flood," and the desolations complete. In A.D. 135, when the Bar Kochba rebellion broke out, "the people of the prince that shall come" (referring to the Romans under whom Christ was crucified) completed the work of destruction. They renamed both the country and the city of Jerusalem and banned Jews from coming anywhere near their ancient land.

We come now to the *final period* (9:27). It may well be that the reference to "the people of the prince that shall come" refers to the people of the revived Roman empire. We recall that Daniel had already been instructed about the course of gentile world empire, about the terrible might of the fourth one, and the end-time events associated with the little horn, the antichrist. What he learned in this conversation with Gabriel were the long periods of time involved. But even so, he could have had no idea of the two-thousand-year agony of the Jewish people brought on by the crime of Calvary. All Daniel knew was that, after the cutting off of the messiah, there was to be an interval before the events associated with the final seven-year period. Daniel also knew that the final seven-year period was linked with the antichrist.

"The prince that shall come" is almost certainly the antichrist. He will be the warmonger of the endtimes, desolator of the earth, and enemy of the Jews. The prophecy foresees many Jews settled in their own land, under duress, and glad of a powerful ally. In the west, the antichrist will have consolidated his hold on the revived Roman empire, the now united nations of western Europe. He may well have brought the western hemisphere also into a new Atlantic alliance controlled by himself from Rome. Standing astride his path to complete world rule will be the Soviet Union. The antichrist will be an opportunist, one well tutored by Satan. He will see in the state of Israel a useful pawn, a means to get rid of Russia and its empire.

Accordingly, he will offer to sign a seven-year pact with the state of Israel—the final "week" of Daniel's prophecy. Under the terms of the treaty the Jews will be encouraged to rebuild their temple. The antichrist will have his own nefarious designs on that temple, which he will certainly not divulge to the Jews. He will also unconditionally guarantee the security of the state of Israel. The Israelis will be delighted with this treaty, even though it is called by God "an agreement with hell" (Isaiah 28:15-18).

Ever since the rebirth of the state of Israel in modern times, the Jews have had to fight fiercely for its survival. It will seem like a dream come true to have a powerful dictator actually offer to sign such a treaty with them. The Arab-Muslim-Soviet threat, an ever-present menace to them, will be curbed. The Jews will be delighted with their new friend.

But not all Jews will be so easily duped. God will have his remnant who will oppose signing that convenient treaty. Zechariah points to both the majority and to the dissenting minority: "And it shall come to pass, that in all the land, saith the Lord, two parts therein shall be cut off and die; but the third shall be left therein. And I will bring the third part through the fire, and will refine them . . . they shall call upon my name, and I will hear them: I will say, It is my people, and they shall say, The Lord is my God" (Zechariah 13:8-9).

Under cover of the treaty, religious Jews will seize the temple site and finance the speedy construction of a new temple, though God is certainly not in the project (Isaiah 66:3). Probably, at this time, with its suddenly favorable political climate for the state of Israel, millions of Jews will move back to their ancestral home.

All this will alarm and infuriate the Arab-Muslim bloc. The Soviet Union will also be alarmed by the power of the revived Roman empire of the west and by its evident intention of moving in power into the Middle East. The west will have a vital interest in securing the flow of oil from the area. Russia will either occupy Iran, Libya, and Ethiopia or be in firm alliance with these countries (Ezekiel 38:5) and will be in a position to threaten western oil interests. To counter this move, the west ("Tarshish") will occupy the Arabian peninsula (Ezekiel 38:13). This saber-rattling in the Middle East will hasten hostilities in the area. The antichrist's treaty with Israel will spur Russia and the Muslim states to act.

The story of the Russian invasion of Israel and its disastrous ending is told in Ezekiel (chapters 38 and 39). The removal of the Soviet Union and the swift submission of the rest of the world to the antichrist's power will make him a world emperor, the last Roman emperor, and the only one of the world emperors of the prophetic scriptures actually to attain the world dominion inherent in God's bestowal of universal rule on Nebuchadnezzar.

Accession to the throne of the world changes the antichrist's attitude toward Israel. His treaty suddenly becomes redundant (9:27a). The Jews will have reinstituted animal sacrifices, something that will be an abomination to the Lord because of its inherent rejection of Christ's atoning work at Calvary. Referring to these provocative sacrifices God says: "He that killeth an ox is as if he slew a man: he that sacrificeth a lamb, as if he cut off a dog's neck; he that offereth an oblation, as if he offered swine's blood; he that burneth incense, as if he blessed an idol" (Isaiah 66:3).

Halfway through the last week of Daniel 9, that is, after three-and-a-half years, the antichrist will make the move he has been planning secretly all the time. He will tear up the treaty with Israel and will seize their rebuilt temple. Doubtless he will have troops garrisoned in Israel as part of his treaty arrangement—there, so he will say, to help protect the country. Then he will install his image in the temple, command all to worship it, require all to receive his mark, and proclaim himself God (2 Thessalonians 2:4; Revelation 13:11-18). The antichrist's seizure and pollution of the Jewish temple will bring "the oblation," the freshly revived sacrificial system, to a sudden stop.

Daniel's prophecy refers to "overspreading of abominations." The translation of this last part of Daniel 9:27 has been troublesome. One or two translators have adopted the reading, "And upon the wing of abominations he shall come desolating." Among the Jews, "abomination" was a common appellation for a pagan idol (1 Kings 11:5-7). Behind all idolatry are evil spirits, as Paul later reminded the Corinthians: "The things which the Gentiles sacrifice, they sacrifice to devils, and not to God" (1 Corinthians 10:20). The antichrist was carried to the throne of the world by the power of evil spirits. The "abomination" (the image of himself) which he will set up in the holy of holies in the Jewish temple will epitomize his defiance and ridicule of God.

In the second temptation, the devil took Jesus to the pinnacle of the temple and urged him to cast himself down. Far below, the usual crowds were milling around the temple courts. Satan referred Christ to the promise, "He shall give his angels charge concerning thee: and in their hands they shall bear thee up, lest at any time thou dash thy foot against a stone" (Matthew 4:5-6). The thought seems to have been this: If Jesus had listened to the tempter's voice, then Satan's angel subordinates would have carried him down in triumph on their wings. He would have been hailed by the people as Christ—Satan would have proceeded to give him all the kingdoms of this world and their tinsel glory. But there was no possibility of God's holy one's succumbing to that daring and blasphemous invitation. The fact, however, that the devil hoped for such a triumph shows how completely the Lord had emptied himself of his glory when He became a man.

What the Lord Jesus refused, the antichrist will seize. Satan will bear him miraculously on the wings of angelic beings to his triumph in the temple. We know from Paul's words that the antichrist will come "after the working of Satan with all power and signs and lying wonders, and with all deceivableness of unrighteousness in them that perish" (2 Thessalonians 2:9-10). From other scriptures we learn that at some point in his career the antichrist will be slain and then brought back to life (Revelation 17:8). In the apocalypse he has two comings. The context of this prophecy, incidentally, is the antichrist's seizure of the temple (2 Thessalonians 2:4). When he first appears he is "the beast out of the sea" (Revelation 13:1). He is an ordinary, though extraordinarily gifted and wholly demon-possessed, individual. But he has a second coming. He is raised from the dead and thereafter is known as "the beast out of the bottomless pit" and "the beast that was, and is not, and yet is" (Revelation 17:8). It will be in this character, as a supernatural being, the willing partner of Satan, that the antichrist will demand and receive the worship and homage of the world.

Those who refuse to worship his image and to receive his mark imprinted on their flesh will be persecuted with a ferocity never equalled in the history of atrocity.

For three-and-a-half years the horrors will continue (especially against the Jewish people) "until the consummation, and that determined shall be poured upon the desolate." The Lord will use these terrible persecutions to prune and purge the nation of Israel and to fill up the ranks of the noble martyrs of the faith. Then He will act against the terrible world system and against the great desolator himself. This particular prophecy is silent as to the antichrist's doom, but other scriptures, notably the apocalypse, fill in the details about that.

Thus Daniel, who was so concerned about the desolation of Jerusalem and the temple, was given a view of things far beyond anything he could have imagined.

B. The Secret War (10:1-21)

The decree of Cyrus ending the Babylonian captivity saw the more spiritual Jews pack their bags and leave Babylon for the promised land. Many Jews remained behind, including Daniel, who was too old by now to go on such a hazardous journey. We can picture his farewells to Zerubbabel, his kinsman, and to Joshua, the rightful high priest. Many who went must have been acquaintances of his, the children and grandchildren of those who had been taken with him to Babylon many years before. Those who went back were not many, relative to the total Jewish population in exile, but they were the very salt of the earth. We can picture Daniel going down to see them off, embracing his friends, calling down his blessings on them all, assuring them his prayers would be with them.

Babylon was lonelier without them. Doubtless Daniel remained on good terms with the Jews who chose to remain behind. Some like himself were too old or incapacitated by ill health. But the majority were too much at ease in Babylon. They had been born there. Babylon was their home and they had business interests there. They mistakenly believed that their money, donated to the cause, was a good substitute for themselves.

So we can imagine an old man wandering the streets of Babylon, that great city with its high walls that nevertheless could not keep out the foe, with its broad river, with its man-made mountain and hanging gardens in a spot perhaps not far from where Eden's flowers once bloomed. Daniel's home was in Babylon; his heart was in Canaan. We see him wend his way home, lonely, shut up now to his books, memories, and prayers.

So comes another vision, a long vision, one that begins with this chapter and continues to the end of the book. We have noted that Daniel 9 and 10 chronicle two critical delays. The delay in chapter 9 revolved around the now-famous seventy weeks. The one in chapter 10, though less spectacular, focuses on the secret war.

In chapter 9 Daniel learned how God's purposes were delayed; in chapter 10 he learned how our prayers are delayed. This chapter gives us an extraordinary glimpse into the mechanics of prayer and a look at the spiritual forces that take sides for and against God's people in the unseen world. This chapter is a prelude to the astonishing vision of chapter 11; chapter 12 is a postscript to that vision.

1. The Delay Experienced (10:1-11)

a. *How the Test Was Endured* (10:1-3). Our attention is drawn to Daniel, now very old. His closest friends were dead or distant. His physical strength may well have abated. But Daniel was alert spiritually, as alive as ever to the ministry of the Holy Spirit. Thus we see him *feasting on a divine revelation* (10:1).

The long and detailed forecast of the wars and ways of Egypt and Syria during the intertestament period (Daniel 11), from the coming of Alexander the Great to the coming of Antiochus Epiphanes, is so remarkable, so accurate in its fulfillment, so evidently supernatural, that the destructive critics have been hard put in their efforts to explain it away. Their favorite claim is that the prophecy was written in the days of Antiochus Epiphanes. Thus it would not be genuine prophecy at all but a forgery—history posing as prophecy, written by some Jew living after the events had happened (see Appendix 19).

There are all sorts of reasons why the theory of those critics is untenable. The circumstances recorded in chapter 10 surround the prophecy with the most solemn circumstances. Daniel himself was completely overwhelmed. He affirmed categorically that he, Daniel, was one and the same person as that Jerusalem Jew deported to Babylon by Nebuchadnezzar and given the pagan Babylonian name of Belteshazzar. He thus attested that he was the same person who was carried into Babylon more than seventy years before and that he was the same person concerning whom the earlier portions of the book relate.

Jesus quoted from Daniel and referred to him as an authentic prophet, basing part of his own eschatology on Daniel 12:11 (Matthew 24:15). That settles it for Christian believers. Jesus could not have been mistaken. His imprimatur on "Daniel the prophet" seals him once and for all (see Appendix 3).

The vision came to Daniel "in the third year of Cyrus," not in the days of Antiochus. This is yet another affirmation that what follows is prophecy. Also, Daniel said that he understood the remarkable revelation now given to him and that the prophecy was to cover a long period of time. The promised millennium had already been postponed in some of Daniel's earlier visions. News of the difficulties the repatriated Jews were encountering in the promised land may already have begun to filter back to Babylon. More trouble lay ahead. But how many, varied, and severe were to be the trials ahead for the Jews of Palestine was something Daniel could not have known—until he received this vision.

We see Daniel *fasting with a determined resolution* (10:2-3). Fasting in scripture is never a prescribed ritual. Nor is it some kind of spiritual lever designed to force God's hand. Fasting can be just as much an activity of the flesh as feasting. True fasting is brought on by a spiritual burden, by brokenness of heart before God because of some great need that takes away the desire for food or that overweighs the demands of the physical with the demands of the spiritual.

Daniel's soul was grieved because of the spiritual condition of the Babylonian Jews who were eating, drinking, marrying, and giving in marriage. They had no care for the pioneers in Palestine, for the difficulties besetting them on every hand, for the dangers looming on the horizon, for God's ancient people in an endemically hostile gentile world. The visions of chapters 8 and 9 haunted him. The times of the gentiles were in full force. Who could tell when the Persian

bear or the Grecian leopard or the Roman monster would turn savagely against God's chosen people? They were vulnerable, scattered
abroad, dwelling at ease, careless about God's sovereign grace, which
centuries earlier had opened the gentile seas to allow them to go
dryshod to the promised land. Who could tell how soon those seas
would close in?

And what of the small remnant of some forty or fifty thousand
now back in Canaan? Surely God's good hand on them would secure
their stake in the land. The temple, the city walls, would assuredly
be built. But what then? Daniel knew from the vision of the seventy
sevens that the expiration of the first seven of sevens would mark a
crisis of some sort. There would be some kind of jubilee. But what
then? Daniel knew the uncertain temper of the Persian kings. He
knew that Judah was a province so small as to be barely an administrative district at all. How would tiny Judah fare when faced with
the monstrous gentile forces yet to be loosed on the world? Who
would pray for this people when he was gone? How would they be
protected? And how long would their suffering last? He knew that
483 years, five centuries, lay ahead before the coming of Christ. But
then there was that ominous word about the messiah's being "cut
off." Did that expression turn the old saint's thoughts to Isaiah 53?
What new depths of wickedness would engulf the Jewish people, who
in times to come would so wickedly deal with God's own Christ?

So Daniel fasted and prayed. He lost his appetite. For three weeks
the agony endured. The heavens seemed as brass. No answer came,
and the silence of heaven became an added burden.

b. *How the Test Was Ended* (10:4-11). The test came to an abrupt end
by a divine visitation. Daniel made note of *the time* (10:4).

Daniel's fast had spanned both the Passover and the feast of
unleavened bread, two feasts designed to remind Israel of their
bondage in Egypt and their marvelous emancipation—events that
must have had renewed significance to all devout Jews in view of the
emancipation decree of Cyrus. In Moses' day "not a hoof was left
behind" when the Exodus took place. In Daniel's day the "house of
bondage" had become the home of business. Most Jews preferred
the onions, leeks, and garlic of Babylon to the milk and honey of
Canaan. They kept the great annual feasts, but their observance was
hollow when weighed in the balances of God against their indolence
and their carelessness of the prophetic portent of the times.

So, Daniel was sitting on the banks of the Hiddekel (the Tigris)
when the divine visitor came (see Appendix 17). Both the Tigris and

the Euphrates are connected with the garden of Eden (Genesis 2:14). As of old, when He came down in the cool of the day to talk and walk with unfallen Adam, so now He came again to commune with his aged saint.

Daniel described next *the terror* (10:5-8). He mentioned *the man* (10:5-6). There can be no doubt as to who this "man" was. He was the Lord of glory, the second person of the godhead, the one described in Revelation 1:12-15 as "the Son of man."

On various occasions in the Bible we have preincarnate appearances of the Son of God. A number of these angelic and theophanic visitations are recorded in the book of Daniel (3:25; 4:13,17,23; 6:22; 7:16; 8:13-14, 16-26; 9:21; 10:4-8,10,16,18, 20; 12:1, 5-6). This divine visitor's body was like topaz (beryl or chrysolite), a beautiful gem, transparent, and refulgent as gold. He was arrayed in linen, the garb of Israel's priests (symbolic in scripture of righteousness). His loins were girded with a golden girdle. His face blazed like lightning. His eyes burned like fire. His limbs looked like burnished brass (a symbol of judgment in scripture). Everything about this divine visitor was calculated to strike terror, yet He chose to appear as a man. That is what struck Daniel. Terrible He might well be, but He was no remote thunderer from some pagan Olympus. He had chosen to appear as a man, as one in sympathy with humankind.

Daniel mentioned also *the men* (10:7-8). Daniel was left alone with that awesome presence. The others had not seen what Daniel saw, but the sound of that voice, like the roar of a mighty throng, was too much for them. They fled on quaking limbs, looking for some place to hide.

Daniel had already seen Gabriel, but this visitor was far more terrible and majestic. Daniel himself was overcome. Thus Isaiah, when he saw the Lord high and lifted up, cried, "Woe is me! for I am . . . a man . . . unclean" (Isaiah 6:5). Ezekiel, too, when he saw the terrible chariot of the cherubim and became suddenly aware of God's throne and "the likeness as the appearance of a man above it" fell on his face (Ezekiel 1:26-28). Likewise Saul of Tarsus, when he saw the Lord, "fell to the earth" and was blinded (Act 9:3-4,9). Even the beloved John, when he saw the ascended Lord, "fell at his feet as dead" (Revelation 1:13-17). Daniel's comeliness was turned into corruption. He saw himself as a man unclean in the presence of a holiness before which none could stand. Daniel was a good man, a godly man, a holy man. But who can stand in the presence of God? No child of Adam's ruined race, apart from a special dispensation of grace.

Next, Daniel described *the trance* (10:9). Daniel swooned. The thunder of that voice still sounded in his ears; he could not bear to gaze on that form.

The assumption has been made that the second person of the godhead had once assumed human form to create. Now, as at other times, he assumed human form to reveal. The incarnation was not yet an accomplished fact in historical time. The creator had not yet robed himself in human flesh. It was "a certain man" Daniel saw, but not yet a man born of a woman. There was kinship, but a kinship of form, not of kind. Had He appeared in some guise other than human form the old seer might never have recovered. As it was, Daniel fell into a trancelike state, sapped of strength. Truly we have little concept of the awesome majesty of the one who now has stooped to be our Savior.

But the divine visitor had no intention of speaking to the prostrate form of one lying before him on the ground, little better than an animated corpse. So Daniel next described *the touch* (10:10-11). How like Jesus, to be "touched by the feelings of our infirmities." There was warmth and kindness in that touch. No longer prostrate on the ground, the old prophet now rested on his hands and knees.

But that was still too animal-like a posture, too servile a position. Daniel was told to get up.

It would seem, from what follows, that Daniel was now addressed by an angel, probably the angel Gabriel, who presumably accompanied the divine visitor. It must have been both reassuring and comforting for Daniel to be told he was a man greatly beloved. There was no ground for terror. The visitor had come to comfort and not to condemn, to reveal and not to revile. Daniel was to get up and stand on his feet like the man greatly beloved of God that he was. Daniel stood up, but he could not control his trembling. What a rebuke this is to presumption and spiritual pride. We tremble at the thought of those who think they can command God to do this or that or who use flippant and irreverent terms to address the one who sits on the heavenly throne.

2. The Delay Explained (10:12-21)

The vision of the divine person faded and Daniel was left talking with the angel. A mysterious veil was drawn aside and Daniel was given a glimpse into the extraterrestrial world that crowds in on us from the unseen, that touches human life at every turn and is unsuspected by the masses of humankind. The "extraterrestrials," as we now call them, are there. But, for the most part, those who court dealings with humans are evil and powerful lords of darkness.

a. *Revelation* (10:12-14). There was no delay between the spiritual exercise of Daniel and the response of God. The moment he began to pray he was heard and the answer was on its way.

There are various reasons why we experience delay in receiving an answer to our prayers. Sometimes we are in no spiritual condition to receive the answer God would send. Sometimes we ask amiss and God withholds the answer in order to give us time to see for ourselves how wrong our request is. Sometimes God uses natural means to accomplish his purpose and often it takes time for such results to be brought to pass.

We learn from this chapter that hostile forces at work in the universe attempt to oppose all that is of God. There was nothing arbitrary about this particular delay. The sight of this aged seer diligently seeking answers to the perplexities that overwhelmed him brought an immediate response from God. God is delighted when his children set their hearts to understand.

Now Daniel learned what it was that impeded the response to his prayer. There was no tardiness in heaven. There was another factor in the equation. Verse 13 reveals the true nature of the spiritual forces that have power in the unseen world.

First, it is evident that the "prince of Persia" was no human prince. One angel in one night could slay Sennacherib's armies (2 Chronicles 32:20-21). No human prince could hinder a herald angel from discharging a commission from the throne of God. The "prince of Persia," then, was an angelic being opposed to God. He was a fallen angel, a powerful member of Satan's hierarchy. We learn from the New Testament that there are various orders among those spirit powers that owe allegiance to Satan. We engage them in war when we pray. Paul reminded us that "we wrestle not against flesh and blood, but against principalities, against powers, against the rulers of the darkness of this world, against spiritual wickedness in high places" (Ephesians 6:12). There are also countless hosts of demons, creatures (it would seem) of a different order from the fallen angels.

We learn here that the Persian empire was ruled by a human prince (Cyrus, king of Persia, v. 1) but also, in the unseen world, by a fallen angelic prince. He wielded such enormous power that he was able to hinder God's herald angel from delivering his message to Daniel for three weeks of human time. We gather from this that tutelary angels preside over the affairs of the various nations of earth. Also, there is conflict, in the heavenlies, between these fallen angels and the sinless angels who seek to further the interests of God's kingdom on earth.

In this case, the obstructing prince of Persia was able to hinder God's herald. In the end another angel came to help the messenger. He is described as "Michael, one of the chief princes," More is said about him at the end of the chapter. We learn from Revelation 12 that Michael is the martial angel who commands the armies of heaven. His arrival swung the balance of the conflict. "I had superiority over the Prince of Persia," the herald angel explained. With the arrival of Michael, the herald angel was able to continue with his mission. Michael was more than a match for the prince of Persia.

The vision to which the angel referred is the long vision of the next chapter. As we shall see, this remarkable vision covers the entire intertestamentary period from Malachi to Matthew. It then leaps over the church age and focuses on what the angel calls "the latter days." This is one of the focal points of all prophecy.

Old Testament prophecy, while its light falls on many a distant hill, really illuminates two mountain peaks: the first and second comings of Christ—his coming to redeem and his coming to reign. Similarly, New Testament prophecy focuses on two mountain peaks: the two future comings of Christ—the "appearing" and the "advent." The "appearing" is when Christ comes *for* his church, an event we usually call the rapture; the "advent" is when Christ comes *with* his church to set up his millennial kingdom on this planet. This climactic event is the final focus of both Old and New Testament prophecy. We can depict what the prophet saw thus:

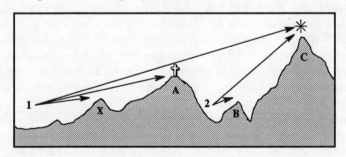

In this diagram:

1 = The Old Testament Prophet
2 = The New Testament Prophet
A = The First Coming (to Redeem)
B = The Rapture of the Church
C = The Second Coming (to Reign)
X = The Era of Antiochus

The valley between peak A and peak C depicts the present age of grace, the church age in which we live—something not revealed in the Old Testament, although it was concealed there in certain of the types.

In Daniel 9 the prophet was given a clear view of peak A. In Daniel 11 he was given his clearest view of peak C. Between where the Old Testament prophet stood and peak A, the chart marks one of the lesser peaks along the way with an X. This smaller peak represents the era of Antiochus Epiphanes, who looms so large in Daniel's prophecies. In Daniel 10 the angel refers the aged seer, in anticipation, to peak C ("the latter days").

This is indeed a key prophetic peak. It was first referred to in Daniel in the interpretation of Nebuchadnezzar's dream (2:38). It has an important bearing on the prophecy of chapter 11. The phrase first occurred in Jacob's remarkable deathbed prophecy (Genesis 49:1). (For a fuller exposition of this prophecy, see my forthcoming book, *Exploring Bible Prophecy*.) In all, it occurs fourteen times in the Old Testament (Genesis 49:1; Numbers 24:14; Deuteronomy 4:30; 31:29; Isaiah 2:2; Jeremiah 23:20; Hosea 3:5; Micah 4:1). In ten of these references it is rendered "latter days" in the King James version.

b. *Reaction* (10:15-19). Again *Daniel's weakness was revealed* (10:15-17). It is not certain whether the one who touched Daniel was his divine visitor or the attending angel. From Daniel's continuing sense of weakness and inadequacy it is likely that the second person of the godhead was still present, that He was the one who graciously touched the prophet who still did not dare to lift up his eyes. His awesome presence rendered even the articulate Daniel silent.

The divine visitor again graciously touched his beloved servant and restored his power of speech. Daniel's first words were an apology for his inability to converse intelligently with his visitor. In the first place, he was quite overcome by the sorrows that were to afflict the world in general and his own people in particular. Also he was weakened, doubtless by his prolonged fast and, perhaps, by the infirmities of old age and certainly by the proximity of the divine being who had condescended to visit him.

Next *Daniel's weakness was removed* (10:18-19). Again, it would seem that this action was taken by the divine visitor. Three times He is said to have touched Daniel (10:10,16,18).

The words, "Peace be unto you" have a familiar echo in our ears from the resurrection appearances of the Lord to his own in the upper room (John 20:19,21,26). But it was not the touch of the visitor that strengthened Daniel, though the act was as gracious as when, in the days of his incarnation, he would touch lepers. It was his words that strengthened Daniel. Again Daniel was assured of the place he held in the heart of God. Daniel was now ready to listen to what these visitors from that other world had to say to him.

c. *Resolution* (10:20-21). It would seem at this point that the angel resumed the conversation—unless, of course, it was the angel throughout. It is not likely that the Son of God spoke the words that followed, for what need would He have of the help of an angel in dealing with satanic foes? One word from him and they would have fled. On the whole, it seems more likely that the attendant angel resumed the revelation begun earlier (10:12-14), which was interrupted by Daniel's collapse.

The angel was about to show Daniel the terrible and ceaseless conflicts that would take place on the earth in the years ahead, conflicts that would ravage the promised land again and again. Judah would be a pawn in the power plays of two rival kingdoms, one to the north and the other to the south. That little land would become a battleground as hostile kingdoms marched back and forth, one against the other.

But behind all this turmoil are unseen spiritual and sinister forces. Satanic princes keep the world in upheaval. People wonder why it is that peace on earth is such an impossible goal. There are persons of good will, persons in power, who long for peace. But all the world has is war and the rumor of war. One reason is that Satan hates the human race. He hates mankind because man was made in the image and likeness of God. Ever since the fall, the world has lain in Satan's lap and he delights in its torments and terrors. He will not allow the human race to achieve peace on any terms but his own: All must crown his man king, all must bow and worship the dragon, the beast, and the image of the beast. It is toward this end that he works. There are powerful forces of evil who secretly rule the world from an extraterrestrial dimension. The angel had already told Daniel that. Now he added something more.

The satanic "prince of Persia" was having his day, since Persia was the ruling world superpower on earth. Whatever rivalries may exist between Satan's hierarchical powers they are united in their opposition to God and his rule. Thus we learn that the struggle between Gabriel and the prince of Persia was by no means over. But first the herald angel would deliver to Daniel what was already written in "the scripture of truth." The future was written on an "unerring tablet." Nothing could fail to be fulfilled. All must come to pass. The future was not in the capricious and malicious hands of Satan's dark lords but in the hands of an omniscient and omnipotent God who, in the end, will make all things work together to accomplish his divine beneficent purpose.

The "prince of Persia" was having his day and the "prince of Greece" was coming. The unseen war was not over. But Gabriel was not alone. He had already spoken to Daniel of Michael the archangel. Now he mentioned him again. He had already described him as "one of the chief princes," thus revealing rank among the angels of God (10:13). Now he called him "Michael your prince" (10:21). Later he was called "the great prince which standeth for the children of thy people" (12:1). Judah was not left defenseless and unprotected from hostile angels in the extraterrestrial world, with no angel to champion its cause. They had Michael, a warrior angel of great rank and power. He took his stand for them.

The unseen world is a real world, and modern men and women are particularly vulnerable to that spirit world because of their ignorance of it and their inquisitiveness about it. The average person today is like a person living in the Middle Ages, trying to fight disease while ignorant of bacteria. During the plague that decimated London and parts of Britain in 1665, people knew next to nothing about the simplest principles of sanitation. An open city sewer ran down the middle of each street. Rats multiplied. What caused the plague? The Royal College of Surgeons said it was carried by the air. People shut themselves in their houses; stopped up doors, windows, and chimneys. They burned noxious and evil-smelling compounds to battle the enemy, fresh air. Suppose someone had told them that the plague was carried by a bacillus, that the invisible microbes were carried by fleas, and that rats were the chief hosts of the deadly fleas. That person would have been regarded as insane. The notion was nonsense.

Modern man no longer scoffs at microbes. But demons? Evil spirits? Fallen angels ruling the nations from an unseen world and delighting in the miseries of mankind? In wars and famines, earthquakes and persecutions? Nonsense. It is considered incredible by most people that behind our destructive ideologies, foolish "scientific" hypotheses, and false religions, there are vast intelligences, organized principalities, who are working to a master plan, who are implacable in their hatred of the human race, and who feast their diabolical appetites on human sufferings and souls. No wonder the world cannot achieve peace, when it not only rejects the prince of peace, but denies the existence of Satan and his minions.

But equally, destructive is modern man's inquisitiveness. Madame Curie in her day explored the mysterious world of x-rays, but she did so without full knowledge of the dangers of radioactivity. She took no precautions—but what precautions could she have taken to protect herself from the forces of nature, the existence of which she knew little? In the end she perished, a victim of forces she could not control.

But there is also danger in tampering with the occult world. Through the ages, evil spirits have induced people to investigate psychic mysteries. They produce certain phenomena, they materialize apparitions, they rap and mutter and chant. They bestow certain powers on those who obey their rules.

All ages have had their occultists and spiritualists, their witches and satanists. The phenomena manifested are almost as old as man. The deceptions remain unchanged. The price for playing with these psychic toys is high: deception, character deterioration, and, if pursued too far, damnation. The spirit deceivers give just enough enticement to lure the unwary farther and farther from the truth. They want human dupes and envoys and tools. Hitler was such a tool. The havoc he wreaked on the world can never be measured.

Eastern religions and cults specialize in the occult. In our spiritually bankrupt day, more and more people are seeking answers in New Age and other occult-oriented movements, unaware of the hard-core realities that lie behind trivial psychic experiences. Only those like Hitler and his kind really touch at last the terrible powers who rule in that other world. By then it is too late to withdraw.

The only safe guide we have to these things is the Bible. The scriptures make no attempt to hide the fact that evil spirits exist. There are mischievous and malicious demons which crave embodiment, delighting in possessing their dupes. They propagate philosophical and religious lies, promote wars and disasters on earth. They are all dangerous, and the Bible tells us all we need to know about them. The Bible warns us against them; it forbids witchcraft, astrology, necromancy, and all such attempts to make contact with them. The Bible tells how we can break free of their influence, pray against them, and be protected from them.

They are there. They are real. They torment individuals and rule nations. It is a sobering thought, ignored by the world's political pundits, never considered as a factor in any analysis of national affairs. Those who rule the nations do not know that behind human government are "the rulers of this world's darkness." Behind the Soviet Union, China, Britain, France, Canada, the United States of America, and all other nations are Satan's princes. The world's best protection against these extraterrestrials is a praying believer, Bible in hand, indwelt by the Holy Spirit of God.

III. Two Complete Disclosures (11:1–12:13)

We approach chapter 11 convinced that it is pure prophecy (see Appendix 18). We shall follow the unerring footsteps of the Holy Spirit as He leads us down the centuries.

Peter described prophecy as "light that shineth in a dark place" (2 Peter 1:19). Prophecy sheds light on human events by foretelling them and on the scriptures by affirming their divine inspiration. Only God can prophesy. This chapter must have comforted that believing remnant among God's ancient people who lived in those dark days between the Testaments. They could put their fingers on verse after verse and say, "Here's where we are." For four hundred years God remained silent, and it was not until John the Baptist raised his voice that the silence was broken. Yet those silent centuries were not without echoes, and those echoes sound loudly in this chapter. This chapter was written to be a lamp to the feet of God's people and a light on their path in the intertestamental period.

A. Specific Details about the Future (11:1-45)

There is a clear-cut break in this remarkable prophecy between Daniel 11: 35 and 11:36. The prophetic history is continuous right down to the days of Antiochus Epiphanes. Then it leaps over the ages (as does the prophecy of Daniel 9:25-26) and comes back into focus at the time of antichrist, of whom, as we have seen elsewhere, Antiochus was a type.

Before exploring the prophecies of this chapter, note the intricacies of the history to which they refer as diagrammed on the following chart. You will find it helpful to refer from time to time both to the outline and diagram. The cold recitation of the facts of history summarized in this chart should not bore us. They should thrill us when we remember that when Daniel 11 was written they were not history but *prophecy*. We see them as history; Daniel saw them still ahead in the unborn ages. No other chapter in all scripture gives us such an awesome exhibition of God's power to foretell the future.

1. The Coming of Antiochus (11:1-35)

The period covered by these verses can be divided into three. The first of these introduces us to:

a. *The World of Alexander the Greek* (11:1-9). We see Alexander's rivalry with Persia and his vast conquests. Who would have thought in

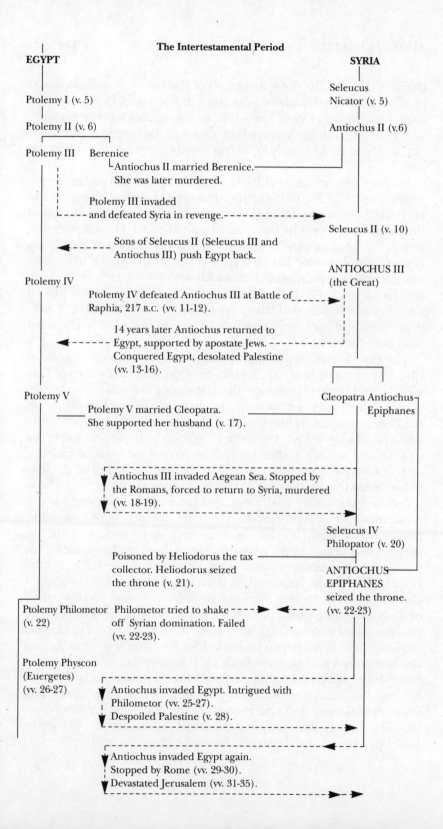

The Intertestamental Period

EGYPT   SYRIA

Ptolemy I (v. 5)   Seleucus
                                          Nicator (v. 5)

Ptolemy II (v. 6)   Antiochus II (v.6)

Ptolemy III   Berenice
                └Antiochus II married Berenice.
                  She was later murdered.

                Ptolemy III invaded
                and defeated Syria in revenge.

                                          Seleucus II (v. 10)
                Sons of Seleucus II (Seleucus III and
                Antiochus III) push Egypt back.

                                          ANTIOCHUS III
                                          (the Great)
Ptolemy IV
                Ptolemy IV defeated Antiochus III at Battle of
                Raphia, 217 B.C. (vv. 11-12).

                14 years later Antiochus returned to
                Egypt, supported by apostate Jews.
                Conquered Egypt, desolated Palestine
                (vv. 13-16).

Ptolemy V   Cleopatra Antiochus
                Ptolemy V married Cleopatra.   Epiphanes
                She supported her husband (v. 17).

                Antiochus III invaded Aegean Sea. Stopped by
                the Romans, forced to return to Syria, murdered
                (vv. 18-19).

                                          Seleucus IV
                                          Philopator (v. 20)

                Poisoned by Heliodorus the tax
                collector. Heliodorus seized
                the throne (v. 21).   ANTIOCHUS
                                          EPIPHANES
                                          seized the throne.
Ptolemy Philometor Philometor tried to shake   (vv. 22-23)
(v. 22)   off Syrian domination. Failed
                    (vv. 22-23).

Ptolemy Physcon
(Euergetes)
(vv. 26-27)   Antiochus invaded Egypt. Intrigued with
                    Philometor (vv. 25-27).
                    Despoiled Palestine (v. 28).

                    Antiochus invaded Egypt again.
                    Stopped by Rome (vv. 29-30).
                    Devastated Jerusalem (vv. 31-35).

Daniel's day that the disunited states of the Greek peninsula would produce a conqueror who would grind the powerful Persian empire to pieces? Daniel already knew this, of course, because he had previously been given the vision of the ram and the he-goat. The vision of chapter 11 touches only lightly on prophecies already given to the seer.

We have first *his success* (11:1-4), beginning with *the concluding period of Persia* (11:1-2). The statement in verse 1 really belongs at the end of the previous chapter. It records the concluding comment of the herald angel on his cooperation with Michael. He was referring to a previous occasion, at the time when the prince of Persia was coming into his own. The first year of Darius the Mede, of course, was the year that Babylon fell to the Medes and Persians. We are not told in what way Gabriel assisted Michael at that time. It is just an added confirmation that "the powers that be are ordained of God," that Satan and his fallen angelic princes do not have undisputed sway over the destinies of nations.

The first three kings the herald angel referred to were Cambyses (the Ahasuerus of Ezra 4:6), Pseudo-Smerdis (the Artaxerxes of Ezra 4:7-23), and Darius Hystaspes (the Darius of Ezra 4:24). This particular prophecy makes no attempt to chronicle all the vicissitudes of the Persian empire. It hurries on to the fourth Persian emperor, the one who was significant from the viewpoint of Bible prophecy: the wealthy and mighty Xerxes (the Ahasuerus of the book of Esther).

This king was quite willing to sell to Haman the lives of all the Jews in his realm for ten thousand talents of silver. He was a king whose unbridled sensuality, ambition, and pride paved the way for the downfall of the Persian empire. For years this king kept Asia in turmoil as he stirred up his vast realm against Greece (as foretold in this prophecy). He assembled an army of over three million men for his invasion of Greece, and stirred up Phoenician Carthage against Greek colonies in Italy and Sicily. The Carthaginians, seeing a chance to plunder a rival maritime power, raised some 300,000 men of their own along with a naval force of two hundred ships. So, as the prophecy states, Xerxes did "stir up all" against the realm of Greece.

He seemed invincible as he hurled his land and sea forces against the tiny country of Greece. Both at Thermopylae and at Salamis, however, he suffered crushing defeats and his power was broken. All he could do was to sneak off, overwhelmed and humiliated. The invasion of Greece by Xerxes proved in the end to be Persia's Waterloo. The empire lingered on in history for another century and a half, but its glory was departed. Although there were other Persian kings, the Bible ignores them because the handwriting was now on the wall for Persia, as it once had been for Babylon. The day would come when Greece would exact full retribution for Xerxes' folly.

The prophecy turns next to *the coming punishment of Persia* (11:3-4). Here Alexander the Great's debut on the stage of history is foretold, noting *his conquests* (11:3). We have already chronicled the astonishing history of Alexander the Great (Daniel 8), so it will not be necessary to retell that story.

No Persian emperor after Xerxes was powerful enough to attack Greece. When Darius Codommanus demanded why Alexander was invading his kingdom, he was told that the Persians had formerly done the same to Greece without cause or provocation. Alexander had come to punish them, he said. So, between Xerxes and Alexander there is the closest connection. The prophecy was accurate. The Persian kings in between simply did not count.

Alexander did "according to his will." His first resolve was to invade Persia and avenge Greece for the attacks made on the country years before by Xerxes, but he did not stop there. Within a dozen years he had brought Asia, India, and parts of Africa and Europe under his sway. He never met a foe he could not conquer, a city he could not subdue, a people he could not subjugate.

He was willful in all things, but his career was a short one. He died in his early thirties, leaving behind him an empire over which his minions squabbled and fought. Thus the prophecy spoke also of *his collapse* (11:4).

Alexander died in Babylon at the zenith of his power. He lived only thirty-two years and eight months and reigned for a mere twelve years and eight months. None of his posterity received any lasting inheritance. His half-brother, Philip Aridaeus, succeeded him, but after six years was murdered, along with his wife Euridice, at the instigation of Alexander's mother, Olympias. His illegitimate son Hercules was not recognized by the generals and was murdered by Polysperchon, along with his mother Barsine, Alexander's former mistress. His wife Statira, daughter of the ill-fated Darius, was murdered by Roxane, another of Alexander's wives. His posthumous son Alexander Aegus, born to Roxane, was put under a guardian and then murdered by the order of Olympias through the treachery of the general Cassander. Alexander's mother, Olympias, was murdered. His sister Cleopatra, queen of Epirus, was murdered. Within fifteen years of his own death, none of his family remained alive. Thus exactly was the word of God fulfilled.

After the death of the conquering Alexander, confusion reigned for twenty years. Then, after the battle of Ipsus, the empire was carved up by the generals Lysimachus, Cassander, Ptolemy, and Seleucus Nicator. Ptolemy took Egypt and became "the king of the south." Seleucus took Syria and became "the king of the north." The seesaw battles, feuds, and intrigues of these two dynasties kept the land of Palestine in turmoil. It is because the history of these two countries affected God's people Israel and the little land of Palestine that they become the center of prophetic interest.

So the prophetic focus turns to *his successors* (11:5-9). The first focal point of interest is *the Egyptian prince* (11:5). This verse had a literal fulfillment. One of Alexander's successors, Ptolemy Lagus, (from which name the designation Legidae is derived) founded a new dynasty in Egypt. His son, Ptolemy Soter, is the strong "king of the south" referred to here.

In the meantime, one of Alexander's generals, Seleucus Nicator, had been appointed vice-regent of Babylon. He was driven out of his province by the ambitious Antigonus. He fled to Egypt, where he was hospitably received by Ptolemy. In the battle of Ipsus he was one of Ptolemy's commanders and the real architect of victory (301 B.C.). Antigonus was defeated and Seleucus seized the lion's share of Alexander the Great's empire. He took Cappadocia, part of Phrygia, upper Syria, Mesopotamia, and the Euphrates Valley, and reigned from the Hellespont to the Indus—an empire second only to that of Alexander himself. Thus, as the prophecy said, the king of the south was strong, but one of his princes (captains) was stronger than he. The Seleucid kingdom was greater than the other three put together.

The next point of prophetic interest centers on *the Egyptian princess* (11:6). The two kings who now occupy the prophetic stage are Ptolemy II Philadelphus, king of the south, and Antiochus III Theos, king of the north. The "king's daughter of the south" was Berenice.

There was peace between the two kingdoms during the reigns of Ptolemy Soter and Seleucus Nicator. Eventually Ptolemy abdicated and gave the Egyptian throne to Philadelphus, the son of his second wife Berenice. Not long afterward, Antiochus Soter became the Syrian king and war broke out between Syria and Egypt. A half-brother of Ptolemy Philadelphus, a son of Berenice, named Magas, married Apame, the daughter of Antiochus. This marriage became the cause of the first war between the two kingdoms. Magas had been appointed governor of Cyrene. Not content with that, he tried to make himself king of his province. Further, he plotted to seize Egypt from Ptolemy, his half-brother, and he persuaded his father-in-law Antiochus to support him by declaring war against Egypt. So began the interminable wars between north and south, which clutter up this prophetic history. Only God could have foreseen and foretold the kaleidoscopic changes of fortune that now followed.

Antiochus Soter died and was succeeded on the Syrian throne by Antiochus II Theos, who continued the war against Egypt. At last "in the end of years" Ptolemy offered Antiochus a bribe for peace. He would give him his daughter Berenice in marriage and a large dowry besides. However, Antiochus must divorce his wife Laodice and declare her two sons, Seleucus and Antiochus, to be illegitimate. When Antiochus, who was weak and profligate, agreed to this arrangement, Ptolemy bestowed a fortune on his daughter and sent her to Syria with great pomp. Both rulers imagined that this despicable agreement would bring in lasting peace.

All seemed to go well until the death of Ptolemy Philadelphus, when Antiochus promptly repudiated Berenice and took back Laodice as his wife. Laodice, however, distrusted her husband and, eager to secure the throne for her son, poisoned Antiochus, clearing the way to the throne for Seleucus Callinicus. Then it was the turn of Berenice, the unfortunate Egyptian princess. Laodice persuaded Seleucus to have her assassinated. "They that brought her" perished in this coup for, according to Polyaenus, most of her women attendants were slain before her eyes while trying to protect her. Her child who, by terms of the original marriage agreement, was heir to the throne, was also killed.

Thus the abominable treaty ended in a welter of treachery and death. Ptolemy II Philadelphus, author of the treaty, died. The unprincipled Antiochus II Theos was murdered. The poor Egyptian princess did "not retain the strength of the arm" nor did the scheming Antiochus "stand." All who had any connection with this unscrupulous treaty—father, child, husband, most of the Egyptian courtiers—came to a speedy downfall. So end treaties that are based on expedience, treachery, and dishonor.

The next prophetic picture follows on quite naturally. It tells of *the Egyptian protest* (11:7-9). "One of the branches of her roots" refers to one of the other children of Berenice's parents—in fact, to her brother Ptolemy Euergetes ("benefactor"), who succeeded his father Philadelphus on the Egyptian throne. He was outraged at the treatment of his sister. Seleucus II Callinicus, now on the throne of Syria, soon had to face the consequences for what he and his parents had done. Ptolemy raised an army and marched north to wipe out with blood the insults and crimes of the Syrian rulers. He captured Seleucia, "the fortress of the king of the north," subjugated the country, put Laodice to death, and treated the Syrians as he pleased. Indeed, he captured most of the Syrian empire. His armies took Babylon and marched to the boundaries of India.

Nor did that quench his thirst for revenge. The prophecy foretold that immense booty would be his, and so it was. He brought back to Egypt 4,000 talents of gold, 40,000 talents of silver, 2,500 molten idols and their sacred vessels, including many that had been captured and taken from Egypt by Cambyses some 300 years before. The prophecy specifically mentions the capture of these gods. Pagan conquerors invariably made off with the gods of defeated nations because that proved their gods were stronger than those of the conquered people. The recovered Egyptian idols were installed back in their temples with great ceremony, and the Egyptian priests rewarded their heroic king with the title "Euergetes."

His thirst for revenge slaked, Ptolemy made no further attacks on Syria. He left Seleucus on the throne, satisfied that he had taught him a lesson he was not likely to forget. A truce was signed, it seems, which lasted for ten years. Then the foolhardy Seleucus made an attempt to invade Egypt. His fleet was lost in a storm, his forces were routed, and he was driven back to Syria in humiliating defeat.

This, then, was the world of Alexander the Greek. His great empire was divided into four parts, two of which assumed prophetic significance. Syria and Egypt occupy the center of the stage for the succeeding centuries. The opening rivalry between these two countries becomes the pattern of the years ahead.

b. *The Wars of Antiochus the Great* (11:10-20). We look now at *his first campaign* (11:10-12) in which Antiochus was first *victorious* (11:10) and then vanquished. Seleucus Callinicus died as a result of injuries suffered when he fell off his horse. He was succeeded on the Syrian throne by two of his sons, first by Seleucus III Ceraunus, and, on his death three years later, by Antiochus III, afterward surnamed Magnus (the Great). These two sons of the weak Callinicus were determined to restore the glories of Syria and to avenge their father's defeats at the hand of Ptolemy. The fortified port city of Seleucia, only sixteen miles from Antioch, was still in the hands of an Egyptian garrison, and was therefore a constant reminder of their nation's humiliation and a threat to Syrian independence.

But that menace would have to wait. Seleucus Ceraunus was barely enthroned when he received news that Attalus, king of Pergamum, had seized all the country beyond the Taurus mountains. Ceraunus assembled a sizable army and marched over the mountains to recover his imperiled domains, but misfortune dogged his steps and he was murdered by mutinous troops. He was succeeded on the Syrian throne by his brother Antiochus III, the Great, a man of far more determined character. The story of his reign was one of incessant warfare.

The first concern of Antiochus was to defeat Attalus, even though Hermias, his chief adviser, urged him to strike at Egypt. But the king's attention was diverted from both these objectives by another dangerous uprising, this one raised by Molon and Alexander, governors of the upper provinces in the east. The rebels defeated the generals Antiochus sent against them and were not quelled until he in person took the situation in hand.

Thus both brothers, Seleucus Ceraunus and Antiochus the Great, collected great armies, as the text foretold. However, it was Antiochus alone who marched against Egypt. This is reflected in the text by the change of the verbs from the plural to the singular.

Meantime, the throne in Egypt had passed to Ptolemy Philopator who had succeeded his father Euergetes. Philopator was not cut from the same piece of cloth as his father. Weak, indecisive, dissolute, and advised by vile ministers, he was to be no match for the determined Syrian now on the throne of the northern kingdom.

Having secured Seleucid power in the upper provinces and having put his uncle Archaeus on notice that he had not forgotten the revolt in the west, Antiochus began to direct his developing might against Egypt. His first goal was to recover the fortress port Seleucia. This he accomplished swiftly. Then he seized Tyre and Ptolemais, which put him in territory ruled by Philopator. Like an overflowing flood, he burst through Palestine, seizing Dora, a strong fortress north of Caesarea.

Ptolemy's ministers, Sosibius and Agathocles, were preparing for the coming onslaught; to win more time they negotiated a truce, whereupon Antiochus garrisoned the towns he had already captured and retired for the winter to Seleucia. In the following spring he renewed hostilities and captured numerous cities, especially in Phoenicia and eastern Palestine. He decisively defeated Nicolaus, the Egyptian general, whose shattered forces retired into Sidon. By this time, another winter season was approaching, so Antiochus took up residence in Ptolemais. The next year he advanced farther south until he arrived at Gaza, described in the text as the "fortress" of the king of the south, the limit set by the prophecy. Syrian ascendancy was now established.

But the prophecy foretold that the king of the north would not only be victorious, he would be *vanquished* (11:11-12). The voluptuous and dissolute Philopator was finally aroused to the seriousness of his situation. He was enraged by the threat of invasion and by the contempt of his subjects. His ministers, Sosibius and Agathocles, had put together an army of mercenaries and volunteers, and Philopator, like the conquering pharaohs of old, along with Arsinoe his consort, marched forth to battle.

Antiochus was ready. He had massed a great army of some 70,000 infantry and 5,000 cavalry and, confident of more speedy victories, he besieged the Egyptian border fortress of Raphia, not far from Gaza. The battle of Raphia resulted in the total and unexpected defeat of Antiochus. Thus the "great multitude" was "given into his hand," the hand, that is, of the king of the south. The king of the south was exultant, as the text foretold, but being essentially a weak man, he failed to follow through on his resounding victory. "He shall not be strengthened by it," ran the prophetic word. Nor was he. He annexed Palestine but threw away the fruits of his victory by failing to invade Syria. Instead, he made peace with Antiochus and returned to his dissolute ways.

Nor was that all. Before returning to Egypt, in his pride and self-will he profaned the Jewish temple in Jerusalem, to the indignation of the Jewish people. He demanded entrance into the holy of holies but was struck down to the ground speechless before he could actually enforce his plan.

The Jewish people now come increasingly into the prophetic focus of this chapter. All history on earth, from the divine standpoint, centers on Israel.

Philopator was by no means through with the Jews. All the way back to Egypt he brooded over his mysterious humiliation in the Jerusalem temple and doubtless imagined that the Jews had used some kind of magic against him. But back in Egypt he had thousands of Jews who would be in his power. Accordingly, once back in his own land he launched a wholesale persecution of the Jews. Some 40,000 were martyred for refusing to embrace the idolatrous Egyptian religion. Thus he did "cast down many myriads." This, however, was but another proof of the weakness of this evil king.

We look next at *his further campaign* (11:13-17). Thirteen years passed after the battle of Raphia, during which time, in spite of his defeat, Antiochus reorganized and plunged into new wars. He recovered Asia Minor from his rebel uncle Achaeus, settled affairs in Parthia, Bactria, and Hyrcania to his satisfaction, and received the submission of various princes on the western side of the Indus. On his march back from the east he followed the route taken by Alexander the Great and made numerous conquests in Arabia. Now, with his empire at peace and firmly in hand, he reigned from the Caspian Sea to the Indus River. Wealth flowed into his coffers and he was able to raise a vast army, splendidly equipped and with no lack of men. He could again turn his thoughts toward Egypt. Now he could "set forth a multitude greater than the former, and . . . come . . . with a great army and with much riches."

In the meantime, his old enemy Philopator had died, along with his queen. The assumption seems to be that they were poisoned. Egypt was now in disarray because the new king of the south, Philopator's son, Ptolemy Epiphanes, was only four years old. Throughout Egypt, various factions took full advantage of the weakness of the central authority. The foolish actions of the infant Ptolemy's chief minister of state, Agathocles (later to be murdered), provoked riots and insurrections in the provinces. One formidable riot, for instance, broke out in Alexandria and was directed against Agathocles and other favorites of Philopator. Then came the conspiracy of Scopas and that of Lycopolis. Throughout the country there was a series of military and civil disorders.

The Jews, too, revolted. Some of the more determined leaders saw in Antiochus a possible savior from the galling yoke of Egypt, with the result that some of the Jews threw in their lot with Antiochus. To do so was the result of unbelief and apostasy, and was also a great folly, because the real foe of Israel was to the north.

The Jews who threw in their lot with Antiochus are referred to as "the robbers of thy people." The phrase has been rendered "the violent among thy people," or "sons of the oppressors." They were apostate Jews determined to meddle now in international affairs. They doubtless hoped to secure their national independence by this alliance with Syria but, if so, they seriously misjudged Antiochus. The Jews gained no advantage from this alliance and many perished in the war.

Whether Antiochus was victorious or vanquished, the Jews suffered in consequence and, in any case, were a convenient scapegoat. Even when Antiochus bestowed some favor on them, it was the favor of a raw pagan. Worst of all, the leaning of some Jews toward Syria inclined some of them, especially in high places, to lean toward Hellenism—a more subtle, long-range, and insidious danger for the Jews than Syria's or Egypt's troops. The subsequent adoption of Hellenism and heathen customs by many Jews helped bring about the horrors in the days of Antiochus Epiphanes, son of Antiochus the

Great. So, as the text says, the Jews who espoused a pro-Syrian policy were "robbers" of God's people.

Antiochus moved south, now resolved to recover Coele-Syria, Phoenicia, and Palestine, territories that had been garrisoned with Egyptian troops by the late Ptolemy Philopator. The Egyptian general, Scopas, was unable to withstand Antiochus's invasion of Coele-Syria. He was roundly defeated at Mount Panium and retreated with some 10,000 of his remaining troops to the fortified city of Sidon, the "well-fenced city" of the text. Desperate attempts were made by the Egyptians to relieve the city. Three famous generals and the best troops were sent in successive waves. It was in vain. The Syrians were too well entrenched. "The arms of the south [could] not withstand." Famine eventually forced the surrender of Sidon, Scopas, and the Egyptian garrison.

Once Antiochus had repossessed Coele-Syria, Phoenicia, and Palestine, there was none who could prevent him from doing whatever he willed (11:16).

As has been noted, the Jews welcomed Antiochus, vainly imagining he was their deliverer. "The glorious land," of course, is Palestine. The Jews, however, had a tiger by the tail. Up until now, Palestine had repeatedly suffered, because it was in the path of the warring armies of north and south and was thus a wretched buffer state kicked this way and that.

Now, however, Antiochus made it a base from which to harass Egypt. Since his troops had to live off the land, they plundered Palestine unmercifully. So "by his hand" the land was "consumed" or "laid waste."

Antiochus now decided to invade Egypt (11:17). He summoned the armed might of his kingdom and collected a vast army and naval force. As a preliminary to the invasion of Egypt he set about reducing to servitude all the cities of Ptolemy along the coast of Casia and Cilicia. The "upright ones" who are associated with him in this enterprise seem to be certain prominent Jews. The descriptive term does not necessarily imply that these Jews were more upright than others of the Jewish people. Rather it was a term applied by Jews to Jewish people in general.

However, Antiochus was about to receive a severe check to his ambitions. The Egyptian regent had appealed to a new and growing power on the stage of history: Rome. The Romans, although not yet a world power, had defeated Hannibal and humbled Carthage in the second Punic War. They had fought and won their second Macedonian War and had taken Greece. The ambitions of Antiochus the

Great, therefore, were beginning to encroach on what the Romans considered to be their sphere of interest. It was no secret that Antiochus wanted to conquer Pergamum, a constant thorn in his flesh; he also wanted to conquer Greece and become a second Alexander. The Egyptian appeal gave Rome its opportunity to confront a king who was now threatening to become a menace. Faced by the likelihood of Roman interference if he invaded Egypt, Antiochus backed off.

He resorted to diplomacy. He proposed to the Egyptians that his daughter Cleopatra be married to the young Ptolemy Epiphanes. Both were only children. Cleopatra is described in the prophetic text as "the daughter of women," an idiomatic expression that signifies a child of tender years still under the tutelage of her mother and nurse. Ptolemy was only seven years old. Antiochus promised the revenue of Coele-Syria, Phoenicia, and Palestine as a dowry (a promise he never kept). The marriage was celebrated at Raphia.

Antiochus had sought to corrupt his infant daughter, as the text says. He wanted her to betray her husband's interests and serve, instead, her father's political ambitions. What a romance could be written about these two children, married to one another at a tender age, drawn to one another, becoming one in heart and purpose. Cleopatra took the side of her boy-husband. She even went so far as to send an envoy to congratulate the Romans on their victories over her father, to urge them to expel him from Greece and to carry the war to Asia. Thus Antiochus was foiled in his plot. He must have been enraged at this betrayal of his interests by his daughter. But he was by no means through.

We now come to *his final campaign* (11:18-20). The text begins with *his vain scheme* (11:18-19). Antiochus now fitted out a fleet of three hundred ships and attacked the coastlands and islands of Asia Minor and Greece. The Romans sent ambassadors to Lysimachia to confront Antiochus, but Antiochus was in no mood to listen to reason. He contemptuously told the ambassadors that the Romans had no vital interests in Asia, that he was no vassal of theirs, and that he had every right to recover the cities and lands which had formerly been under the control of Lysimachus and were part of Alexander's domain.

That was enough for the Romans. The Roman consul Acilius met Antiochus at the pass of Thermopylae, defeated him, and expelled him from Greece. He was next defeated at sea by Livius and Aemilius, but the decisive battle was fought at Magnesia, near Smyrna, in 190 B.C. Antiochus's army of 80,000 men was defeated with terrible loss of life by Lucius Cornelius Scipio. Antiochus was forced to renounce all claim to any part of Europe or Asia Minor west of the Taurus Mountains and was made to accept a humiliating peace treaty. His younger son, Antiochus, was carried off to Rome along with other hostages, to ensure his father's future good conduct, and remained there for about fourteen years. Nor was this all. Antiochus was fined 2,550 talents toward the expenses of the war he had caused and levied an annual tribute to Rome of one thousand talents for the next twelve years.

A few months later, as Antiochus was crossing his eastern provinces to raise money for the tribute, he tried to plunder the temple of Bel (the Elymaian Zeus). Furious local inhabitants killed both him and his attendants. So, as scripture says, he stumbled and fell, and was found no more (11:19).

The story of the wars of Antiochus the Great has a footnote. Reference is made to *his vile son* (11:20). Antiochus was succeeded on the throne of Syria by his eldest son Seleucus Philopator, who was little else but a raiser of taxes. He did not have his father's restless, ambitious spirit. He was more tolerant and easygoing and wanted only to be at peace. The tribute laid on the kingdom by Rome was onerous and most of Seleucus's twelve-year reign was spent in trying to meet the quota.

Toward the end of his reign, being hard pressed for money as usual, he sent his treasurer Heliodorus to Jerusalem (here called "the glory of the kingdom") to raise additional funds. Heliodorus was detested by the Jews because of the merciless taxes he had already imposed on them, and this time he went too far. Having been apprised of the riches of the temple by one Simon (a Benjamite who had a score to settle with Onias, the high priest), Heliodorus tried to plunder it. He was prevented from doing so, however, by a supernatural apparition which rose up before him as he was about to enter the temple treasury.

Not long after this the unfortunate Seleucus Philopator died, probably having been poisoned by his odious tax collector Heliodorus. Thus this unsung king died "neither in anger, nor in battle."

c. *The Wickedness of Antiochus the God* (11:21-35). The prophecy now turned to the infamous Antiochus Epiphanes, whose story is an Old Testament type of the antichrist (see Appendixes 19 and 20). We can divide our study of this king into five parts. First we have the story of *his contemptibility* (11:21-22). We note *his coming to power* (11:21). The last we saw of this Antiochus he was in Rome as a hostage. He

was still there when his brother Seleucus took the Syrian throne after
the death of Antiochus the Great. Seleucus decided that he needed
the younger Antiochus in Syria, probably thinking that his contacts
at Rome could be used to secure better terms for the impoverished
kingdom. So he arranged to send his own son Demetrius to Rome
in exchange for Antiochus. While Antiochus was on his way home
from Rome he stopped off at Athens, where he heard that his brother had been murdered and that Heliodorus the tax collector had
proclaimed himself king.

That claim was immediately contested by Ptolemy Philometor, the
new king of Egypt, who claimed the Syrian throne on the ground
that his mother Cleopatra had been the sister of Seleucus. Antiochus
dimissed both the claim of Heliodorus the usurper and the claim
of his nephew Ptolemy. If anyone had a right to the throne it was he,
and he was determined to get it.

Various ancient historians agree in telling us that young Antiochus
was indeed "vile" or "contemptible," as the text declares. Often his
behavior was eccentric, if not actually mad. He was given to the most
degraded and unnatural vices. He was unscrupulous, cruel, of a savage temper, and fond of the company of the lowest of men. He was
erratic and cunning, but not devoid of courage.

The "honor of the kingdom" was not his. It belonged to his
nephew Demetrius, who was the rightful king. Demetrius, however,
was in Rome, while Antiochus, who was on his way home, had
already made some influential friends, including Eumenes, king of
Pergamum and his brother Attalus. He seems to have joined them
in some conspiracy against Rome, and they appear to have seen in
him an ally in the east. In any case, his friends at Pergamum put up
the money and the troops and, with their aid, he was able to depose
the usurper and secure the Syrian throne for himself. The despicable Heliodorus was put to death. Antiochus, making sure that
Demetrius remained in Rome, made himself pleasant to the Syrians
with clemency and flattery. He used the same cunning in dealing
with the Romans. Thus he came to the throne "peaceably" and
"obtained the kingdom by flatteries," as foretold.

Next we have *his control of the priesthood* (11:22) Some have taken
"the overflowing forces," which sweep away all opposition, to refer
to the armies of Heliodorus, which were swept away by Eumenes and
Attalus in installing their colleague on the throne. Some think that
the expression refers to the routing of the forces loyal to Demetrius.
It seems more likely, however, that the phrase refers to the overthrow
of an Egyptian army near Pelusium. Soon after Antiochus seized the

throne, his nephew Ptolemy Philometor made an ineffective attempt to recover the territory previously lost to Syria. The campaign was a disaster. His forces were swept away as by a flood, as the text states.

But who was "the prince of the covenant"? Possibly it was Onias III, the Jewish high priest. One of the first acts of Antiochus Epiphanes was to depose him because he opposed the pro-Syrian, Hellenized party in Jerusalem, and also because he was a supporter of Ptolemy. He was murdered. His brother Jason, who paid a substantial bribe to obtain the office of high priest, was a thoroughgoing Hellenist. He seduced a considerable number of Jews, some of whom called themselves Antiochians. Some even went so far as to attend the heathen festival at Tyre as Jason's ambassadors, bringing a donation of three hundred drachmas of silver as an offering to the pagan god Hercules. According to the story, however, before they could present the offering they were so overcome in conscience at the sight of the heathen abominations that they diverted the money to something else.

Next our attention is directed to *his craftiness* (11:23-24). Antiochus Epiphanes was crafty in all his dealings. In view of expected war with Rome, he signed a treaty with Eumenes nd Attalus, who had helped him to his throne. But Antiochus had no compunction about breaking the treaty in order to secure the more powerful patronage of Rome in return for a promise to serve Rome's interests. At the same time he fully intended to throw off his Roman connection, just as soon as he was strong enough to do so.

He did "become strong with a small people." When he reappeared in Syria after being a hostage at Rome, he was almost a nobody, but soon he reigned in strength over a great people. History tells how rich he was and how great was his military power. Some idea of his magnificence is given in a description of the procession with which he opened a thirty-day festival and games at Daphne.

There is, however, another way in which Antiochus fulfilled this part of the prophecy. It could be that "the prince of the covenant" was Ptolemy Philometor of Egypt. The crafty Antiochus had designs on Egypt, but signed a peace treaty with the youthful Egyptian king in order to lull Ptolemy into a false sense of security. Antiochus then proceeded with his goal. Still mouthing assurances of good will, he made his way up the Nile as far as Memphis. His army was small but it enabled him to build up his strength. He entered "peaceably even upon the fattest places of the province."

Still assuring the trusting Ptolemy of his friendship, Antiochus suddenly invaded Galilee and lower Egypt and achieved something none of his forebears had been able to do: he made himself virtually the master of Egypt. He also did something else not characteristic of his predecessors: he distributed his booty with a lavish hand, hoping thus to make friends and influence people. What the young Ptolemy thought of all this can well be imagined. For the moment, however, he was mesmerized as a bird is mesmerized by a snake about to devour it.

The secret plans of Antiochus called for the taking of all the major Egyptian fortress cities, especially Pelusium, Naucratis, Alexandria, and Memphis. So, as the text says, he "forecast his devices [devised plots] against the strong holds, even for a time." That final expression, "even for a time," shows that God had already drawn the line beyond which this treacherous man would not be allowed to go. For instance, although he did eventually capture three of the fortresses he deemed essential to the permanent domination of Egypt, the fourth, Alexandria, escaped his grasp.

We come now to *his conquests* (11:25-27). We are told how he *entered the Egyptian kingdom* (11:25-26). When his initial preparations were complete, Antiochus mobilized a large army and marched against Ptolemy. But by now the Egyptian king was aware not only of his danger but also of the character of his adversary. He hastily mobilized an army to match in size that of his enemy. The first encounter was at a place between Pelusium, the great frontier fortress, and Mount Cassius. Ptolemy was defeated. Another battle followed and again Antiochus was victorious. This time he captured Pelusium, marched on to Memphis, and made himself master of most of Egypt, except for the key city of Alexandria.

Many of Ptolemy's woes resulted from the treachery of some of his own trusted advisers, who, as the text says, "forecast devices against him." Antiochus was a master of intrigue and much of his success stemmed from his ability to plant a fifth column inside Egypt. He subverted Eulaeus and Lenaeus, Ptolemy's guardians, and many another of the Egyptian king's courtiers and captains. The unhappy Ptolemy discovered too late that these men had been dealing treacherously with him throughout the course of the war and that, at the last, they had openly betrayed him. It was probably through their treachery that Ptolemy himself was delivered into the hands of his enemy.

Next we are told how he *entertained the Egyptian king* (11:27). It seems that for some time the Egyptians had been growing tired of their ineffective and gullible king. Already many had transferred their allegiance to Ptolemy Philometor's brother, Physcon (Euergetes), whose successful repulse of Antiochus at Alexandria had greatly increased his prestige. This rivalry between the two brothers gave Antiochus his pretext for his continuing interference in Egyptian affairs. He was coming, so he said, to strengthen Philometor's grip on the throne. In reality, of course, he intended to depose him too, once he had used him to vanquish Physcon.

So, unable to take Alexandria, Antiochus returned to Memphis and sat down at the conference table with his youthful nephew, Philometor. He pretended friendship for him, acknowledged him as Egypt's king, promised to help establish him firmly on the throne, and conferred with him as to the best way to deal with the usurper there in Alexandria.

But Philometor had learned craftiness from his uncle. He pretended to go along with all this. Secretly, however, he was just waiting for Antiochus to go back to Syria; then he hoped to outwit him. Thus, as the text says, they spoke lies at one table. It all came to nothing, however, because God was not in either their promises or their prevarications. As soon as Antiochus was gone, Philometor made overtures to Physcon and proposed a form of joint sovereignty. His brother received him into Alexandria and then the two issued a proclamation against Antiochus. As the text declares, the end of these wars was not yet. Man proposes; God disposes. Further, the land of Judea had not yet learned its lesson. It still had to suffer as the buffer state between Egypt and Syria because of its sins.

Having foretold the contemptibility, the craftiness, and the conquests of Antiochus Epiphanes, scripture also foretold *his cruelty* (11:28).

As has been noted, in Judea a number of Jews had become apostates from Judaism. Rationalizing their beliefs, they were adopting Greek ways, philosophy, and unbelief, something that must have pleased Antiochus. But as he was marching homeward, laden with spoil and plunder, he heard news that enraged him. A rumor had run through Palestine to the effect that he was dead and many Jews were celebrating and rejoicing at the news. Further, Jason, whom Antiochus had deposed from the high priesthood, had decided that this was a propitious time to recover the office by force from Menelaus, who had bribed Antiochus to give it to him.

Jason mobilized a thousand mercenaries and marched on Jerusalem, capturing the city and forcing Menelaus back into his castle. Antiochus chose to regard this as a revolt against himself and determined to teach the Jews a lesson they would never forget. So his heart was "against the holy covenant," the holy land and all it stood for. He fell on Jerusalem with his seasoned veterans, killed forty thousand of its inhabitants, sold another forty thousand into slavery, and plundered the temple, carrying off treasure valued at eighteen hundred talents. Jason fled and Menelaus was confirmed as the puppet of Antiochus.

"He shall do exploits," the prophecy said; that is, "He shall act effectively" or "accomplish his pleasure." Antiochus was not yet finished. He horrified most of the Jews by sacrificing a sow on the brazen altar in the temple court and, not content with that insult to the holiness and majesty of the living God, he made broth of swine flesh and sprinkled it all over the temple. No wonder Antiochus Epiphanes is regarded as one of history's major types of the coming antichrist.

But the Holy Spirit has not finished yet with this prophecy, since Antiochus was by no means through. Laden down with booty, he returned to Syria, still smarting over the fact that the Jews hated him and had rejoiced to think him dead. Now he had given them just cause to hate him more.

So we come to the prophecy of *his crimes* (11:29-35). We begin with *his rebuff* (11:29-30a). In Egypt the reconciled pharaohs agreed to a joint regency, made common cause against their mutual foe, and prepared for a fresh onslaught. Antiochus thereupon undertook a second campaign against Egypt, a campaign ignored in the prophetic text, probably because it was so much overshadowed by the memorable events to be connected with Antiochus's third and final campaign. This third campaign not only had dire consequences for Syria but also for Judea.

After Antiochus's second campaign, the pharaohs decided they had suffered enough from the oppressions of their terrible uncle. Because they needed a strong ally, they hired Greek mercenaries to stiffen their own armed forces and sent an embassy to Rome to appeal for help.

By the spring of 168 B.C., Antiochus was ready. He gave orders for his army to march, demanding the immediate surrender of Cyprus, Pelusium, and other territories. No one could stand before him. Memphis fell, and Antiochus appeared before the city of Alexandria.

But, as the text says, this time it was not to be the way it had been before. The "ships of Chittim" lay at anchor in the bay. The Romans had come. The name *Chittim* originally designated a town in Cyprus; then it denoted the people of the island (Genesis 10:4; Isaiah 23:1, 12). Still later the word became a general term for the island and coastlands of the Mediterranean. Here it evidently means the

Romans, who were now beginning to spread fledgling wings toward acquiring an empire.

Antiochus was met by legates from the Roman senate at Eleusis, four miles from Alexandria. He was handed an ultimatum by Popilius Laenas ordering him to leave the friends of the Roman people alone and to evacuate Egypt immediately. Antiochus, trying his old game of prevarication, replied that he would consult with his advisers as to what should be done. The Roman, however, was not to be deceived by bluff. He took his staff and drew a circle in the sand around the Syrian king. "Before you step out of that circle," he said, "you give me your answer in conformance with the senate's demands." Intimidated, this international bully replied, "If it so please the senate, we must depart." And so the empire of Alexander bowed to the newly emerging masters of the world.

The rage of Antiochus at this public humiliation and his urgent need to save face called for some kind of scapegoat. Tiny little Judea appealed to him as a place where he could safely take out his frustrations and do something to soothe his injured pride. The Jews had no formidable ally to defend them against his wrath.

The prophetic text tells of Antiochus and *his revenge* (11:30b-35). Antiochus was not without friends and accomplices in Judea. We are told how he *invaded Jerusalem* (11:30b). The apostate Jews, led by Menelaus, were doing all in their power to rid the Jews of circumcision and other distinctives of Judaism, and were trying to persuade their countrymen to adopt Hellenism. Antiochus decided to give them a helping hand.

He sent the Syrian general Apollonius and a force of some 22,000 men to attack Jerusalem. Their massacre of worshipers in the temple was only the beginning of sorrows.

The text tells next how Antiochus *insulted Jehovah* (11:31). The attack on Jerusalem took place on the sabbath day, when thousands were attending to their religious duties. The troops ravished the city, tearing down buildings and spreading terror. They occupied the citadel overlooking the temple and repaired it, building massive walls and garrisoning it with Syrian troops.

Then Antiochus issued a decree calling on everyone, on pain of death, to join in a universal religion and obey universal laws. All had to conform to the Greek religion. The Jewish temple was consecrated to Jupiter Olympus, and Antiochus, identifying himself with this pagan god, demanded that he himself be worshiped also. He ordered an immediate cessation of all Jewish sacrifices, all observance of the sabbath and ceremonial observances. He destroyed copies of the scriptures. He replaced the annual feast of tabernacles with a feast to Bacchus, and he perverted the youth of the city with vile practices.

Worst of all, he desecrated the temple. He built an idol-altar over the brazen altar. Then he installed above it what the sacred text calls "the abomination that maketh desolate," which some take to be an image of Zeus, the pagan thunderer of Olympus. That would have been bad enough, but there are those who think the image he erected was an Asherah, the sex symbol associated with the groves and high places of pagan canaanite religion. Whatever it was, it was "an abomination," a term commonly used in the Old Testament to refer to idols.

The desecration of the sanctuary was the crowning calamity for Israel, and the fact that God had permitted it the proof of his displeasure with his people. In addition, idols with accompanying chapels were set up all over the land and everyone was commanded to burn incense to the gods of Greece. To disobey, or to be caught with a copy of the scriptures, was to be killed without mercy.

Finally we are told how Antiochus *inflamed Judea* (11:32-35). But now he had gone too far, and massive resistance to his oppression broke out—but not by all. We are told, first, of *those who deified him* (11:32a). Antiochus Epiphanes was not without admirers and followers among the apostate Jews in Judea. These went along willingly with his decrees. It meant nothing to them that they were serving false gods since they had long since apostatized from Jehovah and abandoned his word. Many of them held positions in places of influence in the country and they were the enemies of God and of those who loved his name. Others were halting between two opinions. They were attracted by the sophistries and brilliance of Greek rationalism yet they were still tied to the truths and traditions of conservative faith. Now they were forced to decide one way or other. Many took the easy way out and allowed themselves to be Hellenized.

But God always has his remnant, so we are told of *those who defied him* (11:32b-35). There were those in that unhappy land who knew their God. Theirs was an experiential knowledge, not just an intellectual knowledge. They took a brave stand against the wickedness that was now inundating the country and which would continue unabated for three years. They braved the storm, defied the wicked king and his decrees, dared to endure all consequences in order to be true to Jehovah. Among these were Mattathias and his sons, and their followers. These men revived the old spirit of the theocracy and sought to restore both it and independence to the country. They did exploits and, in the end, succeeded in breaking the Syrian stranglehold on their country.

A new class emerged among the downtrodden people, the Maschilim ("the wise"), men who knew the word of God and who struggled to keep the true faith alive in the midst of persecution. They could see how these things had been foretold. They were living in the days about which Daniel had written. As line by line, word by word, the prophecy was fulfilled, they could put a finger on a page and say, "We are right here, right now." These men did no great martial exploits, as did the Maccabees. They performed no heroic deeds on the battlefield. They read the scriptures, believed them, understood them, looked beyond the tribulation of their day, and with sure and certain hope looked for the coming of Christ.

They drew on themselves the wrath of the king. Many perished by fire and sword. The Syrians took advantage of the sabbath, a day when the Jews refused to fight, to fall on them. Some were roasted alive; some were crucified; some were strangled; some were sold into slavery. They were robbed and left destitute to wander in caves and on the mountains. The terrible things listed in Hebrews 11:35-37 are clearly drawn from these days. And on and on it went, for three interminable years.

God's purpose in permitting these horrors is explained: He intended to purify the nation from its apostasies and sins (11:34-35). Even when the persecution was at its height, God was still on the throne, still sovereign over the nations. He had already set a time limit to it all. Not even Antiochus Epiphanes could go one step or one moment beyond the line that God had drawn.

The one small ray of hope and comfort for those who suffered through this ordeal was to be found in Mattathias, a priest living at Modin, and his five sons, who became known as the Maccabees. When Antiochus's officers arrived at Modin to enforce the king's decree, Mattathias and his sons defied them. There was a skirmish and the fiery rebels slew Apelles and others, and so the resistance began.

Upon the death of Mattathias, the struggle was continued by his son Judas Maccabeus. This able guerrilla leader cut to ribbons the armies Antiochus sent against him, first those led by Apollonius and Seron, then those led by Gorgias and Lysias. By the end of six years, Judas had become a power in the land and had put together an army to be reckoned with. Many who had deserted the Judean cause now came back with hypocritical declarations of loyalty, motivated by fear of reprisals by the victorious Maccabeans.

At length the Maccabeans marched on Jerusalem and recovered the city and its fortress. They repaired, cleansed, and rededicated the temple amid the rejoicing of the people. A new feast, known as the feast of the dedication, was instituted, and incorporated into Israel's annual religious calendar (John 10:22).

At this point in the narrative the prophecy leaps over the centuries. It leaves Antiochus Epiphanes to his fate, which it ignores, and focuses on the still future history of the antichrist. There is nothing extraordinary in this kind of prophetic leap. It occurs elsewhere in prophecy, as for instance in the gap between the sixty-ninth and seventieth week of Daniel's prophecy of the seventy weeks.

2. The Coming of Antichrist (11:36-45)

a. *His Blasphemies* (11:36-38). The prophecy concentrates on three things: first on the antichrist's *royal pride* (11:36).

There can be little doubt that this one, who is bluntly labeled "the king," is the antichrist. His shadow has been before us in the story of Antiochus. He now appears on the page himself, in all his pride and arrogance. He will be the last of all the Caesars, Borgias, Machiavellis, Hitlers, and Stalins who have cursed this earth.

Further light is cast on this dreadful person in 2 Thessalonians 2, where he is described as "that man of sin" and "the son of perdition." He is the beast out of the sea in Revelation 13, the dreadful scion of Satan, lord of the west, the final Caesar, head of the revived Roman empire, gifted, brilliant, lawless, cruel, faithless. He will be supported by his soul twin, "the beast out of the earth," the false prophet, the apostate Jewish apostle of the beast. In Revelation 17 he is described as "the beast whose deadly wound was healed" and as "the beast out of the abyss," signifying that, in the later stages of his career, having been killed, he will be brought back to life again and thereafter will be a supernatural being, one utterly devoted to evil.

In his arrogance and pride, the antichrist, in full control of the west, will exalt himself and magnify himself against every god and will blaspheme the true and only God. Paul expanded on this aspect of antichrist's career (2 Thessalonians 2:4). Pagan deities will be opposed by the antichrist just as much as the true God, but it is against God himself that he chiefly rants and raves. The expression "marvelous things" can, perhaps, better be translated "monstrous things" (11:36).

He will carry all before him. He will go from one success to another, uniting the west, deceiving Israel, manipulating the Arabs, baiting Russia, for a while taking over the whole earth. He will be persuasive and charming or terrifying and treacherous as the occasion demands.

Wickedness will get worse and worse. As "the man of sin" the promotion of sin will be his chief aim. He will gratify lust and glorify sin. He will appear as the messiah of the Jews, the mahdi of the Muslims, the krishna of the Hindus. He will be the ideal of the humanists, the Christ of apostate Christendom, the mantra of the eastern mystics. A war-weary, famine-ravished, disease-ridden, plague-infested, panic-stricken world will hail him—"till the indignation be accomplished."

He will think he is doing his own will but he will be accomplishing God's will. The "indignation" referred to here is God's indignation against the nation of Israel, the nation that has persistently rejected Jesus as messiah and called down God's curse on itself: "His blood be on us, and on our children" (Matthew 27:25). This rejection of Christ, which was culminated in the cry, "Let him be crucified," has been endorsed by nearly two thousand years of Christ-rejection by the Hebrew people. It will take the horrors of the great tribulation finally to open their eyes as a people, so that they will recognize in Jesus their rejected messiah.

Then the prophecy mentions antichrist's *religious policy* (11:37). The man who will one day be revealed as the antichrist will be raised in the Judeo-Christian, possibly in the Catholic, faith. G. H. Pember said:

> The expression "the Desire of Women" is placed between two nouns which indubitably refer to concrete gods; it must, therefore, itself designate some individual deity which is more especially sought after by women. And having reached this point, our difficulties are over: the deity intended can be no other than the many-named Goddess of Nature, who has been worshiped, and at all times chiefly by women, from the earliest ages to our own days, by Pagans and by apostate Christians of every land.
>
> She is the Beltis, or Mylitta, of the Babylonians; the Ishtar of the Assyrians; the Astarte of the Phoenicians; the Queen of Heaven mentioned by Jeremiah; the Tanata of the Persians; the Isis of the Egyptians; the Shing Moo, or Holy Mother, of the Chinese; the Aphrodite of the Greeks; the Artemis, or Diana, of the Ephesians; the Venus of the Romans; the Friga of the Scandinavians; the Amida, with her son Xaca, whom Francis Xavier found established as the goddess of Japan; the woman presented for worship by Strauss, Comte, and the Theosophists; and the Virgin Mary of the Eastern and Western Catholics.
>
> This is the goddess of whom we have so often heard as Our

Lady of La Salette, Our Lady of Lourdes—to whom it seems there are temples erected even in China—Nostra Senora del Pilar, Our Lady of Loretto, and Our Lady of Ransom (G. H. Pember, *The Great Prophecies of the Centuries* [London: Hodder and Stoughton, 1895] p. 428).

We learn from Revelation 17 that the Vatican will try to exploit the power of the beast for its own advantage—with dire results for the Roman religious system (see my book *Exploring Revelation* [Chicago: Moody Press, 1974], pp. 211-230). The cynical antichrist will use that system as a ladder to supreme power in the west; then he will destroy it, distributing its wealth to his colleagues.

Next the prophecy reveals his *real purpose* (11:38). His god will be Satan, who will give him his throne and global power. The antichrist will accept what Christ refused—the kingdoms of the world, supreme power under Satan, and worldly glory—all as a reward for worshiping the devil (Luke 4:5-8).

Satan is here described as "the god of forces." This king will not be simply an initiate into occult powers; he will be indwelt by Satan himself. As "the god of forces," Satan is the instigator of war. Antichrist will rise to power over the world in the wake of war. He will glorify war. And when he arrives at the apex of his power, he will acknowledge his debt to his sinister master by establishing Satan worship as the world's new religion.

b. *His Battles* (11:39-45). The section begins with *his great powers* (11:39). No world power will be able to stand against the antichrist. One way or another, all the world superpowers will be forced to acknowledge him. Probably the nations of the western hemisphere will be forced into a new Atlantic alliance, ruled by the beast and centered in Rome. The Soviet Union will be manipulated into striking at Israel and will be swept off the map as a global power. China, Japan, and the other countries of the east will be faced with the ultimatum of surrender or annihilation.

Those who support him will be rewarded with wealth and subordinate power, with honor and position. He will carve up the land of Israel and apportion it to his most trusted followers. Israel itself will be of great importance to him, not only because of its strategic geographical location as the hinge of three continents, but because it will be the homeland of his universal false religion. Control over an administrative district in Palestine will thus be a choice political plum.

So far, all will have gone his way. But now comes the change. The text underlines *his great problems* (11:40-45). First, there is the matter of *his rivals* (11:40a). Those old rivals, Egypt and Syria, are to come back on stage in the last days, united in a hatred of the antichrist. The antichrist's empire will begin to disintegrate. We learn from the apocalypse that the early vials of God's wrath will be directed at the power structure of the beast. As a result he will begin to lose his grip on his universal empire. The eastern half will break away and mobilize against him.

Daniel did not see the entire picture, though this chapter of his prophecy has been mainly concerned with the now historic rivalries between north and south, between Syria and Egypt. In the endtimes, these two countries will join against the antichrist, once they see their opportunity to break free from his rule. The country of Palestine (Israel), occupied by the antichrist, seems to be the focal point of this joint military venture.

Some have seen, in this verse, a reference to the Russian invasion foretold by Daniel's colleague Ezekiel (Ezekiel 38–39). There are good reasons, however, for rejecting this view, some of which have been developed in this book. The Russian colossus will have collapsed long before this time and its role in world affairs taken over by the antichrist. Throughout Daniel 11 the king of the north and the king of the south always are identified as the rulers of Syria and Egypt respectively. There seems no reason to suppose something else here. Both countries will be absorbed into the antichrist's world empire. The loosening of his grip will give these Muslim nations their opportunity to break away. Indeed, probably none of the Muslim nations will be enthusiastic about worshiping the beast's image, located in Israel, given the monotheistic, anti-idolatrous nature of Islam. However, expediency and the terror tactics of the beast will doubtless cow even militant Islam—for a time.

Now come the antichrist and *his revenge* (11:40b-43). The antichrist seems to be at Babylon, one of his capital cities, when this new insurrection breaks out. Ever since his seizure of Jerusalem and the temple, prior to the inauguration of the great tribulation, the antichrist will keep garrisons in Israel to protect the country from attacks by Syria and Egypt. This combined attack will provoke a swift response. The antichrist will mobilize and hurl his forces against Egypt, committing both land and sea forces to secure his vital interests in that strategic corner of his empire. Egypt and Syria, bitter enemies of Israel, will meet their retribution as a result of this final onslaught on that land.

The antichrist's line of march will lie through Israel. It is probable that at this time he will make that onslaught on Jerusalem mentioned by Zechariah (14:2). Perhaps the Jews, by now thoroughly awakened to the character of antichrist, will also seize the opportunity presented by all these turmoils to revolt.

Three peoples, historically the bitterest enemies of Israel—Edom, Moab, and the children of Ammon—will escape his fury. On a modern map we would identify these countries with the country of Jordan. No explanation is given why these countries escape the antichrist's wrath. Probably, however, Jordan will choose to remain aloof from the Syro-Egyptian rebellion. Or perhaps Jordan will be too solidly under the thumb of the antichrist to consider rebellion, or too compliant with his policies to want to. Some think that, as the successor to Edom, Moab, and Ammon (historically Israel's bitterest foes), this area will be reserved for special divine retribution—a hint of this is found in Isaiah 11:14, a great messianic passage.

The antichrist will deal firmly with the countries he overthrows on his westward march. With the countries of the Far East now mobilizing against him, the antichrist will be all the more infuriated by these insurrections in the west. They will hinder his preparation for dealing with the new oriental alliance of "the kings of the east" and they will imperil all his holdings in the west.

Finally, he will reach Egypt, where he will deal summarily with the king of the south. He will systematically plunder Egypt of its wealth. The museums containing the treasures of the pharaohs will be looted. Everything of value will be hauled away.

In the meantime, Egypt's allies, Libya and Ethiopia, will prove to be but fair weather friends. They will hasten to make their peace with the antichrist, abandoning Egypt to its fate. These two countries will now be added to the list of his obedient and subservient allies.

Now comes *his rage* (11:44). This is the beginning of the end. The antichrist's mighty, monolithic, worldwide empire is now rapidly falling apart. It was built on treachery and war, and held together by terror, lies, and every form of wickedness. It was energized by Satan, but it now is tumbling down around the antichrist's ears.

The kings of the Far East, taking advantage of the antichrist's more local troubles in the Middle East, will march. They will cross the Euphrates and deploy rapidly on the plains of Armageddon, or the mountain of Megiddo (Revelation 16:12-16). We can imagine the consternation of the beast and of the west when Japanese technology is married to Chinese manpower and mobilized against the west. The hordes of the east will join the marching millions moving to Megiddo. Nations from the distant north will join the eastern allies—perhaps the nations of Mongolia, Tibet, Siberia, and remnants of the former Russian colossus. The former Muslim lands will add their numbers. The approaching horde will be countless.

Infuriated and enraged, the antichrist will mobilize his western allies. The enormous military and industrial resources of the west will be rapidly harnessed for war. The stage will now be set for the battle of Armageddon.

Finally, the prophecy foretells *his ruin* (11:45). Somewhere between the Mediterranean and the Jordan, in the vicinity of Jerusalem, the antichrist will plant his resplendent pavilion. With what armies he can gather from the west, he will prepare for the final confrontation with the east. But his time has run out. The divine clock of seven years, which began its countdown with the signing of his treaty with Israel, has been relentlessly ticking away. Now it chimes the final hour.

At that moment the heavens will open. The Lord Jesus will come, backed by the armies of heaven and accompanied by his blood-bought bride. Invincible and omnipotent, sweeping all before him, He will descend. The sword will flash forth, and the battle of Armageddon will be over in a moment, in the twinkling of an eye.

"None shall help him" is Daniel's final word on the fate of the antichrist. No one could help him. The apocalypse adds the final details. The antichrist and his soul-twin, the false prophet, will be hurled living into the lake of fire. Satan will be incarcerated in the abyss. And Jesus will take to himself his mighty power—and reign!

B. Specific Dates about the Future (12:1-13)

Daniel 12 serves as a kind of appendix to the book, paying special heed to the coming great tribulation period. We can imagine how overwhelmed Daniel must have been by the scope of the revelations he had received: war and rumor of war, kingdom rising against kingdom, nation against nation, bloodshed and persecution, terror and treachery. And it seemed that it was to go on and on, and his beloved people, God's people, were to receive the brunt of it.

Was there no hope? Was there no help? There was. Across the sweep of this foreseen history God's people could write the words, "Our times are in his hands" (cp. Psalm 31:15).

Daniel 11 ends with the downfall of the antichrist. This chapter begins with the hatred of this sinister sovereign toward God's people.

1. The Tribulation (12:1)

First we must consider the archangel Michael and his distinctive relationship to the nation of Israel. When God created Adam, He said,
"Let them have dominion" (Genesis 1:26). Adam was thus given
sovereignty over all the earth. When he fell, he surrendered that
sovereignty to Satan. Satan today is called "the prince of this world"
(John 12:31) and as such he sets "principalities and powers," his
angelic viceroys, over the nations of the world.

The reality of Satan's sovereignty is evident from what happened
at the time of the Lord's temptation (Luke 4:5-7). The Lord did not
question Satan's sovereignty over the nations. Satan, however, did
not get that dominion from God; he wrested it from Adam. Thus
the world lies in the lap of the wicked one.

When God called Abraham, He gave him a promise: "Get thee out
of thy country, and from thy kindred, and from thy father's house,
unto a land that I will show thee: and I will make of thee a great
nation" (Genesis 12:1-2). Thus God began all over again with a single
individual. He saved him, separated him, and sanctified him. Then,
from that individual, He proceeded to bring into being a new nation,
the nation of Israel. This nation was unique in every way. It was
unique in its origin, in its "special nation" status with God, and in its
treaty relationship by the abrahamic covenant with God. It is unique
in that it stands apart from other nations. The hireling prophet Bal-
aam, under the direct control and inspiration of the Holy Spirit,
declared concerning Israel: "Lo, the people shall dwell alone, and
shall not be reckoned among the nations" (Numbers 23:9).

By creating a new nation from the descendants of a regenerated
man, God sovereignly brought into being a nation over which Satan
had no angelic overlord. Instead, God appointed Michael, the
archangel, field marshall of the armies of heaven, to be this nation's
representative and protector in the spirit realm, a fact that infuriates
the devil. He hates this nation and has done all in his power down
through the ages to eradicate it, corrupt it, and persecute it. This
helps explain the phenomenon of antisemitism, hatred of the Jew,
which is so prevalent in gentile society. From time to time antisemitism becomes epidemic, and results in a holocaust.

Daniel was now told that Michael, Israel's guardian angel, will be
especially active in the endtimes, when the antichrist will launch
against the Jewish people the worst period of persecution in all their
troubled history.

Numerous scriptures speak of this coming time of terror. Our Lord referred to it in his Olivet discourse (Matthew 24:21). Jeremiah wrote of this period: "Alas! for that day is great, so that none is like it: it is even the time of Jacob's trouble" (Jeremiah 30:7). The focus of the persecution will be the Jewish people, hence the description of it as "the time of Jacob's trouble." Revelation 7 makes clear that the gentile converts of the 144,000 witnesses will also suffer martyrdom by the million at this time. Also, the period coincides with the outpouring of God's wrath on this planet: "My determination is to gather the nations . . . to pour upon them my indignation, even all my fierce anger: for all the earth shall be devoured with the fire of my jealousy" (Zephaniah 3:8). Essentially, however, the great tribulation is Jewish in focus and will be permitted by God in order to sift the Hebrew people. The Jewish rejection of Christ must be broken so that the remnant of the nation will be ready to accept the returning Jesus as messiah, Savior, and Lord.

The holocaust of the great tribulation will be precipitated by Satan's expulsion from the heavenlies at the hands of Michael and his angels (Revelation 12:7). Satan's wrath will know no bounds. The antichrist will be a ready tool in his hands to accelerate those endtime events that culminate in the great tribulation. The antichrist's benevolent mask will then be torn away and he will stand revealed at last for what he is: the malevolent enemy of both God and man and, particularly, of the nation of Israel.

When one thinks of the terrible sufferings of the Jewish people in all ages, especially of their sufferings during the Nazi holocaust, it seems impossible that anything could be worse. The Holy Spirit assures us, however, that the great tribulation will be worse than anything ever to take place on this planet.

Think of the sufferings of the Jewish people. Egyptian pharaohs have tried to exterminate them. Assyrian kings, Babylonian emperors, and Persian potentates have turned their hands against them. Xerxes ordered their total extermination from all his realms. Greek tyrants and Roman caesars, neighboring princelings and church officials, Spanish inquisitors and Roman popes, medieval kings and swashbuckling czars and commissars—one and all have persecuted this people. The dungeon and the sword; the thumbscrew and the rack; fagot, flame, and fire; concentration camps and gas chambers; starvation and tortures; sadistic experiments in the name of science—all that fallen men or raging demons could devise—all have been used against this people. But the great tribulation will be worse than them all.

The devil will not succeed, however, in this final attempt to exterminate the Jewish people. A remnant will survive. Michael will see to that, and we can be sure that the devil will be deathly afraid of Michael after his ouster from the heavenlies at Michael's hand. Likely it will be Michael who will lock him up in the abyss while the millennial ages roll (Revelation 20:1-3). In any case, God in heaven will see to it that this time of tribulation serves his immutable purpose. Apostate Jews may indeed perish but enough of Daniel's people will survive to form a ruling nucleus in the following millennial age.

2. The Tomb (12:2-3)

a. *Resurrection* (12:2). Not until Jesus "brought life and immortality to light" was much light shed on the tomb and what awaits us at death. The Old Testament saints believed in an afterlife, believed in bodily resurrection (Job 19:26). But all was sketchy, vague, and dim.

Here in Daniel 12:2-3 we have one of those rare Old Testament statements about the coming general resurrection of the dead. Various views have been advanced as to the correct interpretation of this passage. Some have thought that it refers to a specific and partial resurrection of the Jewish people prior to the millennium. Some have supposed that it refers to Israel's resurrection as a nation in the endtimes. Some have seen the expression "sleep in the dust" as symbolic of Israel's national degradation. It makes more sense to take the verse just the way it is written, at its face value, and accept it as meaning exactly what it says. In this case it was a reminder to Daniel that death is not the end. There is a resurrection from the dead in which all will have a share. Some will be raised to enjoy everlasting life; others will be raised to everlasting "contempt" (the word literally refers to a "thrusting away"). The New Testament pours its greater light on this (John 5:28-29; Acts 24:15; 1 Corinthians 15:23; 1 Thessalonians 4:16; Revelation 20:5-6).

b. *Rewards* (12:3). We learn from Revelation 7 that many will be saved after the rapture of the church, when the 144,000 Jewish evangelists will reap an enormous harvest among people of all nations. These fervent Hebrew preachers, saved and sealed by God and kept from the vengeful hands of the antichrist, will be the latter day *maschilim* (cp. Daniel 11:33,35), wise men, turning many to righteousness in spite of the wickedness of the age and the wrath of the beast. Their reward will be great. Sun and stars are often used symbolically in scripture to depict high position and great power.

3. The Times (12:4-7)

Note the numerous time references in this chapter. Verses 5 to 7 seem concerned primarily with the question, "How long?"

a. *The Sealed Book* (12:4). John was told not to seal up his visions because their time of fulfillment was at hand. Daniel's prophecy, especially concerning the endtimes, dealt with events so remote in the future that the meaning would be obscure until closer to the time. He was therefore told to seal the book. The idea was not to conceal the book's contents, but to preserve the contents until the time came for their fulfillment.

The attacks made on the prophecies of Daniel by unbelieving liberal theologians show the need for this special protection of the book's contents. The devil has brought up his heavy artillery and his deluded intellectuals to attack the book of Daniel. Yet it outlives all its critics, and its contents remain God-breathed, Holy-Ghost-inspired prophecies of the ages. Our confidence in their inerrancy and infallibility remains unshaken. Many of its revelations have already been fulfilled, to the chagrin of the devil's disciples. The rest are about to be fulfilled, to the glory of God and the encouragement of his own.

The words "many shall run to and fro, and knowledge shall be increased" have been taken at their face value by some who have seen here a prophecy of the transportation revolution and the knowledge explosion so characteristic of our times. It is doubtful, however, that this is its primary significance, though the expression "run to and fro" is not altogether foreign to the original. The expression is found, for instance, in Jeremiah 5:1 and Amos 8:12 of literal movement. Zechariah used it to describe the Lord's eyes scanning every corner of the globe (4:10).

One rendering reads, "Many shall search it through and through and knowledge of it shall be increased." If that is a valid translation, then the prophecy implies that at the end when the time comes for the fulfillment of these prophecies, people will diligently examine them, comparing scripture with scripture (running to and fro, so to speak, through the word of God) and arriving at an accurate and expanded knowledge of what the prophecies mean. The prophecies, in other words, would be understood when needed.

Another view is that the words "run to and fro" should be translated "to apostatize." Technical reasons are advanced for substituting one Hebrew word *shūt* ("to rove," "turn about," "despise," hence "to do despite"—Ezekiel 16:57; 28:24,26) with a similar word *sūt* ("to swerve," "to turn aside," "to apostatize," "to revolt"—Psalm 101:3; Hosea 5:2; Psalm 40:4, "such as turn aside to lies"). One edition of the Septuagint (Swete's) reads "till many shall have gone raving mad."

If we collect together these various renderings we get quite a composite picture of the endtimes. We see a world of rapid and easy travel, a world where knowledge is increased. We see a world where apostasy abounds, a world where insanity and the need of psychiatric care are prevalent, a world where people who know God pore over the pages of his blessed book seeking and finding light for the times.

b. *The Spirit Beings* (12:5-7). The river was the Tigris. The actual word used to describe it is an Egyptian one, usually used of the Nile. Some see in this a reminder to Daniel of the Lord's protection over his people and of his changeless purpose. As He had once spread his wings over persecuted Israel in Egypt and foiled pharaoh's plan to exterminate them, so, again, He will spread his wings over beleaguered Israel in the last days and protect them from antichrist's avowed purpose of exterminating them.

God's agents are two angels. Possibly one of them is Michael. We know from the mosaic law that an angel is connected with Israel in God's redemptive and sovereign purpose: "Behold, I send an Angel before thee, to keep thee in the way, and to bring thee into the place which I have prepared" (Exodus 23:20-21).

Daniel not only saw these angels, he heard them. These are "things the angels desire to look into" (1 Peter 1:12). The angelic beings who stand before God, who rush to do his bidding, are intensely interested in human affairs. The fact that the entire cosmic "mystery of iniquity" is to be brought to a head and adequately dealt with on our planet vests this scene with much more than passing interest to the angels. Sin, we must remember, has defiled heaven as well as earth. That man was "made a little lower than the angels," and that he should be the creature for whose sins heaven's beloved would be prepared to die, has vested the human race with more than ordinary significance. So the angels watch every event connected with the redemption of our race. The age-long patience of God with his erring creatures, under blasphemous provocation, in view of the appalling sufferings and disasters that afflict the human race, in the light of what men did to his Son—these things cause the angels to say, "How long?" just as they do us. It is an interesting sidelight on the limitations of angelic intelligence, knowledge, and genius.

The answer came swiftly. With a solemn gesture, raising both his hands to heaven, the shining one, standing above the waters of the Tigris, took his oath by the living and eternal God that an end was in sight. The period "a time, times, and an half" refers to three-and-a-half years. The antichrist will sign his pact with Israel and will guarantee Israeli security for seven years. This marks the beginning of the final "week" of the seventy weeks of Daniel 9. Halfway through the "week" he will tear up his treaty, seize the rebuilt temple in Jerusalem, desecrate it with his image, follow in the footsteps of his ancient type, Antiochus Epiphanes, and inaugurate that ruthless and relentless persecution of the Jews, the great tribulation, to which Daniel 12:1 alluded.

But now we have the oath of the shining one, surely none other than the Christ himself, that a sandglass of three-and-a-half years is all it will take to accomplish God's purpose and bring these things to an end.

And what is that purpose? The scattering of "the power of the holy people." The "holy people" are the Jewish people, still called such by God, in spite of their sins as a nation over many centuries. The Jews today are a small and scattered people, but they are a powerful people. Their influence in the world is enormous, out of all proportion to their numbers. They are a power to be reckoned with in the Middle East. During the first half of Daniel's seventieth week they will enjoy the full patronage of the antichrist and will doubtless seek to extend their already great influence in the world. They will become even more obdurate in their disdainful rejection of Christ.

The great tribulation will break the power of the Jews in the world. Their protector, the antichrist, will turn against them. They will realize, too late, that he has played them for fools, using them as pawns in a larger game. The machinery of his now-worldwide empire will be put into high gear to deprive them of status, wealth, power, and of all human and political rights. They will find themselves alone in a hostile world. The final holocaust will break out and every man's hand will be against them. To shelter or aid a Jew will be an act of high treason against the empire. Here and there a brave, believing soul will dare the wrath of the beast, but the majority of the world's peoples will find it safer and more expedient to betray them to the antichrist's secret police. They will become fugitives and vagabonds on the earth, to be rounded up and shipped to the nearest concentration camp for extermination.

They will be reduced to the extremity of poverty, weakness, fear, and woe. Never will the world have seen such horrors or such helplessness. They will have no influence, no allies, no hope, no power.

They will be brought to an end of themselves. All they have trusted in the past will prove useless. That is what the great tribulation has to accomplish. Then, and not until then, will the Lord act. But He already knows exactly, to the day, how long it will take: "a time, times and a half."

4. The Truth (12:8-13)

a. *Request by the Prophet* (12:8). Whatever the two angels understood by the answer of the one clothed in linen, it all seems to have gone right over Daniel's head. He asked for enlightenment. None was given. These high matters, now being discussed by the angels, were not for Daniel's day. Their fulfillment lay far in the future. New Testament revelation would add more details. It was not necessary for Daniel to know all the factors in the end-time equation.

b. *Reply to the Prophet* (12:9-12). This was in three parts. First there was a statement as to *why* (12:9). Daniel was to ask no more questions. The words were sealed up. God has set his seal on the book of Daniel. Let the liberals come with their Bible-denying, Holy-Ghost defying, unscrupulous, lying philosophies. Let them enlist their "scholars." Let them bring the weight of their united unbelief to bear on this book. God's protective seal is on it, and behind that seal is the omnipotent power of the living God. Their cause is hopeless, their efforts in vain. God has set his seal on both the book and its contents, and no one, however well-schooled in unbelief, can break it.

Daniel, then, need have no fear for the future. All was in God's hands. The times were set, the truth was sealed, the triumph was sure. Why should he ask no more questions? That was why.

There was a statement as to *what* (12:10). This statement is God's gauntlet flung down before unbelieving theologians who have no understanding whatsoever of the book of Daniel. The more pages of false exegesis and foolish explanation they produce, the more they reveal themselves to be both void of understanding and wicked. God knew all about the so-called higher critics and their attacks on the word of God in general and on the book of Daniel in particular. He knew all about their flaunted scholarship. He knew how they would subject gullible students, sitting in their classrooms, buying their books, awed by their degrees, to a barrage of unbelief in the name of Christianity. He knew with what wit and sarcasm, with what devilish skill and authority, they would present their propositions. He knew how many eager young students, called to the ministry, receptive to their blandishments, would be guided onto the rocks by these men, there to make shipwreck of their faith and a mockery of their call. He knew how many of them, thus brainwashed and bewildered, would blunder on into the ministry to pastor churches, preach lies, undermine people's faith, and sow death. He knew about these men and their disciples. He has a word for them. He called them "wicked." The Hebrew word means "lawless" and is used three times in this one verse.

There is more, however, to the verse than that. It points on to the endtimes. The fires of the great tribulation will separate the wise from the wicked. "None of the wicked shall understand." They will remain blind to the truth to the end. The ultimate truth concerning unbelief is that it is not a mental issue but a moral issue. It is not that people can't believe; it is that they won't believe. The truth is there. They refuse to see it through a deliberate act of the will. They will scorn the book of Daniel then as now, even as its final, end-time prophecies are being fulfilled before their eyes. They will hurry on to their doom. The wise, however, will understand and will know what to do when the crisis comes and the beast's image is raised in the rebuilt temple in Jerusalem (Matthew 24:15-21).

There was a statement as to *when* (12:11-12). These time periods are still in the future. There are three of them all together, two mentioned here and one elsewhere. There is an initial period of 1,260 days (three-and-a-half years, using the Jewish lunar calendar of thirty days to the month) to which is added another 30 days, making a total of 1,290 days, to which is added another period of 45 days, making a grand total of 1,335 days. It will be observed that to the initial period is added a lunar month and to that period is added a month and a half.

There is an interesting coincidence between these future dates and what happened in the days of Antiochus Epiphanes. From the time the Syrian king profaned the temple in Jerusalem until the restoration of divine worship by Judas Maccabeus was 1,290 days. From that date to the death of Antiochus and the end of his persecutions was 1,335 days. That, however, was only illustrative since Antiochus was not the antichrist. The prophecy, as is true of much Bible prophecy, had a near and far focus of fulfillment. As we have noted, often a prophecy will have an initial, partial fulfillment and then, at a much later date, a second and complete fulfillment.

The period of 1,260 days will begin when the antichrist seizes the Jewish temple and puts an end to Jewish ceremonial worship. It will end with the return of Christ and with the destruction of the antichrist.

No light is shed on the extra two-and-a-half months that follow. It may be that thirty days will be necessary for completing the mopping-up operations against the vast armies that have been deployed both by east and west at Megiddo and for bringing to an end all further hostilities worldwide. Also, the land of Israel will need to be cleansed of the dead. The temple, defiled by the antichrist, will probably have to be demolished too, before true worship can be established. Maybe all this will take up the first month.

Then, too, we learn from other scriptures that the Lord intends to set up his throne in the valley of Jehoshaphat, near Gethsemane, and to judge the nations in accordance with the criteria of Matthew 25. Possibly it will take the extra month and a half to gather the surviving people of the world, from earth's remotest bounds, to this great assize. The sheep will be separated from the goats. Swift doom will overtake those who sided with the antichrist, who wore his mark, and who cooperated with his antisemitic laws. The remnant of the Jews and the redeemed from among the gentiles will go on into the millennial kingdom, the nucleus of the new kingdom.

In any case, God pronounces them "blessed." The word, as usual, is in the plural. It can be rendered, as in Psalm 1:1 and elsewhere: "O the blisses of the person who . . . " or "Happy, happy is the one who . . . " The millennial kingdom will be worth waiting for.

c. *Rest for the Prophet* (12:13). Daniel's days were drawing to a close. The angel turned to him with a final prophecy, one for him personally. He would continue on his way. Death would overtake him and he would rest. Time would pass. The things he had seen and heard would be fulfilled. Empires would rise and fall. The Christ would come, only to be cut off. The ages would pass. The antichrist would come. The messiah would come again.

Yes, Daniel would rest in death, but that was by no means all for him. He would stand in resurrection. He would receive his "lot" of inheritance. He would enter into his reward and have his share in the glories yet to come. Thus, abruptly, the book ends.

When I was a boy, I often stood by the blacksmith's forge in my father's shop. I would watch him heat his iron until it glowed. He would hold that burning metal over his anvil and down would come his hammer. The sparks would fly like miniature meteors. The glowing iron would change its shape. Sometimes the hammer would break. But the anvil remained impervious to it all.

Just so the book of Daniel and its foes. They hammer away. The sparks fly. Their hammers break. They make a lot of noise. They impress some who change shape beneath their attacks. But the old anvil remains as strong, firm, solid, and infallibly true as ever. God's seal is on this book.

Century after century the book stands. It cannot be broken. In the end archaeology and history vindicate the accuracy of its background scenes. Philology and linguistics endorse its claims. The onward march of events relentlessly fulfills its predictions. The arguments of the critics break down before the answers of their critics. The book needs no defense. It is able to defend itself because it is God-breathed, God-sealed, God-endorsed, by the Son of God.

So, we believe this great book of Daniel. We thank God for it.

> Within this awesome volume lies,
> Mystery of mysteries . . .
> Happiest they, of human race
> Who from their God have gotten grace
> To read, to learn, believe, and pray,
> To lift the latch, to face the way:
> But better had he ne'er been born
> Who reads to scoff, who reads to scorn.

APPENDIXES

APPENDIX 1
Two Witnesses in Defense of Daniel's Authorship

Although we are not undertaking here a defense of the book of Daniel, some notice needs to be taken of the attacks the book has suffered. We shall call two witnesses for the defense, a layman and a theologian. The layman is Sir Robert Anderson, in his day the respected head of Britain's prestigious Scotland Yard. He was not only a well-taught Bible scholar with a number of thought-provoking books to his credit, but he was a man well versed in interrogating witnesses, detecting falsehood, and exposing the sophistries of error. He described himself as a man "long accustomed to deal with evidence in difficult and intricate inquiries." The Hebrew scholar and theologian is Edward B. Pusey. (For another theologian's defense of Daniel, see Appendix 18, where reference is made to the remarkable insights of Prof. Robert Dick Wilson. Let us begin here with Sir Robert Anderson:

> Let it not be forgotten that the present inquiry is altogether judicial. The question involved is precisely similar in character to issues such as are daily decided in our Courts of Justice. And one of H. M. Judges with a good "special jury" would be a fitter tribunal to deal with it than any company of philologists, however eminent. Due weight would of course be given to the evidence of such men as experts. But the *dictum*, so familiar to the lawyer, would not be forgotten, that the testimony which least deserves credit is that of *skilled* witnesses, for the judgment of such men becomes warped by their habit of regarding a subject from one point of view only.
>
> · The critics maintain that the definiteness of the predictions of Daniel is due to the fact that the book was written after the events referred to; and further, that its "visions" cease with the reign of Antiochus Epiphanes. The main issues of fact therefore, to be decided at such a trial would be these:—
>
> (1) Was the Book of Daniel in existence in pre-Maccabean days? and

(2) Was any one of its visions fulfilled in later times?

And if either of these issues should be found against the critics their whole case would be shattered.

The discovery of Neptune was due to the fact that astronomers found reason to assume the existence of such a planet. And if the Book of Daniel had been lost, true criticism would assume the presence of a Daniel at the Court of Babylon. For otherwise the story of the exile and return of the Jews would be intelligible only on the assumption of miracles such as those which marked the Exodus. And further; if the advocates of the pseud-epigraph theory of Daniel were versed in the science of evidence, they would recognise that, on their own hypothesis, the presence of the book in the canon is evidence of the existence of the man. For the Sanhedrim [sic] would never have accepted it unless they had had knowledge of the historical facts on which it is based.

But while the existence of Daniel was *indisputable* when Dr. Driver wrote his *Introduction*, it was only "probable" when he came to write his *Book of Daniel*—a deplorable lapse from true criticism to "Higher Criticism," and from rational belief to unreasoning scepticism. On this point I have already cited the testimony of Ezekiel; and that testimony is conclusive unless the critics can find some adequate answer to it . . . the same remark applies, though in a modified degree, to the testimony of I Maccabees.

Even if the testimony of these witnesses stood alone, it would prevail with any impartial tribunal. But when we come to consider the general question of the canon, the weight of proof becomes overwhelming. Apart from the disturbing influence of these controversies, no reasonable person would reject the clear and definite tradition that the completion of the Old Testament canon was the work of the men of the Great Synagogue. In an age when scepticism of a singularly shallow type has been allowed to run riot, it is the fashion to reject that tradition because of the myths and legends which have attached themselves to it. But a soberer scholarship would recognise, first, that this very element is a proof of its antiquity, and of the hold it gained upon the Jewish mind in early times; and secondly, that if historical facts are to be ignored on this ground the whole volume of ancient history must shrink to very small proportions.

But all that concerns me here is to establish that the canon was complete before the Maccabean epoch. And upon this point I might almost rest the case upon the evidence of a single witness.

As mentioned in an earlier chapter, *Ecclesiasticus* was written not later than about B.C. 200. The object of the book is thus explained by the grandson of the writer, who translated it into Greek not later than B.C. 132:[1] "My grandfather Jesus, seeing he had much given himself to the reading of the law, of the prophets and the other books of the Fathers, and had gotten therein sufficient proficiency, was drawn himself to write something pertaining to learning and wisdom." Now it is acknowledged even by hostile critics that the words "the law and the prophets and the other books," or as he calls them again, "the rest of the books," refer to the sacred writings, and that they imply the existence at that time of a recognised canon.

"I think it quite incredible," says Dr. Ryle, "that the thrice repeated formula should have been an invention of the Greek translator, and not rather the description of the Hebrew Scriptures commonly used among the Jews." *The Law, the Prophets, and the Writings*—these same words stand upon the title-page of the Jewish Bible of today, and no fair and competent tribunal would hesitate to find that that title has covered the same books for more than twenty-three centuries.

Ben-Sira was "a poetical paraphraser" of the Old Testament, and his book abounds in passages which are imitations of the canonical writers. And, "as clear examples of such imitation can be found of *all* the canonical books, with the doubtful exception of the Book of Daniel, these books must, as a whole, have been familiar to Ben-Sira, and must therefore be much anterior to him in date." These words are from Dr. Schechter's *Introduction*, already quoted, and they are substantiated by a list of the passages referred to. That list includes three quotations from Daniel; these however are, of course, rejected by the critics.

Now I confidently maintain that upon the evidence any impartial tribunal would find that the canon was complete before Ben-Sira wrote. But assuming, for the sake of argument, that the inclusion of Daniel is doubtful, the matter stands thus:—It is admitted, (1) that the canon was complete in the second century B.C.; and (2) that no book was included which was not believed to have been in existence in the days of Nehemiah. For the test by which a book was admitted to the canon was its claim to be inspired; and the Sanhedrim held that inspiration ceased with the prophets, and that no "prophet"—that is, no divinely inspired teacher—had arisen in Israel after the Nehemiah era.[2] When, therefore, Josephus declares that the Scriptures were "justly believed to be Divine," and that the Jews were prepared "willingly to die for them,"[3] he is not recording merely the opinion of his contemporaries, but the settled traditional belief of his nation.

How, then, can the critics reconcile their hypothesis as to the origin of the Book of Daniel with its inclusion in the canon?

As regards point (1) above indicated, the Bishop of Exeter's testimony carries with it the special authority which attaches to the statements of a hostile witness. "If," he says, "all the books of 'the Kethubim' were known and received in the first century A.D., and if, as we believe, the circumstances of the Jewish people rendered it all but impossible for the canon to receive change or augmentation in the first century B.C., we conclude that 'the disputed books' received a recognition in the last two or three decades of the second century B.C., when John Hyrcanus ruled and the Jews still enjoyed prosperity."

This ought to decide the whole question. For mark what it means. The critics would have us believe that after the death of Antiochus some Jewish *Chasid* incorporated a history of his reign in a historical romance, casting it into the form of a prophecy supposed to have been delivered hundreds of years before; and that, at a time when this was still a matter within living memory, the work was accepted as divinely inspired Scripture, and bracketed with the Psalms of David among the sacred books of the Hebrew nation!

We are dealing here, remember, with the acts, not of savages in a barbarous age, but of the religious leaders of the Jews in historic times. And the matter in question related to the most solemn and important of all their duties. Moreover, the Sanhedrim of the second century B.C. was composed of men of the type of John Hyrcanus; men famed for their piety and learning; men who were heirs of all the proud traditions of the Jewish faith, and themselves the sons or successors of the heroes of the noble Maccabean revolt. And yet we are asked to believe that these men, with their extremely strict views of inspiration and their intense reverence for their sacred writings—that these men, the most scrupulous and conservative Church body that the world has ever known—used their authority to smuggle into the sacred canon a book which, *ex hypothesi*, was a forgery, a literary fraud, a religious novel of recent date.

Such a figment is worthy of its pagan author, but it is wholly unworthy of Christian men in the position of English ecclesiastics and University Professors. And were it not for the glamour of their names it would be deemed undeserving of notice. But our respect for Church dignitaries of our own times must not make us forget what is due to the memory of Church dignitaries of another age, men whose fidelity to their trust as the divinely appointed custodians of "the oracles of God" has earned for them the gratitude and admiration of the Church for all time. Their fitness, moreover, to judge of the genuineness and authenticity of the Book of Daniel was incomparably greater than could be claimed for any of those who join in this base and silly slander upon their intelligence or their honesty. For if the critics are right, these men who were, I repeat, the divinely appointed custodians of the Hebrew Scriptures, and from whom the Christian Church has received them, were no better than knaves or fools. Let no one start at this language, for it is not a whit too strong. They were utter fools if they were deceived by a literary forgery of their own time; they were shameless knaves if they shared in a plot to secure the acceptance of the fraud.

For let it be kept steadily in view that no book would have been thus honoured unless it was believed to be ancient. The "avowed fiction" theory of Daniel is puerile in its absurdity.[4] If the book was not genuine it was a forgery palmed off upon the Sanhedrim. And like all forgeries of that kind the MS. must have been "discovered" by its author. But the "finding" of such a book at such a period of the national history would have been an event of unparalleled interest and importance. Where then is the record of it? When it suits them, the critics make great use of the argument from the *silence* of witnesses; but in a case like this where that argument has overwhelming force they ignore it altogether.

Moreover, the suggestion of the critics that the Sanhedrim admitted a book to the canon in the way a library committee adds a volume to their catalogue is grotesque in the extreme. "They never determined a book to be canonized the sense of introducing it into the canon. In every instance in which a writing is said to have been admitted to the canon, the writing had already been in existence for generations, and had for generations been claimed as canonical before the discussions arose in regard to it. In every instance the decision is not that the book shall now be received into the collection of sacred writings, but that the evidence shows it to have been regarded from the first as a part of that collection."

One point more. While books of great repute, such as Ecclesiasticus and I Maccabees, were absolutely excluded from the canon, and even canonical books, such as the Book of Proverbs, Ecclesiastes, and even Ezekiel were challenged, *"the right of the book of Daniel to canonicity was never called in question in the Ancient Synagogue."*[5]

In disparagement of Daniel the critics point to the extraordinary additions which mark the Septuagint version. But owing to their want of experience in dealing with evidence, they fail to see what signal proof this affords of the antiquity of the book. The critics themselves allow that the Greek version of Daniel was in existence before I Maccabees was written.[6] According to their own case, therefore, the interval between the appearance of the book and its translation into Greek must have been within the memory of the older members of the Sanhedrim. And yet they ask us to believe that though during that interval it was under consideration for admission to the canon, it was guarded so carelessly that these additions and corruptions were allowed.[7] The Septuagint version is evidence that Daniel was a pre-Maccabean work: the corruptions of the text which mark that version are evidence that it was in existence long before the Maccabean era.

In view of all this it is not surprising that even a writer so cautious and so fair as Canon Girdlestone should assert that "there is not an atom of ground for the supposition that any of the books or parts of books which constitute our Old Testament were the work of men of that age." "Of one thing," he adds, "we may be quite certain: nothing would be introduced into the 'Sacred Library' which was not believed to be 'prophetic,' and therefore in some sense Divine, and though there were occasionally men after Nehemiah's time who had semi-prophetic gifts, the Jews do not acknowledge them as prophets.[8] We look in vain down the remains and traditions of Hebrew history between the age of Nehemiah and the Christian era for the appearance of any men who would venture to add to or take from the sacred library or canon which existed in Nehemiah's days."[9]

Upon the first of the issues above specified I therefore claim a decision in favour of the Book of Daniel. . . . "[10]

Such is the answer given to the critics by a man well equipped to sift and weigh the evidence and expose falsehoods.

Now it is the turn of the trained theologian. Dr. Edward Pusey took up the challenge of these liberals on their own ground. He discussed their arguments at length. He exposed the flaws in their attacks on the Bible. Page after page he wrote, showing how little the destructive critics agree even among themselves:

> And so the weary changes were wrung [sic], each refuting his predecessor, the last awaiting his refutation from his successor, or ofttimes taking up that which he had before condemned. Lengerke refuted Rosch, and Wieseler refuted Lengerke, and Hitzig, Wieseler; or they mutually exchanged with each other. Wieseler took up with Corrodi; and Hofmann exchanged his theory for Ewald's; and Ewald gave up what Hofmann took, for Hitzig's; and, at last, since the assumption, that the prophecy is no prophecy but a description of Antiochus, was to be infallible, and yet the periods given by Daniel were hopelessly irreconcilable with that assumption, the fault is to be thrown, not on the infallible theory, but on what, (whether men will it or no,) abides what it was, the word of God. Hitzig, in his arrogant way, says, "If, in this way, the reckoning does not agree, then Daniel has erred, and the only question is to explain the error. . . ."
>
> Such then is the result of this "scientific" criticism. It fixes the interpretation beforehand, at its own will; then it endeavors, in every way it can, to adjust with its theory the clear and definite statements of the text as to the seventy weeks of years, as divided into the periods of 7, 62, 1, and this one into its two halves. It adjusts the numbers, adapts the descriptions of those spoken of, as it wills; no one for the time interferes with it; it has free scope; it adjusts, re-adjusts, turns, re-turns, in every way it wills. It gives its explanations authoritatively; no failure damps its confidence; it has but to please itself; and it cannot. After 80 years of twisting, untwisting, hewing at the knot, the knot is to them as fast and indissoluble as ever. "Except the Lord build the house, their labor is but lost that build it." They form a rope of sand, and wonder that it does not cohere; that, twist it how they will, it is but sand. And so at last they throw up the problem; and, like insolent scholars, accuse not their own ignorance, but their Master's. "It is not we who erred, but Daniel. The problem is insoluble in our way; therefore it cannot be solved at all."
>
> And yet, in this very charge of error on the writer of the book

of Daniel, they forget their own previous charges. This school objects to the book, that the writer had too minute a knowledge of the history of Alexander's successors. "God does not," they say, "so minutely reveal the future." Good. So far then it is conceded that the account is accurate. Again, it says, that the writer was ignorant of the Persian history; that he believed that there were only 4 Persian kings in all, and that the Persian empire lasted but 54 years; that the empire of Alexander was divided immediately after his death. Good, again. It concerns not us, whether God revealed to Daniel more of the future, than he has actually set down. But how this is to help the adaptation of the 70 weeks to the period from Jehoiakim or Cyrus to Antiochus Epiphanes, these theorists have to explain. According to them, the writer knew accurately the period from the battle of Ipsus, B.C. 301, to B.C. 164. This gives 137 years. Add the 54 years, during which these assume the writer to have believed the Persian Empire to have lasted, and the 10 of Alexander's Asiatic wars. This gives us 201 years, which the writer is supposed to have believed to have elapsed from Cyrus to the death of Antiochus Epiphanes. And yet they would have us to accept this as an explanation, why the writer of the book of Daniel should have supposed 63 weeks of years or 441 years to have elapsed from the 4th year of Jehoiakim or, if they would be but decently honest, from Cyrus, when a decree did go forth to *restore and to build Jerusalem*, to Epiphanes. They assume that the writer of the book of Daniel supposed the period from Cyrus to Antiochus Epiphanes, to have been *little more than half of what it was*, viz., 201 years, instead of 374, and then, retaining the general term, "inaccuracy of chronology," they urge this as an argument why the writer may have fixed a period, *more than twice the length of time* which they themselves suppose him to have imagined the actual time to be. Their charge of "inaccuracy of chronology" tells against themselves.

And yet what one, the more bold because the least believing, speaks out, must have been in the conscience of many. "After the death of Jesus, the Son of man, it was inevitable that they, to whom He was the Messiah, should refer to Him the words, *Messiah shall be cut off.* "One might easily be tempted to interpret *Messiah*, v. 26, who was to die by a violent death, of Jesus and His Death; and if one thought of this *Messias*, notwithstanding the absence of the Article, as *the Messias*, (as *Christ* stands in Greek for *the Christ*,) they with whom the Name had weight, naturally understood *Messias*, v. 25, also to be Jesus Christ." Yet with a strange inconsistency, *any* chronological difficulty was a solid ground not to believe that Jesus was foretold; *no* chronological difficulty was any ground against believing any one else to be spoken of.

The harmony of unbelieving criticism has been contrasted with the disagreements among believers. It were no harm, were these disagreements as great as they allege; for the exposition of particular texts, closely or incidentally as it may at times bear upon the faith, is not in itself, matter of faith. Not the meaning of texts in detail, but the truths, on which they bear, are mostly matters of faith. But the alleged unanimity of this unbelieving criticism has been in pulling down, not in building up. It has been agreed in rejecting Christ. It would, if it could, blot the mention of Him out of the Old Testament. But when the question is, how to replace it, quot homines, tot sententiae. All agree in bearing witness against Him. But it is still, as of old, *their witness agreed not together* (Mark 14:56). If they waited, until they found those whose witness would agree together, the old faith would not have been parted with till now.

In regard to the 70 weeks, agreement on certain points was a necessity of the case. It was essential to any exposition which should exclude our Lord, that the Messiah of v. 25, should be Cyrus; it was their axiom that the last week should be part of the reign of Epiphanes; they had then next to no choice as to the *Messias* who was to be *cut off*. Without religious indifference they could not have lighted upon more than one. The table in the appendix will show their unanimity as to the rest.[11]

---

1. The evidence clearly points to an earlier date for both the book and the translation of it. But as I wish to avoid all "collateral issues," I adopt for the sake of argument the dates accepted by the critics. See, however, Dr. Ginsburg's article in *Kitto's Cyclopedia*; also Edersheim's *Life and Times of Jesus the Messiah*, vol. i, pp. 26ff.

2. The question of the justice of such beliefs and claims in no way affects the force of my argument.

3. *Against Apion*, i. 8.

4. Imagine a meeting of the upper House of Convocation to discuss a proposal to add Dr. Farrar's *Life of Christ* to the canon of the New Testament! Quite as ridiculous is the suggestion that the Jewish Sanhedrin in the second century B.C. would have entertained the question of adding "an elevating romance" of their own age to the canon of the Old Testament.

5. Edersheim's *Life and Times of Jesus the Messiah*, vol. ii., App. V.

6. The presumption is strong that the LXX version was in existence at the date to which the critics assign the book itself. But here, as on every other point, I am arguing the question on bases accepted by the critics themselves.

7. And Professor Cheyne adopted the suggestion that the Hebrew original of ii. 14 to vii. was allowed to be lost! (Smith's *Bible Dict.*, art. "Daniel").

8. In proof of this he referred to I Maccabees iv.46; ix.27 (which puts the prophets in the far past); and xiv.41.

9. *The Foundations of the Bible*, ch.ii., pp. 8 and 10.

10. Sir Robert Anderson, *Daniel in the Critic's Den*. (London: James Nisbet and Co. Ltd., 1902), pp. 96-111. See also his book The Coming Prince (Grand Rapids: Kregel Publications, 14th ed.; reprint 1954).

11. See Appendix 2.

APPENDIX 2

Pusey's Table Showing the Disagreements of the Destructive Critics among Themselves

	70 WEEKS BEGIN B.C.	FIRST 7 END	MESSIAH V. 25	62 WEEKS BEGIN	62 WEEKS END	MESSIAH V. 26	LAST WEEK BEGINS	LAST WEEK ENDS
Harduin	606	507	Cyrus, typically	606	172	Onias (type of Christ)	171	165
Marsham	607	538	Cyrus	607	175		175	168
Collins followed Harduin.			Cyrus and, better, Judas Maccabeus					
Eckermann	537	537	Zerub-babel	536	536	Jewish high priest, suspended by antiochus	174	165
Corrodi	588	none	The Christ	588	170	Onias's death, 172	170	164
Eichhorn Ammon	536	588	Nebu-chadnezzar	606	175	Onias de-posed, 175 hiatus 5 years	170	165
Paulus	536	588	Zede-kiah	588	154	Jewish high priesthood between Onias and Jonathan, 175-157	175	165
Bertholdt Rosenmueller	588	536	Cyrus	536	170	Alex-ander	170	164
Bleek	588 or Jere-miah's time of prophesying generally	536	Cyrus	536	175	Seleucus Philopator (at first Nicator)	175	164
Maurer	588	Cyrus	Cyrus	Cyrus	176	Sel. Phil.		165
Hitzig, 1st	588	539	Cyrus	588	175	Sel. Phil.	170	164 hiatus 5 years
Hitzig, 2d	606, but the 7 at 588	536	Cyrus	606	172	Onias	172	165
Rosch	609	560	Cyrus	609	175	Sel. Phil.	175	164
Lengerke	588	538	Cyrus	588	220	Sel. Phil.	178	164
Wieseler, 1st	606	none	Onias iii	606	172	Onias	172	164, Feb.
Wieseler, 2d	606	none	The Christ	606	175	Onias	172 hiatus 3 yrs.	165, Dec.
Ewald, 1st	607	Cyrus	Cyrus	Cyrus	176	Sel. Phil.	Philop.	166/167
Ewald, 2d	588	539	Cyrus	539	176			
Bohmer	654	605		605	171			
Hilgenfeld as Harduin but dropping the types								
Herzfeld	587	538	Joshua	538	170	Priesthood 170 after Jason		

Edward B. Pusey, *Daniel The Prophet* (New York: Funk and Wagnalls, 1886), p. 219.

APPENDIX 3
The Testimony of Christ

In a letter to a Christian magazine many years ago, a believer wrote:

> The sceptical critics of modern Germany, in their discussion of the Old Testament, completely ignore the opinions of Christ, as they do also the indubitable opinions of the Jews of New Testament times. These German critics deliberately leave out of view a whole mass of vital evidence bearing on the subject, which—sceptics or infidels though they may be—it is most unscientific for writers, professing to be serious historians, to rule out of court and treat as if it had no existence (Andrew Craig Robinson, *Church Family Newspaper*, March 24, 1921).

No one has had a loftier or more thorough acquaintance with the Old Testament than Christ. Especially important, from the critical point of view, should be his views of the book of Daniel, since He lived within a couple of centuries of when the critics claim the book was written. To ignore Christ would be as though a historian ignored Herodotus on the Greek and Persian wars or Plutarch on the lives of the caesars. That the critics do so is evidence of their dishonesty.

The critics treat the book of Daniel as a religious romance, its title as pseudonymous, and its prophecies as an apocalypse written after, not before, the events.

To Jesus, Daniel was a real person. He gave him his proper title, "Daniel the prophet." He quoted him three times in his own prophetic discourse (Matthew 24:15,21,30).

In this great advent prophecy, He quoted first from Daniel 9:27 (11:31; 12:11) where He endorsed Daniel's warnings about the coming abomination of desolation with a special added warning of his own that people should pay heed to this warning.

He quoted from Daniel 12:1 in adding his own confirmation of the coming woes of the Jewish people in the impending great tribulation.

He quoted from Daniel 7:13 to describe his own second coming, both in his Olivet discourse and again when put upon his oath by the high priest as to whether or not He were the Christ, the Son of God (Matthew 26:64). From this quote we learn it was from Daniel 7:13 that the Lord took his own favorite title for himself, "The Son of man." His use of the definite article, prefixed to the title, intimates that He himself was indeed the mysterious being seen by Daniel, "one like the Son of man."

In addition, the Lord's description of the resurrection is an endorsement of Daniel 12:2 (John 5:28-29). His description of the coming glory of the righteous is a paraphrase of Daniel 12:3 (Matthew 13:43).

Such was the Lord's endorsement of Daniel, a book the critics dismiss as religious fiction.

Further New Testament endorsement of the book of Daniel can be found in the book of Revelation, described specifically by the Holy Spirit as "the Revelation of Jesus Christ" (1:1). The apostle John, under the inspiration of the Holy Spirit, echoed his beloved master's reverence for the book of "Daniel the prophet": Daniel 1:12,15 and Revelation 2:10; Daniel 3:6 and Revelation 13:15; Daniel 4:30 and Revelation 14:8, 17:5, 18:2,10,21; Daniel 5:23 and Revelation 9:20.

APPENDIX 4
The Chaldeans

The term *Chaldeans* is used frequently in an ethnic sense in the Old Testament as, for instance, when we read of "Ur of the Chaldees." It was used in this sense by Daniel, but also in a quite different sense. By Daniel's day the word had come to denote a special privileged class, the chief of the five classes of the wise men of Babylon.

Historically the Chaldeans were always hostile to Assyria. Nabopolassar, father of Nebuchadnezzar, was a Chaldean. Jeremiah described Nebuchadnezzar's army as "the army of the Chaldeans." Herodotus mentioned the Chaldeans as comprising part of the multinational army of Xerxes; and Stabo, centuries later, could still find traces of them in their own homeland which he described as part of Babylonia bordering on Arabia and on the Persian Gulf.

So the Chaldeans were not, strictly speaking, Babylonians, though they often ruled Babylon. In Daniel 5:30 Belshazzar is called "king of the Chaldeans." His father, Nabonidus, though a usurper, was united by marriage, it appears, with the Chaldean dynasty of Nabopolassar.

Herodotus confirmed Daniel's use of the term *Chaldeans* to denote a special caste of the wise men of Babylon. He said that during his visit to Babylon (probably sometime prior to 447 B.C., when he went to live at Athens) the Chaldeans were his tour guides of the temple-tower and of the precincts of the sanctuary of Bel. It has been noted that "when this chatty old historian leaves his description of the temple and its precincts and goes on to speak of the city of Babylon and the strange customs of its inhabitants we hear no more of the 'Chaldeans,' but only of the 'Babylonians.'"

It is, then, an error to claim that the use of the word *Chaldean* dates from a time when Chaldean had become synonymous with Babylonian. On the contrary, Herodotus confirmed that the Chaldeans were the priests of the great temple of Bel-Merodach-Esagila, "the house of the towering summit," the chief Babylonian temple and the place where Nebuchadnezzar had deposited the golden vessels taken from the house of God at Jerusalem.

Diodorus Siculus (first century B.C.) called Belesys (Nabopolassar, founder of the New Babylonian empire) "the most distinguished of the priests, whom the Babylonians call Chaldeans." (See Boutflower, pp. 35-46.)

So, the Chaldeans were a privileged class, numbered among the notables of Babylon. They come confidently forward in the book of Daniel, jealous of their position and prerogatives. It must have been with a jaundiced eye that they saw Daniel, a foreigner and a Jew, raised above them.

APPENDIX 5
Kingdoms "Inferior" to Babylon

It is a fact of history that the Medo-Persian kingdom was not inferior to that of Babylon, nor was the Greek kingdom inferior to the Medo-Persian, nor the Roman inferior to the Greek. How then can it be said that they were inferior?

The answer lies in the two aramaic words, which are translated "inferior to thee." They literally mean "lower than thou." That is, they were lower down on the image than Nebuchadnezzar. (For a defense of this position as against the Septuagint rendering of Daniel 2:39, see Boutflower, pp. 19-21.)

It is noteworthy that, in explaining to Nebuchadnezzar the meaning of his dream, Daniel expanded on the head of gold. It was the then-existing kingdom of Babylon, and we can well imagine that Nebuchadnezzar would be gratified to hear himself so described.

Daniel, politically perhaps, but under divine restraint, said nothing about the second kingdom. The subject was one on which, unless expressly questioned, he would do well to tread lightly. Nebuchadnezzar was not likely to be delighted to hear that his empire was to be replaced by the Medo-Persian power, of which the Babylonian kings were always apprehensive.

As to the third kingdom, Daniel also said little. He was back on safe ground when it came to the distant fourth world power. He spoke at length about its strengths and weaknesses and the ultimate end-time dissolution of gentile world power. But then, this revelation was evidently one of the chief burdens of the vision.

APPENDIX 6
The Stone Mountain

The flatness of Babylon was relieved by ziggurats, manmade mountains, used as temple towers in much the same way as the Aztecs used their pyramids. Add to that the famous hanging gardens, built by Nebuchadnezzar to remind his favorite wife of the mountains of her native Media, and we can see how great an impression was made on this king by a dream of a mountain.

Babylonian mythology had long since established a sacred mountain ("the mountain of the lands") as the home of the gods. In time, the chief god of Babylon became "the god of the mountain" and eventually became so completely identified with the mountain he was actually called "the Great Mountain."

When the priests of the Great Mountain (i.e., the god Merodach) heard Daniel tell Nebuchadnezzar that the kingdom of the God of heaven would become "a great mountain" (2:35), or "the Great Mountain," they must have been arrested at once.

It was the common practice to identify kingdoms with their patron gods. They would readily understand that, as supremacy had been taken away from the god of Nippur and bestowed on the god of Babylon, so it would be taken away from Babylon. It would be bestowed on a succession of kingdoms until, at last, it would be given to the kingdom of the God of heaven. This would be reinforced by the fact that their chief god was called "the Great Mountain."

Some surprise might have been engendered by the idea of a stone kingdom. Stone would seem weak and worthless when compared with gold, silver, copper, and iron. On the other hand, it was cut out of the mountain (out of the deity) and "without hands" (that is, by God himself). Further, the stone would smash the image in pieces and itself become a great mountain, filling the earth.

The entire symbolism was designed to convey to these pagans the concept of the messianic kingdom. (See Boutflower, pp. 45-49.)

APPENDIX 7
The Vision of the Tree

Nebuchadnezzar was very fond of the great cedar forest in Lebanon. He was in Palestine at least four times. On his second and third visits he made a special expedition to the cedar forests to cut down timber for his public works back home.

The tree Nebuchadnezzar saw in his vision resembled one of the giant cedars with its far-flung branches. These trees were the natural habitat of a variety of birds; their branches offered shelter and shade for animals and humans. The cedar, then, was a fitting symbol for a strong, central government, supporting a widely extended sway, such as Nebuchadnezzar's Babylonian empire.

That the tree in his vision was cut down would have ominous significance. Nebuchadnezzar had watched many a forest giant fall beneath the woodsman's axe.

APPENDIX 8
The Use of Foreign Words in Daniel

The view of the critics is that the language of Daniel mandates a date for its authorship after the conquest of Palestine by Alexander the Great. The argument turns on the use of various Persian, Greek, Aramaic, and Hebrew words found in the book.

About half the book is written in aramaic (2:4-7:28). The critical view is that the entire book was originally written in Aramaic and that the Hebrew section is a translation.

The Arameans are the Syrians of our Bible. Like the Chaldeans they seem to have originated in Arabia, "that prolific hive of Semitic peoples." We meet them in the Bible in Laban, for instance, and in the Aramean states, to the north and east of Israel, which figure in the wars of David (Damascus, Zobah, Beth-rehob, and Maacah as well as the Aram-naharaim to the east of the Euphrates). Some of the early Assyrian kings mentioned them (Shalmaneser I and Tiglath-pileser I). So we can look for them from northern Palestine to Haran in the east. Amos said they came from Kir, which is taken to refer to a region east of Babylonia bordering on Elam (Isaiah 22:6).

It was from these eastern Arameans that the western or Syrian branch came. Tiglath-pileser III warred against them. In recounting his first campaign he mentioned some thirty-five tribes and summed them up as "the Arameans." Earlier Assyrian references spoke of Chaldea, Elam, Namri "and the land of the Arameans" as being allies of Babylon. It is evident that Babylonia was encircled by Arameans. They occupied territory between Assyria and Media in the north and Babylon and Elam in the south.

This vigorous people left the impress of their language everywhere. Dr. Albert Sanda pointed out, "The Aramaic language came more and more into acceptation at Babylon, and made its way upwards from the villages into the towns, and from the lower classes to the magistracy and into the higher circles of society." Along with this upward current there would also be a downward current, since Aramaic was already the language of diplomacy and of commerce. This was due to its being so widely extended, and spoken in districts bordering on Elam, Babylonia, Media, Assyria, Asia Minor, Phoenicia, and Palestine.

When the Assyrians invaded Judah in the days of Hezekiah, Aramaic was already the language of oriental diplomats. When Rabshakeh began his propaganda offensive against Jerusalem, Hezekiah's representatives urged him to speak in Aramaic (2 Kings 18:26).

There can be little doubt that Daniel, a Jewish courtier and diplomat under both Babylonian and Persian kings, was at home in Aramaic. Why should he not use this *lingua franca* of the ancient world in recording sections of his book intended for a much larger audience than his Jewish readers? And why should he not restrict himself to Hebrew for those portions addressed to the Jews and which mostly concerned them?

Professor Robert Dick Wilson had the last word. His writing is the authority on the linguistic argument about the book of Daniel and how language bears both on the date and place of writing. He is the expert when it comes to comparing the foreign words found in it with other aramaic documents, the age of which is more or less known. He said:

> The Zakir inscription of 850 B.C. has no foreign elements, except perhaps Hebrew. The Sendsherli inscriptions of the latter part of the eighth century B.C. have Assyrian ingredients. The Egypto-Aramaic of the fifth century B.C. has Persian, Babylonian, Hebrew, and Egyptian terms, and perhaps one Latin and three Greek words. The Nabatean has Arabic in large measure, one predominantly, some Arabic, and two Sassanian or late Persian words. The Targum of Onkelos has mainly Greek words, five Persian words, and some Hebrew and Babylonian elements. The Targum of Jonathan has yet more Greek nouns and three verbs likewise, Aramaic in form, derived from Greek nouns, at least one Latin word, apparently no Persian words, and only one Babylonian word or form, except such as are found in the Scriptures, and a considerable number of Hebrew words. The Syriac (edessene) has hundreds of Greek words, a considerable number of which are verbalized; a little Sanskrit, and in later works many Arabic nouns, especially names of persons and places. In New Syriac the foreign elements are predominantly Turkish, Arabic, and Kurdish loan-words.
>
> Therefore it being thus apparent that on the basis of for-

eign elements imbedded in Aramaic dialects, it is possible
for the scholar to fix approximately the time and the locality in which the different dialects were spoken; all the more
then, as has been shown in the case of Daniel, such a date
and locality are required by the vocabulary of the pure Aramaic substratum and favoured, or at least permitted, by its
grammatical forms and structure, we are abundantly justified in concluding that the dialect of Daniel, containing
as it does so many Persian, Hebrew and Babylonian elements, and so few Greek words, with not one Egyptian,
Latin, or Arabic word, and being so nearly allied in grammatical form and structure to the older Aramaic dialects
and in its conglomerate vocabulary to the dialects of Ezra
and Egypto-Aramaic, must have been used at or near Babylon at a time not long after the founding of the Persian
empire. ("The Aramaic of Daniel," *Biblical and Theological
Studies*, p. 304. Quoted by Boutflower, pp. 227-228.)

Linguistically speaking, no book of the Old Testament more clearly
advertises its age than the book of Daniel. Of course Daniel used foreign words. His nationality, education, governmental rank, high position in society, his daily contact with foreigners from all parts of the
world, his close contacts with the kings of Babylon and with the
Medo-Persian emperor and his officials, all make it likely that Daniel
would use the foreign words he did. He was a cosmopolitan with a
longing for his boyhood Zion.

One of the favorite points with the critics in attacking the book of
Daniel has been the mention he made of certain musical instru-
ments. The use of Greek names for these was supposed to prove that
Daniel was composed at a late date.

It is an acknowledged philological principle that "the name travels
with the thing." In Nebuchadnezzar's Babylon there was an extensive
trade with the west. Long before the Greeks began to make and write
history, they came into contact with the eastern empires of Assyria
and Babylon. In the eighth century B.C. Sennacherib fought and
overcame a Greek army. Considerable commerce existed between
Greece and the Assyrian provinces of Asia Minor, especially with
countries bordering the Mediterranean and the Black Seas. They
traded with Lydia and with Cyprus. The first Assyrian ruler Esarhad-
don had Greek mercenaries in his army and Greek soldiers accompanied him on his Asian expeditions. The name Javan (Greece)
occurs in the inscriptions of Sargon as one of the countries from

which he received tribute. Who is to say that Sargon and other monarchs, who transported a monolith obelisk from Armenia, who moved those colossal bulls, and who brought cedars from Lebanon could not also import a few musical instruments?

The claim of the liberals is frivolous and ludicrous. "As spoils of war or articles of commerce, Greek instruments might easily have found their way to Babylon." (See Pusey, pp. 95-96.) The tragedy is that, so eager are the skeptics to get rid of Daniel, they will resort to extremes to do so. A worse tragedy is that their unsuspecting disciples believe these "assured results" of the so-called higher criticism.

APPENDIX 9
Nabonidus

Nabonidus was the son of the high priest of the temple of the moon-god in Haran. The city of Haran was not far from Media, which perhaps accounts for the fact that he is sometimes called the "son of a Median woman." Early in life Nabonidus seems to have developed a strong attachment for the cult of Sin, the moongod, and for Shamash. Nearly all of his inscriptions are taken up with work he did for Sin, Shamash, and Anunit in Haran, Ur, and Sippar, rather than, as might have been expected, for Merodach and Nebo in Babylon and Borsippa. His first great work was to rebuild the temple of Sin in Haran and to this work he harnessed the energies of his far-flung armies as well as the services of princes, priests, and people.

Nabonidus not only liked to rebuild temples. He was an eager antiquarian and historian. It may be he acquired his love for antiquity from his aged father, who could remember the days of Ashurbanipal and who liked to talk about the past.

Nabonidus was chosen by his fellow-conspirators to succeed Labarosoarchod, the young son of Nosiglissar. He appears, at the beginning of his reign, to have been a popular favorite. But from his seventh to this seventeenth year he seems to have retired to Tema. Moreover, year after year, he refused to come to Babylon to renew his royal authority by taking the hands of the image of Bel. Indeed, he seems to have been content to allow his son Belshazzar to assume responsibility for the affairs and defense of Babylon.

Some explanation for this odd behavior has been sought in the king's age. He was getting on toward sixty when he became king; he was about sixty-five when he went into retirement, and seventy-five at the time Babylon was taken by Cyrus. That, plus his natural antiquarian tastes, gives a partial explanation. But why stay away from Babylon when every demand of common political sense would mandate at least a token annual appearance at the great feast Marduk? The only explanation is that Nabonidus was so besotted by his devotion to Sin and Shamash that he stayed away from Babylon in order to diminish the supremacy of Merodach and Nebo by stopping the customary procession. In other words, he was a religious fanatic and his obsession led him into head-on collision with the powerful priestly castes of the capital. Nothing he could have done could have so ensured his unpopularity.

But Nabonidus didn't care, not until the last year of his reign when, too late, he woke up to his folly, came out of his self-imposed retirement, ventured to Babylon for the New Year celebrations, and sought to take a belated interest in the defense of his country. A blunderer to the end, one of his final acts of folly was his effort to ensure the security of Babylon by gathering into the city the gods of other cities. Such an act would infuriate the people of those cities who would imagine that Nabonidus had taken away their defense for the sake of Babylon. And it would enrage the priests of Merodach who would imagine that Nabonidus had slighted their god by implying that he was unable to defend his own city. (For a more complete discussion see Boutflower, pp. 97-110.)

·APPENDIX 10
Belshazzar's Drunkenness

It was the night of the 11th of Marchesvan (October/November), 539 B.C. Babylon's last night had come. Belshazzar's last night had come. Excavations have exposed the scene for us. We not only know what the throne room was like but we can locate the double-recessed niche, opposite the central entrance where the throne stood and where Belshazzar sat.

The Chaldeans were fond of wine. That night Belshazzar had drunk himself to the point of bravado. To the cheers and applause of his cronies and courtiers, he decided to teach the Jews a lesson in religion. He would prove that the gods of Babylon were superior to the God of the Jews. So "whiles he tasted the wine" he "commanded to bring the golden and silver vessels, which his father Nebuchadnezzar . . . had taken out of the temple which was in Jerusalem."

Nebuchadnezzar had deposited those vessels in the temple of his favorite god, Merodach, in Esagila. Esagila had now fallen to the enemy, but we have no trouble there because, doubtless, Nabonidus, who showed little reverence at the best of times for Merodach, had removed the treasure from the temple to the palace in Babylon before Esagila fell into enemy hands.

As Belshazzar gazed around the throne room in his intoxicated state, his eye, it would seem, fell on the motley collection of gods, "gods of gold, and of silver, of brass, of iron, of wood, and of stone" which his father Nabonidus had recently imported from the provinces. The emphatic idiom of the text leads to the conclusion that these images "must have been in the room at that critical moment when 'the King eternal, incorruptible, invisible, the only God,' saw fit to assert his supremacy." (See Boutflower, pp. 133-134.) So the drunken bravado of Belshazzar and the ribald acquiescence of his lords, his wives, and his concubines combined to set the stage. Even as they raised those sacred vessels to toast the assorted idols all about them, out of the sleeve of the night came the hand of God—and death walked in the door.

· APPENDIX 11
The Writing on the Wall

If we were to use our own letters, what appeared on the palace wall was this: NISRPU LQT ANM ANM. Or, since we read from left to right: MNA MNA TQL UPRSIN (the "A" and the "U," however, were not vowels).

The king and his stricken court saw on the palace wall the aramaic words for three units of money: "A mina, a mina, a shekel, and half minas." These words have been met with frequently in archaeological finds. Since Aramaic was the commonly spoken language of western Asia, the people at Belshazzar's feast would at least be familiar with the words. The Babylonian kings, and Belshazzar in particular, saw nothing wrong with the monarch being a merchant. Indeed, the atmosphere of Babylon was one of false religion on the one hand and business on the other.

One of the mysteries, however, connected with these eerie words now blazoned on the palace wall was the unusual order in which they occurred. The shekel, which was only one-sixtieth of a mina, was placed in between the mina and the peres (the half mina) instead of coming at the end. The king could read the words, but they made no sense. But the ominous way in which they had appeared made it obvious that they were intended to convey some message.

Daniel, having read the guilty king a sermon, turned to the words on the wall:

> He treated them, not as substantives, but as the past participles of three Aramaic verbs, which have their very similar equivalents in Babylonian; and thus interpreted them as he went along: "*MNA*," pronounced *mena*, "God hath numbered thy kingdom and brought it to an end"; "*TQL*," pronounced *tegal*, "thou art weighed in the balances, and art found wanting"; till at last, coming to the final word, he gave it in its singular form, *PRS*, and treating it also as a past participle, accounted for its plural form, PRSIN, by declaring that it carried with it a further reference to the

Persians, who, along with the Medes, were besieging the
city at that time: "*PRS*," pronounced *peras*, "thy kingdom
is divided, and given to the Medes and Persians." The message, then, as read by Daniel, may be written thus—

NUMBERED NUMBERED WEIGHED AND DIVIDED

The repetition of the first word marks the certainty of the
coming judgment, and is, as it were, the solemn death-
knell of the Babylonian king; the third word gives the reason of it; and the last word, which because of its double
meaning it is impossible to do justice to in an English
translation, shows the course which that judgment will
take. (Boutflower, pp. 138-140,151.)

One other fact is of interest here. The word *peres* was used by Daniel
to signify the kingdom being divided and given to the Medes and Persians. He used the word, therefore, according to its primary meaning, "divided into two parts." Cyrus did just that. One part of the
Babylonian empire he added to the countries already under his rule;
the other part was given as a subordinate kingdom to Darius the
Mede.

APPENDIX 12
Shushan

Tradition has selected Shushan as the place where Daniel's bones lie, awaiting resurrection. Looking eastward, beyond the Tigris, tower range upon range of lofty limestone mountains. The mountain passes beyond rise five and six thousand feet and the peaks to over eleven thousand feet. These ramparts stand astride an average width of three hundred miles. The Semitic peoples called the southern portion of this great mountain range Elam (the Upland).

The Elamites were historically the traditional foes of Assyria and the constant allies of the Chaldeans. It was against Elam that Sennacherib mounted five of the eight campaigns described on the Taylor Cylinder. Ashurbanipal thrashed the Elamites twice and on the second occasion took such fearful vengeance as virtually to wipe out the Elamites. The nation recovered, however, and outlasted Assyria in the end. Nineveh fell. Time passed. The prophet Jeremiah lifted his voice against Elam. Time passed and Ezekiel recorded the fulfillment of Jeremiah's word.

In the closing days of the detested Assyrian empire, when the Medes were laying siege to famous Assyrian cities, the Elamites, eager to be in at the kill, joined forces with Nabopolassar, father of Nebuchadnezzar, and marched with him in his attack on the southern borders of Assyria.

Nineveh fell and the ancient Assyrian scourge was removed. The Medes took firm hold of the northern half of the old Assyrian empire, and Babylon seized the southern half. The world was changed. The Elamites were left out in the cold. The Babylonians wasted no time in extending their empire westward. As Jeremiah had foretold (49:36) Elam, isolated, was attacked from all quarters.

Nebuchadnezzar had not been able to extend his power very far eastward, because the small kingdom of Anshan barred the way. Anshan, destined to be the nucleus of the future Persian empire, was a province of Media. Nebuchadnezzar had a healthy respect for Media. In no way would he meddle with a Median sphere of interest. But he could join hands to attack and carve up what remained of

Elamite power. When the dust had settled, that part of Elam closest to Babylon was his reward.

It was in this part of Elam, now a Babylonian province, that the city of Shushan was to be found. It was just two hundred miles east of Babylon. That Nebuchadnezzar's empire terminated on its eastward side near Shushan seems evident from the fact that the Babylonian king drew his timber supplies from far-off Lebanon rather than from the much nearer Elamite forests.

During the Assyrian period, Shushan had been the royal capital of Elam, and the dwelling place of Elam's gods. It was famous for its sacred groves, its royal mausoleum, its statues of thirty-two kings, and the treasures stored up in its palaces.

During the Babylonian era we can assume that the city continued to be an important place. Doubtless it was a strategic military outpost and a key frontier town.

In Persian times (already underway when Daniel wrote) Shushan (Susa) became one of the empire's capitals, along with Ecbatana, Persepolis, and Babylon. It was a popular winter resort, so much so that Darius Hystaspes seems to have made it his chief capital. There he kept his treasure and there terminated the royal road from Sardis mentioned by Herodotus.

The city stood on a narrow island between two rivers. Near the junction of the rivers, standing on a hill, stood the castle or citadel. The famous Persian archers, known as the Immortals, wore badges emblazoned with a picture of the citadel of Shushan.

In the British Museum is a bas-relief of the town and citadel of Shushan, showing the city as it was in the middle of the seventh century B.C. (See Boutflower, pp. 214-216.) Scattered palm trees and houses are in the foreground, between the town and the larger of the two rivers. Many of the houses have rooms on their flat roofs. It was such a chamber that Daniel used for his prayer room.

APPENDIX 13
Antiochus Epiphanes and the Jews

The date of Antiochus's first attack on Jerusalem is given as the 143rd year (of the Seleucids), 169-170 B.C. At that time he plundered the temple to replenish his treasury, and went on his way.

The real threat to Jerusalem came two years later, after his humiliation by Popilius, some time in the fall of 168 B.C., when he sent his tax collector to plunder the cities of Judaea. Jerusalem lay secure behind those massive walls that had withstood so many sieges. Apollonius, the Syrian representative, came with persuasive words. When they gave heed to his deceitful tongue, he suddenly and unexpectedly seized the city, devastated parts of it, fortified mount Zion with a strong wall and mighty towers, and garrisoned it with apostates.

Up until this time (fall of 168 B.C.) there had been no permanent Syrian control of Jerusalem. The persecution began on the fifteenth of Chisleu (December 168 or January 167 B.C.). The temple was desecrated by the idol-altar built on the altar of God, and the first pagan sacrifice was offered on it on December 25. Not until three years later, to the day and month, was it cleansed.

In December 165 (January 164) Judas fortified the sanctuary. Meanwhile Antiochus was preoccupied with a war with the satraps of the upper provinces. News of the new Jewish defiance doubtless reached Antiochus. Judas Maccabeus continued on his victorious way, punishing the petty nations that had harassed Israel. But Antiochus was still far away, trying to plunder the temple in Elymais. He failed in this attempt and was forced into another retreat with news coming in of one victory after another by Judas Maccabeus. But Antiochus's sandglass had run out and he died while still in Persia of a wasting disease, in 164 or 163 B.C.

The death of Antiochus was the signal for renewed Syrian hostilities. In the name of Antiochus's youthful son, Antiochus Eupator, Lysias renewed the war. He and Eupator were subsequently murdered by Demetrius, who continued the war. Nor did rest come until the Jews defeated and slew Nicanor, the second general sent against them by Demetrius, early in 161 B.C. (See Pusey, pp. 220-222.)

APPENDIX 14
The Persian Empire

The Persian empire was sprawling and ungainly. Its vast bulk was forever crumbling through internal disorganization. Even its victories were haphazard affairs, though countless men were employed in the pursuit of its wars. The Persians hurled their human waves, the accumulated hordes of Asia, for instance, against the tiny Greek republics. It seemed as though they must submerge them. Instead the rushing Persian sea broke and receded. All the internal affairs of Persia seem to have been directed more toward collecting taxes in order to pursue expensive wars than toward good government.

The sixty years of its seeming prosperity closed with the defeat of Xerxes. For over 150 years more the Persian empire held together, but that was because Greece was divided and its Alexander had not yet come. Pusey wrote:

> It did nothing for mankind; it left no memorial of itself. There is not a trait in its history upon which the human mind can dwell with interest, save the one scene of the kindness of Artaxerxes to Nehemiah; scarce any, from which human nature does not turn away. Its heterogeneous elements were not more assimilated after two centuries, than at the first. Its connection with its provinces consisted in the appointments of satraps with the state of kings, military governors, and governors of the garrisons which kept them in check; and the contribution, on the part of the provinces, of fixed tribute, of contingents of troops when required, or, in times of peace, of eunuchs and replenishers of the Persian harems. Government by favorite, often revengeful Queens, or by eunuchs, was the order of its policy; fratricide, a path to the throne, or a condition of its tenure. The jealousies or even mutual wars of its satraps, in that they kept each other in check, were thought to be the safety of the government (pp. 166-167).

Its provinces were in a constant state of revolt. The petty prince of Salamis on the island of Cyprus was able to defy Persian power for ten years. Egypt had three brief dynasties of native princes in defiance of Persian rule. The Persian wars were chiefly to quell revolts. Its armies were a hodgepodge of nationalities. Rarely has the dictum been more aptly illustrated than in the Persian empire: "All power corrupts; absolute power corrupts absolutely."

APPENDIX 15
Alexander's Empire

Alexander dreamed of blending east and west into one. Everywhere he went he planted Greek cities to be links in a chain of commerce, bands to tie his dominion together, centers of a new Hellenistic civilization, and a means of colonizing an empire.

He had an eye for location. He instantly saw the value of the site of Alexandria. He founded more than seventy cities, or commanded his generals to do so. Pusey said that such cities:

> . . . have been traced in Asia Minor, Syria, Egypt, Mesopotamia, Media, Hyrcania, Parthis, Aria, Margiana, Drangiana, Arachosia, Paropamisus, Bactria, Sogdiana, India on the Hydaspes, Acesines, Indus; in modern terms, in the whole of Turkey in Asia, Egypt, all habitable Persia, North, East, and South, and beyond it, in Beloochistan, the Deccan, Cabool, Afghanistan, the Punjaub, and yet Northward, in Khorassan and Khondooz to Bokhara and Turkestan (pp. 169-170).

We follow Alexander's line of march. We see his genius at work as he seized each important spot by instinct. In Egypt, in the old civilizations along the Tigris and the Euphrates, he had one goal in view: conquer and colonize. Media was belted with Greek cities. At the pass of the Caspian Gates, at the confluence of the Indus and the Chenab, at the mouth of the Indus, on the Persian Gulf, with unerring genius he seized the points that would become the cords of the social, religious, and commercial intercourse of nations. These cities were the knots of a vast net, intersecting and tying together the lines of communication and the strategic military posts. He died too young. His genius was cut off before he could fulfill his dreams.

APPENDIX 16
Belshazzar

The inscriptions make it clear that Belshazzar was the eldest son of Nabonidus and heir apparent to the throne. No actual blood tie existed between Belshazzar and Nebuchadnezzar, on his father's side, at least. Nabonidus was just one of a band of conspirators who murdered the boy-king Labashi-Marduk, actual grandson of Nebuchadnezzar and last of his line. Why then is Belshazzar spoken of as the son of Nebuchadnezzar, both by Daniel and the queen mother?

We can well believe that, as his own celebrated stele tells us, Nabonidus was eager to legitimize his claim to the throne. He told how he was unanimously elected by the other conspirators to be their delegate on the throne. He appealed to "Nebuchadnezzar and to Nergal-sharezer" as "the kings my predecessors" and adds "their delegate am I: their hosts to my hands they entrusted."

With such a strong urge to secure his throne rights, Nabonidus made sure he married into the royal family of Nebuchadnezzar. It seems probable that at least one of Nabonidus's sons was thus a blood descendant of Nebuchadnezzar.

Belshazzar himself had no such lineage. He was born many years before Nabonidus took the crown. He must be regarded as "the son" (i.e., grandson), or descendant of Nebuchadnezzar only in a technical sense. Evidently it was court etiquette to speak of Belshazzar and to treat him as the legitimate son of Nebuchadnezzar. It would be as much as anyone's life was worth not to keep up the pretense. Thus the queen mother addressed him in a stylized form: "The king Nebuchadnezzar thy father, the king, I say, thy father" (5:11).

Belshazzar's mother was dead; she had died in the camp at Sippora in the ninth year of Nabonidus, as we learn from the Annalistic Tablet. Who then was the woman spoken of as the queen mother (5:10)? The suggestion has been made that she was the widow of Nebuchadnezzar and that Nabonidus had married her as part of his scheme to legitimize his claim to the throne, in which case she would be Belshazzar's stepmother. Nabonidus, on that fateful night, was already a prisoner in the hands of the enemy so, naturally, his queen would assume the position of queen mother. (See Pusey, pp. 115-117.)

APPENDIX 17
The Hiddekel

In scripture, the Euphrates is often called "the great river." The Tigris (the Hiddekel), however, is no small stream. It is shorter than the Euphrates (1,146 miles as compared with 1,670 miles) but it makes up for that in its depth, volume, and flow, all of which are greater than that of the Euphrates. The Hebrew name *Hiddekel* corresponds to the Assyrian *Idiklat*. It is believed that the Persians formed their name for the river, *Tigra*, with a play on their word for an arrow—again coming back to the idea of swiftness.

Why did Daniel mention the Tigris as the scene for the visions of chapters 10 and 11? In chapter 8 he mentioned the Ulai. This important canal suggested traffic and commerce, power dependent on wealth. The Tigris, by contrast, a deep and fast-flowing river, brings to mind the turbulence of the nations, the rush of great armies like the rushing of great waters—but held between their banks, just the same, by a restraining power. This idea, of course, would be familiar to Daniel, who doubtless had mastered Isaiah 6–8 where that prophet had likened the invasion of Israel by the Assyrians to the Euphrates flowing at the flood. For even when a river overflows its banks, it is still subject to higher laws.

The question has been asked, Why the Tigris rather than the Euphrates? The Euphrates is connected in scripture with world power. It is the eastern boundary of the land grant deeded by God to Abraham as the promised land. It is the dividing line between east and west. The four prophetic world empires are all linked geographically with the Euphrates. The four angels who controlled these four empires are imprisoned by God by the Euphrates awaiting the day they will be released to lay their united powers at the feet of the antichrist.

The Tigris, as distinct from the Euphrates, was destined to have a special connection with the Seleucid dynasty. It was on the banks of the Tigris that Seleucus Nicator, who founded the dynasty, built his great city of Seleucia. It was his plan that Seleucia should be a second Babylon and that it would be the capital of the eastern part of his empire.

The Tigris is mentioned by Daniel, rather than the Orontes, on which river stood the city of Antioch, the other Seleucid capital, also built by Seleucus Nicator for an equally good reason. It is true that the Syrian armies marched forth from Antioch. But, unlike Seleucia, Antioch had no link with Babylon, and in any case it was too small a river to symbolize the power and influence of the Seleucids. (See Boutflower, pp. 218, 220-221.)

APPENDIX 18
Robert Dick Wilson and the Critics

The prophecies of Daniel 11 are the most remarkable in scripture. Verse by verse, line by line, phrase by phrase, the predictions unfold. Here we have a foreshortened summary of Persian history, a brief glimpse of the empire of Alexander the Great, a detailed chronicle of the wars between Syria and Egypt, a look at the brief period of Jewish independence, and then a forecast of the coming of Rome to world power. With every detail that is added, another nail is driven into the coffin of liberal theology.

Faced with the multiplied details of prophetic utterance here and the exact and detailed fulfillment of these events in history, what should the so-called higher critic do? All should bow to the inevitable and acknowledge that here indeed we have the finger of God. All should recognize that here, in detailed prophecy and exact fulfillment, we have proof of the inerrancy of scripture, of its divine, God-breathed inspiration. But this rarely happens.

The worn-out answer of liberal theology is that this chapter was not written by a Palestinian Jew, carried captive to Babylon in the days of Nebuchadnezzar and writing as an old man during the reign of Cyrus, the first great Persian king. The claim is that the chapter was written very much later, after the facts and not before; that some pseudo-Daniel wrote history in the guise of prophecy; that, to put it bluntly, this is a pious forgery. The liberal theologian is wedded to his unbelief and is determined to twist the evidence no matter what.

The liberal theologian will not believe, no matter what the evidence. He likes his unbelief, feels comfortable with it and clever because of it. He thinks himself a scholar. No matter that men more learned and devout than he have long since met and exploded his pet theories; he holds on to them just the same. No matter that the church for centuries has accepted these prophecies at face value, and marveled at them. No matter that to brand the book of Daniel as some kind of pseudo-prophetic farce is to attack the deity of Christ who believed in the historic Daniel and who quoted from his book as authentic prophecy. The liberal theologian still will not believe.

He is like the man who did not believe in miracles. A friend tried to convince him. "Suppose," he said, "you were walking past a construction site, and a big piece of timber, carelessly dropped from a floor high up on the job, were to come crashing down, and miss you by inches. You were saved from certain death. Wouldn't you say that was a miracle?" The skeptic thought for a moment. "No," he said, "I would call that an accident."

"Well," said his friend, "suppose you were to go past the same site the next day and exactly the same thing were to happen. Suppose a heavy piece of timber, carelessly dropped by a workman high up on the building, were to come crashing down and again miss you by inches. Wouldn't you say that was a miracle?" "No," said the skeptic, "I would call that a coincidence."

His friend insisted. "Suppose," he said, "that you had occasion to pass that same construction site the next day and exactly the same thing happened. You narrowly escaped death a third time from a falling timber. Wouldn't you say that was a miracle?" "No," said the skeptic, "I would call it a habit!"

No matter what, the liberal theologian has made up his mind—miracles do not happen; the Bible does not foretell the future; it is not a miracle book. It is all coincidence, or it was written after the fact, or history must be rearranged, or the text is corrupt, or conservative interpretation is at fault.

The present book makes no pretense at being a critical commentary on Daniel. Others have long since answered the hollow arguments of the agnostic theologians. Sir Robert Anderson answered the liberals for the rank and file (see Appendix 1), and Charles Boutflower showed the accuracy of the book of Daniel from the standpoint of history and archaeology (see Introduction). Dr. Pusey also dissected the liberal position point by point, leaving no place to hide.

But probably the most telling and damning exposure of liberal theology comes from Robert Dick Wilson.¹ Professor Wilson made it his life goal to prove liberal theologians wrong. He divided his life into three parts. First, he determined to make himself thoroughly at home in the original languages of the Bible, in all cognate languages, and in all the languages in which the liberal so-called "higher critics" had written. His linguistic explorations made him thoroughly at home in Greek, Latin, Hebrew, biblical aramaic, Syriac, Arabic, Babylonian, Ethiopic, Phoenician, all the other aramaic dialects, Egyptian, Coptic, Persian, and Armenian. He studied German, French, Italian, Spanish, Portuguese. Before he was through, he was conversant with some forty-five languages and dialects.

Dr. Wilson then turned his attention to the writings of the critics themselves and again he made himself their master. One example of his painstaking thoroughness will suffice. In order to answer a single sentence of a leading critic, Professor Wilson read all the extant ancient literature of the period under review. This involved reading material in numerous languages. He collated some 100,000 citations from that literature in order to get at the basic facts. His findings proved the critic wrong.[2]

One of the worn-out liberal criticisms of the book of Daniel is based on the fact that the book contains three Greek words. The contention is that this proves that the book could not have been written in the sixth century B.C., the time when Daniel actually lived. On the contrary, say the liberals, it must have been written during the Greek period, probably during the reign of Antiochus Epiphanes. The claim, based on such flimsy evidence, is foolish. The three Greek words (the slender thread on which the destructive critics hang such an enormous weight of unbelief) are the names of musical instruments. It remains unproven by the critics that Nebuchadnezzar, an emperor whose court was continually visited by foreign emissaries, could not have imported some Greek instruments into Babylonia. In any case, if the book of Daniel *had* been written by a pseudepigrapher living in the days of Antiochus Epiphanes, when Greek was already a world language and when many leading Jews were apostatizing from Judaism, seduced by the fascination of Hellenism, the book would contain *many* Greek words, not just three (and those restricted to musical instruments).

The vocabulary of Daniel, indeed, is the basis of Professor Wilson's thorough-going exposure of liberal theology. He wrote: "The time at which any document of length, and often even of small compass, was written, can generally be determined by the character of its vocabulary, and especially by the foreign words which are embedded in it."

A moment's thought will show us how true that is. Suppose you were to find an undated piece of writing in English containing the word *sputnik*. You would know at once that it could not have been written before 1957, because it was not until after the first Soviet space spectacular in that year that this word passed into the English language. It remained a common word until the Americans put a man on the moon, and then it waned in usage. So, within certain limits, the use of the word would date the document.

Professor Wilson's investigations into the vocabulary of Daniel have never been answered by the liberals. "He being dead yet speaketh," and he speaks today with a powerful and authentic voice. Professor Wilson and other conservative scholars have long since exploded the liberal views of the critics. Yet they still keep on serving up the same poisonous brew to successive generations of unsuspecting young theology students who enroll in their classes.

---

1. Robert Dick Wilson, *A Scientific Investigation of the Old Testament* (revised by Edward J. Young; Chicago: Moody Press, 1959). See also Wilson's book *Is the Higher Criticism Scholarly?* (Philadelphia: The Sunday-School Times Co., 1922).

2. See *Is the Higher Criticism Scholarly?* p.9.

APPENDIX 19
The Liberals' Claim That the Four Prophetic Empires End with Antiochus Epiphanes

The liberals argue that the four empires portrayed in Daniel end with Antiochus. Since they claim that the book of Daniel was written about the time of Antiochus, obviously it is in their interest to take this position and thus rid themselves of the formidable and (to them) embarrassing prophecies of Daniel. After discussing their various hopeless efforts to establish their position, Pusey wrote:

> The negative evidence then, that no scheme can be made out, whereby the four Empires portrayed to Daniel can be brought within the limits of the times before Antiochus Epiphanes, coincides with the previous direct evidence that the fourth empire is the Roman. For the Roman was the next world-empire which succeeded the Greek in Alexander and his successors.
>
> Men will hardly turn round and say that, in the times of Antiochus Epiphanes, it could have been foreseen that the Roman commonwealth, with its annually changing Consuls, would become a kingdom, and that, a kingdom of the world. Men's consciences will surely hardly allow them. All these various strivings by Porphyry and his recent followers, to make the four empires end with Alexander's successors, bear witness to their conviction that it was beyond human sagacity, within any time which could be assigned to the book of Daniel, to predict the Roman Empire. Else they would not have invented so many far-fetched and contradictory ways of excluding it.
>
> But look at its state, 164 B.C., the year when Antiochus Epiphanes died. A generation only (37 years) had passed since the close of the old Punic war, when the war had been carried to its own gates; Carthage, its rival, still stood over against it. It was felt by Romans to be a formidable foe. Witness the "delenda est Carthago," and the unscrupulous policy adopted in encouraging the aggressions of Masinissa. Enriched by the

commerce of the West, Carthage was recovering its resources, and fell through its intestine divisions. Egypt and Antiochus had lately mustered powerful armies: Perseus, king of Macedonia, had been but recently defeated, and might have repelled the Romans, but for his timidity and avarice. They had defeated Antiochus the Great, and, by their enormous fine for the expenses of the war, had crippled him. But, true to their policy of dividing and conquering, supporting the weak whom they feared not against the strong whom they feared, they had diminished the empires, which were their rivals, by giving a portion of their possessions to the weaker, to be taken at their own will hereafter.

Who should foresee that all these nations should remain blinded by their avarice; that common fear should never bind them in one; that they should never see, until their own turn came, that Rome used her instruments successively, and flung each aside, and found some excuse of quarrel against each, as soon as she had gained her end? The absence of any such fear on any side shows how little human wisdom could then foresee the world-empire, which as yet existed only in the embryo; and which the nations, whom Rome in the end subdued, were, in God's Providence, the unwilling, unconscious, blinded, instruments of forming. To us it seems inconceivable that no experience should have opened men's eyes, until it was too late. Each helped in turn to roll round the wheel, which crushed himself.

Rome had at that time (B.C. 164) no territory East or, except Sicily, South of Italy. Masinissa held the throne of Numidia; Rome had not a foot of ground in Africa. In Spain, she held only so much as had before been in the power of Carthage, the Western and Southern Provinces, now Catalonia, Valencia, Murcia, Andalusia, Grenada: two centuries almost elapsed before it was finally reduced. Gaul and Germany were almost unknown countries. Even Cis-Alpine Gaul had not been formally made a Roman Province; Venetia was friendly; Carniola unsubdued; Istria recently subdued; (B.C.177). Illyricum had been divided into three, yet left nominally free. The Battle of Pydna had destroyed the kingdom of Macedon four years before, (B.C. 168) but it seemed as if Rome knew not how to appropriate territory. It took nothing which it could not at once consolidate. Macedonia was divided into only four independent Republics. The territory which Rome required Antiochus to cede, it gave to Eumenes: Lycia and Caria, which it took from the Rhodians, it made independent.

Such was the impenetrable mask which it wore; everywhere professing to uphold the weak and maintain justice; everywhere unjust, as soon as the time came; setting free in order to enslave; aiding, in order to oppress (pp. 181-182).

APPENDIX 20
Antiochus and the Critics

The prophecy of Daniel 11 focuses eventually on the sufferings of the Jews under Antiochus Epiphanes. So remarkable and detailed are its predictions that the critics have taken the position that it could not possibly have been written by a Jew living in Babylon in the days of the Babylon-Persian empires. The general claim is that the book was written about 164 B.C. The thing that bothers the infidels most is the remarkable amount of detail in the prophecy.

Included in the prophecy, for instance, are details like these: the coming of Antiochus Epiphanes into the kingdom by stealth and gaining power by flattery (11:21), his prodigality (11:24), his two Egyptian campaigns, the second of which ended so differently from the first because of the intervention of the Romans (11:25-30), his persecution of the Jews when returning from his first Egyptian campaign (11:28), his effort to stamp out Jewish worship when returning in humiliation from his second campaign (11:31), the early triumphs of the Maccabees (11:34), the assumption of divine honors by Antiochus in the later years of his reign (11:36), and (as some take it) the special honor paid by him to Jupiter, "the god of forces" (11:38-39). (See Boutflower, pp. 2-4.)

According to the critics, this remarkable chapter is mere history up to verse 39, and then it passes over to prophecy. But then, nothing fits. History knows of no such invasion of Egypt, supposed to be prophesied in verses 40-42. Moreover, Antiochus, far from having "power over the treasures of gold and of silver, and over all the precious things of Egypt" (11:43), was in financial difficulty toward the end of his life. He did not die in the Holy Land (11:45) but in Elymais, after an abortive attempt to rob a temple of its treasures. Evidently the critics are wrong. These verses, if they are prophecies concerning Antiochus, were never fulfilled.

There is a much simpler explanation of the transition from detail to generalities in Daniel 11. The immense amounts of detail in verses 1-35 were given to the prophet because they concerned the uninterrupted future of the Jews from Daniel's day down to the coming on stage of the Roman power (also foretold in the visions of chapters 2 and 7). It was to be in the days of the Romans that Christ would come (chapter 9). Also a great deal of detail was given prophetically concerning Antiochus Epiphanes, not only because of the horrors of that time, but also because this monstrous king would be one of the supreme historical types of the antichrist.

The change (which really runs from 11:36-45), which is evident in the more general and less detailed style, can be explained simply enough. These verses leaped to a far distant future. They passed right over the 2000-year church age to the post-rapture world of the antichrist. Since the fulfillment of this part of the prophecy was so far distant, there was no need to give more details. These would be added in time by New Testament revelation as in Matthew 24; 2 Thessalonians 2; Revelation 11–13,17 and so on.

The infidel view that the detailed early part of Daniel 11 is history posing as prophecy, and that the more general remainder of the chapter was mere speculation on the part of the author as to what he thought would happen in the immediate future, is not only the kind of thing an unbeliever would say, but it does not fit the facts.

APPENDIX 21
The Minuteness of Daniel's Prophecies

God had his purpose in giving the Jewish people such detailed prophecies as are found in Daniel. Pusey said:

> The partial minuteness of Daniel's prophecies belongs to the transition-state of the period for which those prophecies were given. They are in one sense a link between the Old and New Testament. God was preparing His people to depend more on His invisible presence. In the captivity itself, the three great bodies of His people dispersed among the heathen, those in Assyria, in Egypt, and in Babylon, had still each their own great prophet, Ezekiel among the *captives by the river of Chebar*, Jeremiah in Egypt, Daniel in Babylon. After the captivity, there were but three prophets more. Of these, the prophecies of Haggai, preserved to us, fall in the space of four months in the second year of Darius Hystaspes (Hag. 1:1; 2:1-10,20), 16 years after their return; Zechariah began two months later than Haggai (Zech. 1:1), and has no known date beyond the fourth year of Darius (Zech. 7:1). The prophecy of Malachi is probably contemporaneous with the second visit of Nehemiah, about 400 B.C. Then prophecy ceased in act. It was exceptional, while it lasted. For those five centuries, in the first instance, the book of Daniel was written. God no longer willed to interfere visibly. Israel, a petty nation, hated, envied, on account of its magnificent claims that its God was the God of the whole world, was placed in the highway of the world, to be trampled upon by each in turn. Forerunner of the Christian Church, and itself shortly, the whole true Israel, to pass into it, it lay for the time resting on the unseen Providence of God, and awaiting, with keener expectation, the Deliverer of itself and of the world. It was no longer to have single Prophets raised up, to explain to it or to point out God's dealings with it, to preach submission, or to promise mitigation of suffering or deliverance upon its repentance. But God *did not leave Himself without witness.* Details

of prophecy, such as aforetime had been given by different prophets, in succession, were spread out before them at once, culminating in that great trial of faith, the last before our Lord's first Coming, when Antiochus Epiphanes used all artifice and force to extirpate the worship of the One God. Daniel foreshewed to them his power, his artifices, his partial success in abolishing the public worship of God, his sudden destruction without human hand. They should need no human might; they had but to endure, and the victory was God's.

These more detailed prophecies of Daniel, then, so far from being exceptional in God's dealings with His people, were in conformity with all His ways, as recorded for us, before the captivity; so far from being retrogressive, in introducing a more limited character of, so to speak, civil prophecy, his prophecy was adapted to a state of progress, a condition more like our own, in which, instead of the living, revealing prophet, they were cast upon the written book. But in that book God taught them that, however the world might rage, it was in His hands. He Who beforehand told the course which ambitious, selfish, crafty, oppressive, sensual monarchs would take, and how it would fare with them, shewed that He Himself ruled and overruled the affairs of men which He foreknew. The book of Daniel said in fact, at each stage of its fulfillment, what God said in words by Isaiah 42:9, *Behold, the former things are come to pass, and new things do I declare unto you; before they spring forth, I tell you of them* (pp. 262-263).

APPENDIX 22
Nebuchadnezzar's Dream

The dream of world empire was not given to a Hebrew prophet but to a heathen king; the prophet was merely an expositor. The vision did not center on Jerusalem but on Babylon. The focus of interest was not the kingdom of God but the kingdoms of men. Nothing could more graphically illustrate the fallen fortunes of the Hebrew people nor the world importance of Nebuchadnezzar's conquest of Jerusalem. For with Nebuchadnezzar began a new departure in God's dealings with this planet.

With him began a period called "the times of the Gentiles" (Luke 21:24). Up until the coming of Nebuchadnezzar God had invested the right to rule the world in Israel. The Hebrew people were to establish a theocracy and become a people ruled by God. The Hebrew nation was to be in treaty relationship with God (Genesis 12:1-3).

The country deeded to Abraham stretched from the Nile to the Euphrates (Genesis 15:18) and it was located at the geographic center of the world, situated where it could touch three continents. Moreover, Israel was to establish in Jerusalem a testimony for God to all nations, and Jewish ambassadors were to have been a worldwide witness to the true and living God. No nation on earth would have dared to lift a weapon against them; the coming of Christ would have heralded the establishment of a world empire ruled from Jerusalem.

The appalling and repeated apostasies of Israel brought judgment after judgment, prophet after prophet, warning after warning, but all to no avail. The Assyrians came and marched the northern tribes into captivity. Judah only redoubled its sins. Then came Nebuchadnezzar. Jerusalem was delivered into the hands of the gentiles to be under gentile dominion for an unspecified period of time, but for seventy years at least. The temple was burned to the ground, hopes of a worldwide theocracy vanished, and world power was sovereignly transferred by God from the Jews to the gentiles.

This vision of Nebuchadnezzar is to be seen in this light. God's millennial promises to Israel were now deliberately postponed and, after the crime of Calvary, they were postponed again. Now, in our age, the configuration of world events seems to herald the count-down to the endtimes, seen in the vision of this pagan king, and to serve notice on the world that the long "times of the Gentiles" are about to end.

APPENDIX 23
Prophetic Exposition of Daniel 2

I. The King and the Babylonian Professionals (2:1-16)

In spite of the delight with which the critics seize upon imagined errors in the book of Daniel, we can be sure that Daniel's dates are accurate. After all, he was there when these things happened and we can be quite sure he knew how to read a calendar. Moreover, he was much better informed about Babylon affairs than any of his critics. The events in Daniel 1:1 occurred when Nebuchadnezzar was co-regent with his father Nabopolassar. The date in Daniel 2:1 refers to his second year as sole king of Babylon (2:6). That year God spoke to the pagan king in a dream.[1] The rest of the night he spent in a state of sleepless agitation.

The various classes of the Chaldean priesthood were summoned before the king. There were the magicians, those who wielded the rod of office. Their function was to repel demons and evil spirits by means of special spells and incantations. In other words, they dealt in magic, an art reaching back into the mists of antiquity. The astrologers were prophets who cast horoscopes and studied the stars, announced the will of heaven and predicted the future. The sorcerers were wizards; pharaoh kept similar advisers in his court (Exodus 7:11). In the law, God commanded that the Hebrews have no dealings with such people: "Thou shalt not suffer a witch to live" (Exodus 22:18). The death penalty pronounced by God on all witchcraft is proof enough of the reality of intercourse with fallen angels, evil spirits and demons. The Chaldeans were a special class, distinct from the ordinary Babylonians (Jeremiah 22:25; Ezekiel 23:23), and belonged to southern Babylonia. They seem, also, to comprise a special class within the priesthood. They were the elite, a group made up of those exclusively of Chaldean lineage, and they seem to have had a special relation to the temple of Bel-Merodach in which Nebuchadnezzar had put the temple vessels plundered from the temple of Jerusalem.

These were the powerful leaders of the Babylonian religion who were summoned by Nebuchadnezzar. They were the professionals. Their specialty was the world of the unknown. Nowadays we would call them "psychics."

Now comes *the king's demand* (2:4-11). The *first demand* (2:4-6) embodied a *rational request* (2:4) by the magicians. From here to the end of chapter 7 there is a marked change in the choice of language. Daniel draws our attention to it. A study of the Hebrew sections and aramaic sections of Daniel readily reveals the reason for this language dichotomy. The aramaic section deals primarily with gentile world power ("the times of the Gentiles"). Aramaic was the *lingua franca* of the ancient east and was a fitting vehicle for God to use when speaking to and about the gentile world. The very first words written in Aramaic are the words, "O king." The Hebrew portions of the book of Daniel are more concerned with matters of special import to the Jewish people.

The Babylonian professionals asked for details of the dreams which had so troubled the king. If he would provide the subject matter of the dreams, they would provide the secret meaning. They were quite sure that, between them, they could concoct some sort of an "interpretation" which would satisfy him. They were old hands at such mumbo-jumbo. They made their living at it.

But this king was too clever to be caught by such tricks. We note the *reasonable response* (2:5-6) by the monarch. We are struck by the practical common sense of this king. This was the same king who, instead of wasting the talents of his Jewish captives by banishing them to the Babylonian equivalent of Siberia, decided instead to train them and use them in the administration of his empire. The farsighted king could not see any reason why his psychics and soothsayers, if they had the powers they claimed, should not be expected to recount his dream for him. Whether or not he had actually forgotten it is beside the point. The test of their supposed powers was the same.

Now comes the *further demand* (2:7-11). The Babylonian professionals were outraged. This further request was instantly refused. The king saw through their ploy.

Perhaps these soothsayers were hoping for a more propitious day, this day being unlucky. It certainly was an unlucky day for them! The king was merely annoyed and angered by this attempt to gain more time. Lucky day or no, he wanted proof, once and for all, of their pretended powers (2:8-9).

Truly this king was no fool. He had long suspected his professional magicians and astrologers of fraud and he seized a golden opportunity to put them to the test.

It is said that Chaka, the powerful Zulu "Napoleon," once sought to rid himself of the witchdoctors, whose power was rivaling his, in a similar way. The story is that he secretly smeared his hut with blood and then, in well-simulated rage, demanded that the doctors "smell out" the evildoer who had so dared desecrate his abode. The day was set for the culprit or conspirators to be exposed. Chaka's witch doctors, more daring than the Babylonian wizards, tried to bluff the thing through. They arrayed themselves in the ghastly accouterments of their trade and went through their rituals and dances "smelling out" this one and that one. Instead of being instantly slain, as was usually the case, the victims were simply made to stand to one side until the exhausted witch doctors had finished. Chaka then revealed to his witch doctors that he had smeared his hut with blood himself. They were frauds. They had "smelled out" hundreds of innocent men. They deserved the death they had ordained for others. The fraudulent witch doctors were handed over to their victims for execution.

Nebuchadnezzar was evidently about to purge his kingdom of the whole college of magicians in much the same way. The Babylonian psychics were outraged (2:10-11).

Let all people in our day who are fooled by psychics and astrologers take note of *that*—the confession, of the founders of their own fraternity, of the utter inability of such people to tell the truth about the future. Only God can prophesy. Hitler and Germany were lured by evil spirits into occult practices. Before they were through they had devasted Europe, destroyed Germany, and left the world a prey to the evils which now beset it. For whatever "gods" there are, above and beyond the horoscopes and ouija boards and incantations of black magic, they are dark, satanic "gods." They make dupes of men. The Babylonian magicians confessed there were such "gods." They also confessed that they were far beyond their beck and call.

Now comes *the king's decree* (2:12-13). The king's patience with his court magicians was exhausted. He was angry, "very furious," as the text has it. His slender stock of patience was exhausted. He rightly judged that his soothsayers, psychics and astrologers were impotent to help him in his need, so he "commanded to dsestroy all the wise men of Babylon." Good, bad and indifferent, so far as he was concerned, the whole college was tarred with the same brush. The death warrant was signed: "and they sought Daniel and his fellows to be slain" (2:13). Because of their education, Daniel and his friends were lumped together with all the others.

The arresting officers arrived. As soon as Daniel found out what was happening, he made a prudent approach to Arioch, captain of the bodyguard: "Why is the decree so hasty from the king?" Evidently Daniel and his friends had not been at court when the previous drama unfolded. Now he made personal application to the king for a stay of execution, promising something the court psychics could not promise—to tell the king his dream. Indeed, the king could set his own time. The king was impressed, and agreed to give Daniel something he categorically refused to give the magicians—more time. Evidently there was a ring of certainty and assurance in Daniel's request, missing entirely from the prevarications and protestations of the others.

II. THE KING AND THE BELIEVING PROPHET (2:17-49)

In this section, the focus of interest is Daniel himself. He is God's man, the man who will take a stand for God even at the risk of his own life. The man, indeed, whose confidence in God is so great that he personally does not feel he is taking any risk at all. This is the young man who "purposed in his heart" that he would not defile himself with the king's meat (1:8). That is the secret of Daniel's life. We can be sure that we would never have heard of him again if he had compromised when confronted by the first challenge to his faith. He would have become just one more anonymous face in the crowd. But now, in this crisis, he is God's man. He has put God to the test, God has put him to the test; between Daniel and his God there is a perfect understanding.

We note *Daniel's prayerful trust* (2:17-23). He went home. There is something appealing about that. He did not go to some lonely hermitage in the wilderness or seek out some shrine where he could fast and pray. He went home. Daniel's religion was of the everyday, homey variety. He gathered some like-minded friends around him—Hananiah, Mishael and Azariah—and urged them to "desire mercies of the God of heaven concerning this secret; that Daniel and his companion should not perish with the rest of the wise men of Babylon" (2:18). He called for a prayer meeting.

It is significant that he referred to God as *the God of heaven*. Daniel's God was a personal God. He was a God of "mercies" (i.e., "great mercy"), unlike the remote demon gods of the Babylonian stargazers. He was "the God of heaven." The title occurs for the first time in 2 Chronicles 36:23 (the last verse in the last book of the Jewish Bible). It was a name introduced into the Bible because God's earthly people had become *Lo Ammi* ("not my people") and because

God had withdrawn from their midst. It is a title belonging to the times of the gentiles, the time when God acts from heaven rather than from between the cherubim in the temple as the God of Israel.

Then Daniel went off to bed. Such was his confidence in God. It was a good thing he did not pace the floor of his room all night agonizing in his soul. He would have missed the answer to his prayer. As it was, his sweet and simple trust in God was rewarded instantly. As Daniel slept, God gave his trustful servant the same dream he had given to Nebuchadnezzar the night before!

Prayer (2:17-19) gave way to praise (2:20-23). God is both omniscient and omnipotent. He is able to remove sovereigns or to reveal secrets with equal ease. He rules over "times and seasons," over the rise and fall of empires, over those tides in the affairs of men which mark the destiny of nations.

The dawn broke at last. Daniel had cheerful news for Arioch. All was well! "Destroy not the wise men of Babylon: bring me in before the king . . ." (2:24). We are not told whether the soothsayers, psychics and stargazers of Babylon were moved with gratitude for Daniel's intervention, which undoubtedly saved their lives, or whether they were full of jealously at his sudden popularity and promotion and because he had shown up their false gods for what they were.

Now comes *Daniel's personal testimony* (2:24-30). The captain of the guard escorted Daniel into the royal presence. In the process he tried to feather his own nest by claiming to be the one who had "found a man of the captives of Judah" who would "make known unto the king the interpretation" of his dream (2:25). The king at once demanded of Daniel if he was indeed able to make known to him both the dream and its meaning (2:25).

Daniel did not give an immediate yes or no. It was important that this king understand the difference between a prophet and a psychic, between a seer and a soothsayer, between the true and living God of the Hebrews and the false gods of the Babylonian priesthood. He therefore put some distance between himself and the court magicians: "The secret which the king hath demanded cannot the wise men, the astrologers, the magicians, the soothsayers show unto the king" (2:27). This was not a question but a statement of fact. We can be sure that Daniel did not endear himself to the powerful Babylonian priesthood by thus underlining their importance. Daniel had long since learned not to fear men, however exalted or however powerful the fraternity to which they belonged.

Having underlined the incompetence of the Chaldean priesthood, Daniel introduced Nebuchadnezzar to the true and living

God. This was in stark and deliberate contrast with the feeble protest of the wise men the day before. In the place of those distant, impersonal and capricious demon "gods" of the Babylonian religion, Daniel proclaimed the true God of heaven. That God was the very one who, two nights before, far from being remote and unmoved by human frailty, had actually drawn near to the king and spoken to him concerning things to come. The king was quite right in suspecting that his dream was no ordinary dream, but one freighted down with divine portents.

The dream had been given to the king to show him "what shall come to pass" (2:29). Then , faithful to his God, Daniel disclaimed all personal merit for his ability to make known to the king the meaning of his dream.

Having thus cleared the stage, Daniel was ready to proceed. We have next *Daniel's prophetic teaching* (2:31-45). He begins with *the substance of the kings dream* (2:31-36). This king had subdued all his foes. He had built a virtually impregnable fortress-city on the Euphrates; one, indeed, which contained two of the seven celebrated wonders of the ancient world. He was now at rest. He was no fool, this king. He knew that other empires had arisen to rule over other nations but in time these empires had fallen. The most recent and notable example, one fresh in his mind, we can be sure, was the Assyrian empire. He wondered what would be the fate of his empire. What other empires would arise from the dust of the earth to dominate the nations of the world? Would any empire be greater than his?

In his sleep, he had seen a colossus in human form. Its appearance was terrible to behold and it glowed with a brightness all its own. It was made almost entirely of gleaming metal. The head was of fine gold, its breast and arms were of silver, its belly and thighs were of brass, its legs were of iron, its feet were of iron and clay. The king was contemplating this image in wonder and awe when he saw a stone, cut without hands, descend from on high. It smote the feet of the image (2:35).

"This is the dream," said Daniel (2:36), as he finished describing it to the astonished king. We can imagine the awe with which Nebuchadnezzar gazed upon the young Hebrew who stood before him. He had done what all the soothsayers, psychics and sorcerers of Babylon had declared impossible, something which, indeed, was impossible for anyone not in touch with God. But Daniel gave the king no time for comment: "And we will tell the king the interpretation thereof," he continued.

Before we begin to follow Daniel's explanation of the significance of the dream, there are several things we need to observe about the image. In the first place, the vision was given to a gentile king, the first of many such kings who would hold the Jews in bondage and Jerusalem in thrall. With Nebuchadnezzar began, as we have seen, the now famous "times of the Gentiles." It was fitting, therefore, that the course of those "times" should be revealed to him. And, since the times of the gentiles concerned the destiny of the Hebrew people in exile, it was fitting that the significance of the dream should be revealed to a Jew.

When we consider the relationship of gentile, Jew, and the church of God, the light of the prophetic scriptures, there are two periods of immense importance we must keep in mind. When God raised up Abraham, and promised him that through him and his seed all nations would be blessed (Genesis 12:1-3), He entrusted to him and his descendants two things: secular and spiritual supremacy over all people. If Israel, as a nation, had been true to its calling, both would have been realized. One day, in the sovereign purpose of God, both will be realized, for during the millennial reign of Christ, God's original purpose will be brought to full flower and fruit by the Lord Jesus Christ. The millennial kingdom will embrace a world empire ruled from Jerusalem, and all the dynamics of secular and spiritual power will be concentrated in the hands of Jesus.

Israel failed. The long history of the nation of Israel in the promised land was one of rebellion, idolatry and apostasy. At length God abruptly terminated Israel's secular supremacy. He handed Jerusalem, which was to have been the world's capital, over to a gentile world power, Babylon. The temple, which was to have been a house of prayer for all nations, was given over to the flames. There began the first of the two periods of prophetic significance, the "times" of the gentiles. During this period world empire is to remain solidly in gentile hands along with the city of Jerusalem. For "Jerusalem," Jesus said, "shall be trodden down of the Gentiles, until the times of the Gentiles be fulfilled" (Luke 21:24).

In 1967 the Jews regained possession of Jerusalem and have made it the capital of the reborn state of Israel. They have vowed they will never give it up. This had led to some foolish statements that the "times of the Gentiles" are now over. This cannot be. The times of the gentiles will terminate with the coming, career and collapse of the antichrist. For at least three and a half years he will hold Jerusalem in bondage and will be ravishing the city at the very moment Christ's feet touch down upon the mount of Olives. The present control of Jerusalem by the Jews is only temporary. It does

indicate, however, how close we are to the endtimes and the termination of the times of the gentiles. But those times are not over yet
and will not be until the descent of that stone cut without
hands—until the return of Christ, that is, and the establishment of
the millennial kingdom.

The Jews had temporary possession and control of Jerusalem in
the days of the Hasmoneans, until the Roman power took it away
from them. We judge the same will happen again. The Arabs, the
United Nations Organization, and many gentile powers refuse to
acknowledge Jerusalem as Israel's capital. Many of those who maintain diplomatic relations with Israel keep their embassies at Tel Aviv.
So Jerusalem will fall into the hands of the antichrist, the last Roman
emperor, and be "trodden down of the Gentiles" yet again before
it is all over.

The "times of the Gentiles," then, has to do with God's purpose
to give Israel secular power over the nations. The period began with
Nebuchadnezzar and will end with the antichrist. To this day the
bulk of the world's Jewish population is still in exile, some voluntar-
ily, some in forced exile.

An equally important period in God's dealings with the nation of
Israel is that spoken of as the "fullness of the Gentiles." During this
period spiritual ascendancy also is no longer in Hebrew hands but
in gentile hands. For two thousand years, from Abraham to Pentecost, if God had anything to say, He said it in Hebrew and He spoke
through a Jew. After Pentecost, if God had anything to say, He said
it in Greek; the New Testament was written in Greek. He began to
speak to the gentile world in a gentile language.

Portents of this were not lacking even before Pentecost. Hebrew
had already become a dead language by the time of Christ. The ver-
nacular of the people of Palestine was Aramaic. The commonly used
Bible was the Septuagint, a Greek Bible. The fact that half the book
of Daniel was written in Aramaic was a warning in itself, the first
shadow on the moon of Israel's spiritual ascendancy, warning of a
coming eclipse. The murder of their Messiah was the last straw. God
tore away their spiritual supremacy from the Jews, as centuries before
He had torn away their secular supremacy; He gave spiritual ascendancy to the gentiles as well.

In due course, because of their bitter rejection not only of the Son
of God but also of the Spirit of God, not only of the Christ of God
but also of the church of God, God again uprooted and scattered
the Jewish people. For a further two thousand years they have been
homeless strangers in gentile lands. Religiously they are blinded by

the Talmud, and, instead of sending missionaries and ambassadors to gentile lands as God intended they should, gentile believers in Christ send missionaries to them.

Both these periods, the times of the gentiles and the fullness of the gentiles will end. The "fullness" of the gentiles will end with the rapture of the church. Then, again, God will begin to speak to the world through Jews. He will raise up two Jewish witnesses (Revelation 11) and then 144,000 Hebrew evangelists (Revelation 7) to porclaim the gospel of the kingdom and the imminent coming of Christ to a world gone mad. The "times" of the gentiles will end with the return of the Christ to set up his millennial kingdom on this planet, centered at Jerusalem.

All this is part of the general background of the remarkable prophecy now given to Nebuchadnezzar.

Another fact of general significance, evident from even a cursory glance at the image in Nebuchadnezzar's dream, is that, although it gleamed and glowed in the eyes of the astonished gentile emperor, it was really top heavy. Gold has a specific gravity of 19.3; silver has a specific gravity of 10.51; brass has a specific gravity of 8.5; iron has a specific gravity of 7.6 and clay has a specific gravity of 1.9. So, right from the first, the whole thing was doomed. Thus, although God ordained and allowed gentile world empires to wax and wane and rule and dominate the earth, He never intended this innovation, made necessary by Israel's sins, to be permanent. The thing would have collapsed of its own ungainliness in any case, except that God had decided on a far more spectacular end to gentile world domination than that.

The remaining fact of preliminary significance is that Daniel's interpretation of the image concentrated on the head and the feet of the image; that is, on the beginning and on the ending of gentile world rule. The inbetween stages were passed over in silence and became the subject of later visions given by God to Daniel himself.

Now we are ready to examine Daniel's prophetic teaching. The interpretation of the dream revolves around three factors: domination, deterioration, and disintegration. World *domination* (2:37-38) was given to Nebuchadnezzar.

The right to rule the whole world, up to now the prerogative of the nation of Israel, was thus transferred to Nebuchadnezzar. He was "a king of kings," an emperor. Language could not be plainer in describing the right, now vested in this Babylonian monarch, if so desired, to conquer the whole world. In actual fact, the Babylonian empire was relatively small; it was the smallest of all the world powers of prophecy. Nebuchadnezzar could have gone on to subdue the whole world. Moreover, it was only as the subsequent empires took and held Babylon that this world-rule factor entered into the equation of their power. The only empire which will, in fact, rule the whole world will be the last one, the empire of antichrist. In his day, too, all gentile world rule will cease at the coming of Christ. There have been other great gentile empires, notably the British empire and the French empire, and, more recently, that of the Soviet Union. These empires, however, were not part of this prophecy.

Nebuchadnezzar was the head of gold. The head is the most important single member of the body and gold is the most precious of all metals. This dual symbolism spoke of an absolute monarch. Other kings sat upon the throne of Babylon, but the vision ignores Nebuchadnezzar's father, Nabopolassar, for it was Nebuchadnezzar who conquered Jerusalem and also Nebuchadnezzar's successors. Evil-Merodach, the son of Nebuchadnezzar, sat on the Babylonian throne for a scant two years, after which he was murdered. Neriglassar held the kingdom for three years but he accomplished little beyond the building of a palace, soon to fall into Persian hands. Nabonidus reigned for fifteen years, but his whole reign was overshadowed by the growing might of the Medes and Persians. As for Belshazzar, he was a dissolute young prince who imagined Babylon to be impregnable. Only Nebuchadnezzar was the head of gold.

Now comes *deterioration* (2:39-43). Daniel touches but lightly on the next two kingdoms: "And after thee shall rise another kingdom inferior to thee, and another third kingdom of brass, which shall bear rule over all the earth" (39). It is generally accepted that the four kingdoms envisioned in Nebuchadnezzar's dream are the same as those seen by Daniel in his vision of the four wild beasts (Daniel 7). That the second kingdom was the Medo-Persian and the third the Grecian is made clear (Daniel 8). The prophet Daniel, many years later, when he was an old man and had learned much more prophetic truth, bluntly told the drunken Belshazzar, the last ruler of Babylon, that his kingdom was given to the Medes and Persians (5:28).

The deterioration in the succeeding world powers is seen in the way the vision moves from the head to the breast and arms, from the breast and arms to the belly and thighs, from the belly and thighs to the legs and lastly to the feet which walk in the dust. It is also seen in the decline in value from gold to silver, from silver to brass, or bronze, from brass to iron and from iron to clay. The successive empires were not marked so much by a decline in the vastness and

extent of their territorial gains as in the real power of the head of
state. Nebuchadnezzar was an absolute monarch ("whom he would
he slew" 5:19). The government of Medo-Persia was a government
by law. The king could not change edicts once they were read into
law (6:1,14). The Greek empire was irresistible in the days of Alexander though even he, brilliant and successful as he was, was curbed
by his generals. Moreover they wasted no time in carving up his
empire among themselves once their lord was dead.

The fourth kingdom was the one, however, which was of supreme
interest. The legs were of iron, the feet were an admixture of iron
and clay. There is no doubt that the fourth empire was the Roman
empire, though that empire is not actually named in Daniel's
prophecies. The legs formed much the longest portion of the image,
an indication that the duration of the fourth empire would far
exceed that of the preceding empires. Rome was as strong as iron
(2:40).

Thus it was with the Roman empire. Rome ruled the world of its
day with an iron hand. No mercy was shown to rebels—witness the
terrible doom meted out to Jerusalem in A.D. 70 and the even more
forceful measures taken against the promised land by the Romans
after the Bar Kochba rebellion in A.D. 135. Though she ruled with
great cruelty, Rome left the impress of her language and laws permanently on western civilization.

In the final phase of the empire, the iron was mixed with miry clay
(2:42). The clay clearly symbolizes the democratic element which
was prominent in the Roman empire. In spite of the admixture of
clay, the strength of the iron remained right down to the feet and
toes. Wherever the iron rule could be maintained strength would
be in evidence; wherever the whims and wishes of the people could
prevail weakness would result. Efforts to weld the two, dictatorship
and democracy, would fail, just as all efforts to weld iron to clay must
fail. The prophet declared: "And whereas thou sawest iron mixed
with miry clay, they shall mingle themselves with the seed of men:
but they shall not cleave one to another, even as iron is not mixed
with clay" (2:43). Those who maintain the principles symbolized by
the iron will try in vain to amalgamate themselves with those who
uphold the principle symbolized by the clay.

The final focus on the world gentile powers is on the ten toes. The
significance of these is later amplified in Daniel's vision of the wild
beasts, the last of which had ten horns. The ten toes are similarly
described as kings (2:44). The final form of the Roman empire is still
future. The Roman empire will reemerge on the stage of history as

a ten-nation European coalition dominated as we learn from later prophecies, by the dictator known as the antichrist.

Finally will come *disintegration* (2:44-45). In describing the over-throw of the image, Daniel told the king its end would be "like the chaff of the summer threshingfloor which the wind carrieth away, and there is no place found for them" (2:35). Pusey well said: "The intense nothingness and transitoriness of man's might in his highest estate, and so of his own also, and the might of God's kingdom, apart from all human strength, are the chief subjects of this vision as explained to Nebuchadnezzar" (p. 118).

The image is seen standing complete in all its parts when the stone strikes. The final phase of gentile world empire will embrace all the features of the Babylonian, Persian, Greek and Roman empires and the ten kings will dominate all the territory once held by these empires. More, the antichrist, for a brief period, will control the whole world. The last of the gentile kings will inherit fully the principle of world empire given to Nebuchadnezzar, the first of the gentile kings.

Destruction will overwhelm the final gentile empire. That the last empire of all, the empire of Christ himself, was likened in his dream to a stone empire, must have astonished Nebuchadnezzar. The soil of Babylon produced no stone. Most Babylon buildings were built of highly adhesive clay and brick. A stone kingdom, a kingdom descending from on high, would certainly impress the Babylonian monarch of the different nature of the final kingdom. Similarly, the idea of a stone mountain must have been impressive to Nebuchadnezzar.

Thus, Christ's kingdom will come, not by evolution, not by a grad-ual leavening of mankind by the gospel, but by divine intervention. It will be sovereignly imposed on the world by God. The returning Christ of God, the "stone cut without hands," will crush all his foes. He will raise up a kingdom which will embrace the whole world: the glorious millennial kingdom heralded by Isaiah and other Old Tes-tament prophets.

The chapter closes with *Daniel's public triumph* (2:46-48). First the king *praised* Daniel (2:46-47). He was overawed. He looked upon the young Hebrew as some sort of god. He ordered honors be rendered to him similar to those offered to a god. He acknowledged Daniel's God. As he himself, in the dream, had been proclaimed a king of kings, so he now proclaimed Daniel's God a "God of Gods." He praised him as "Lord of Kings, as a Revealer of secrets"—everything, in short, the false gods of Babylon were not. One can hardly doubt that Nebuchadnezzar was sincere. That this impression wore off is evident from the next chapter. That he came at last to a wonderful knowledge of the true God is seen in chapter four.

Then the king *promoted* Daniel (2:48-49). He made him "a great man." He opened the royal treasury and bestowed upon him wealth beyond the dreams of avarice. He made him "ruler over the whole province of Babylon, and chief of the governors over all the wise men of Babylon." How they liked that we are not told. Whatever resentments they may have felt toward the young Hebrew who worshiped a God other than theirs and who held enormous power in his hands, they were unable to do him any harm. He rested beneath the shadow of Jehovah's wings and in the secret place of the most high.

There is at least a good possibility that Daniel wrote Psalm 119. If that is so, then we learn not only what implicit trust Daniel had in God's word and the place it held in his heart, but also the persecution and opposition he had to face in his life. The problems which come with advancement may be different from those which come with adversity, but they are equally trying to the child of God.

Nor did Daniel forget his friends. He was too wise to promote them himself. He did, however, bring their names before the king and the king, convinced of Daniel's integrity and insight, did not hesitate to promote them, too. How they handled the special snares of advancement is told in the chapter that follows.

I. THE KING AND THE BABYLONIAN PROFESSIONALS (2:1-16)
    A. The King's Dilemma (2:1-3)
        1. His Dream (2:1)
        2. His Decision (2:2)
        3. His Doubts (2:3)
    B. The King's Demand (2:4-11)
        1. The First Demand (2:4-6)
            a. A Rational Request (2:4)
            b. A Reasonable Response (2:5-6)
                (1) What the King Professed (2:5a)
                (2) What the King Promised (2:5b-6)
                    (a) Execution (2:5b)
                    (b) Exaltation (2:6)
        2. The Further Demand (2:7-11)
            a. The Request Renewed (2:7)
            b. The Request Refused (2:8-9)
                (1) What the King Saw (2:8)

(2) What the King Suspected (2:9)
c. The Request Rephrased (2:10-11)
   (1) The Human Impossibility (2:10)
   (2) The Heavenly Improbability (2:11)
C. The King's Decree (2:12-16)
   1. The Death Warrant Signed (2:12-13)
      a. No More Excuses (2:12)
      b. No Man Excepted (2:13)
   2. The Death Warrant Stayed (2:14-16)
      a. What Daniel Discovered (2:14-15)
      b. What Daniel Did (2:16)
         (1) His Courage (2:16a)
         (2) His Commitment (2:16b)
II. THE KING AND THE BELIEVING PROPHET (2:17-49)
   A. Daniel's Prayerful Trust (2:17-23)
      1. Prayer (2:17-19)
         a. What Was Shared by Him (2:17-18)
         b. What Was Shown to Him (2:19)
      2. Praise (2:20-23)
         a. Praising God for His Wisdom (2:20)
         b. Praising God for His Ways (2:21-22)
            (1) In Removing Sovereigns (2:21a)
            (2) In Revealing Secrets (2:21b-22)
         c. Praising God for His Willingness (2:23)
            Daniel's sense of:
            (1) Historical Continuity (2:23a)
            (2) Humble Contentment (2:23b)
   B. Daniel's Personal Testimony (2:24-30)
      1. Before the Babylonian Soldier (2:24-25)
         a. The Promise (2:24)
         b. The Presentation (2:25)
      2. Before the Babylonian Sovereign (2:26-30)
         a. The Question Asked (2:26)
         b. The Question Answered (2:27-30)
            (1) An Exposure (2:27)
            (2) An Explanation (2:28-29)
               (a) The Source of the Vision (2:28)
               (b) The Substance of the Vision (2:29)
            (3) An Exclamation (2:30)
               Why the vision was given:
               (a) To the Humble Believer (2:30a)
               (b) To the Haughty Babylonian (2:30b)
   C. Daniel's Prophetic Teaching (2:31-45)
      1. The Substance of the King's Dream (2:31-36)

a. The Details of the Image (2:31-33)
b. The Destruction of the Image (2:34-36)
2. The Significance of the King's Dream (2:37-45)
   a. Domination (2:37-38)
      (1) The Source of Nebuchadnezzar's Power (2:37)
      (2) The Scope of Nebuchadnezzar's Power (2:38)
   b. Deterioration (2:39-43)
      (1) The Future Kingdoms (2:39)
      (2) The Final Kingdom (2:40-43)
         (a) The Might with Which It Commences (2:28)
         (b) The Mixture with Which It Concludes (2:41-43)
   c. Disintegration (2:44-45)
      (1) A Divinely Conquered World (2:44)
         (a) The Coming of the Heavenly Kingdom (2:44a)
         (b) The Continuance of the Heavenly Kingdom (2:44b)
      (2) A Divinely Confirmed Word (2:45)

---

1. Before the completion of the Old and New Testaments, God often spoke to people in dreams and visions. Now that we have a completed Bible we do well to be skeptical of people who imagine they hear from God in this way, although where the Bible is still an unknown book, God may still speak at times by visions. Where people have ready access to God's word, however, God's normal method of speaking is through the Bible. It would be presumptuous to say that people never have impressive dreams or visions, but such extrabiblical revelations need to be tested by the word of God.

IMPORTANT DATES

(All dates are B.C.)

626 Nabopolassar becomes king of Babylon on death of Ashurbanipal, king of Assyria.

614 Nineveh besieged by Cyaxares of Media.

612 Fall of Nineveh before the combined forces of Cyaxares the Mede, Nabopolassar of Babylon, and the Scythians.

608 Josiah, king of Judah, slain at Megiddo.
Pharaoh Necho defeats Babylon at Carchemish.
Pharaoh Necho installs Jehoiakim on the throne of Judah in the place of Jehoahaz.

605 Nabopolassar, now in poor health, sends his son Nebuchadnezzar to Carchemish to confront pharaoh.
Necho defeated. Nebuchadnezzar conquers all Syria and Palestine.
Nebuchadnezzar takes Jerusalem. The seventy-year captivity begins. Daniel taken to Babylon.
Jehoiakim bound in fetters but seems to have been released after swearing allegiance to Nebuchadnezzar.
Nebuchadnezzar presses on to Egypt.

604 Nebuchadnezzar hears of the death of his father and returns to Babylon to claim the throne.
Jehoiakim cuts up Jeremiah's scroll.

603 Daniel interprets Nebuchadnezzar's dream.

598 Jehoiakim dies.

597 Nebuchadnezzar's second attack on Jerusalem.
Jehoiachin taken to Babylon along with 10,000 captives, including Ezekiel. Mattaniah installed as king of Judah; his name is changed to Zedekiah by Nebuchadnezzar.

594   Army revolt in Babylon crushed by Nebuchadnezzar.
          The western provinces, including Judah, under Zedekiah, revolt.

593   Ezekiel begins to prophesy.

587   The final siege of Jerusalem begins.
          The golden image set up in Babylon.

586   Fall of Jerusalem. The temple destroyed, The walls of Jerusalem
          broken. Zedekiah's sons killed before his eyes. He is blinded and
          deported to Babylon.

585   Nebuchadnezzar begins a thirteen-year siege of Tyre.
          Astyarges becomes king of Media. His daughter, Mandane,
          marries Cambyses I, a vassal Persian king (their son was Cyrus the
          Great).

573   Fall of Tyre.

568   Nebuchadnezzar invades Egypt.

562   Death of Nebuchadnezzar.
          Evil-Merodach becomes king of Babylon.

561   Evil-Merodach frees Jehoiachin from prison.

560   Neriglissar, son-in-law of Nebuchadnezzar, murders Evil-
          Merodach and seizes the throne of Babylon.

559   Cyrus the Great succeeds his father as king of the small Persian
          kingdom of Anshan.

556   Labashi-Marduk, young son of Neriglissar, becomes king.
          He reigns two months. He is murdered by conspirators, including
          Nabonidus, who seizes the throne.

553   Astyages delivered up to Cyrus by the Median army. Cyrus spoils
          Ecbatana, and returns to Anshan.
          Nabonidus leaves the administration of Babylon to his profligate
          son Belshazzar.
          Daniel's vision of the four beasts (7:1).

551   Daniel's vision of the ram and he-goat.

547   Cyrus called "king of Persia" for first time.

546 The wealthy Croesus of Lydia refuses to acknowledge the
lordship of Persia. Is defeated by Cyrus.

539 Fall of Babylon. Cyrus entered Babylon on October 29 as a
liberator. Belshazzar slain.
The administration of Babylonia, Syria, and Palestine entrusted
to Darius the Mede (Gubaru).

538 Cyrus reverses the cruel deportation policy of the Assyrians and
Babylonians. Proclamation for return of Jews.

537 Jews set up altar at Jerusalem (Oct 5).

536 Foundation of temple laid (April or May).
End of seventy-year captivity.
Daniel's last vision (10:1).

535 Opposition from pagan neighbors forces Jews to stop work on the
temple.

530 Cyrus dies. Cambyses becomes Persian emperor.

522 Pseudo-Smerdis becomes emperor (March-Sept).

521 Darius I Hystaspes becomes emperor.

520 Haggai urges resumption of work on temple.
Zechariah begins his ministry.

519 Tettenai, a Persian governor, writes to Darius I to challenge the
rebuilding of the temple.
The decree of Cyrus is found in the library at Ecbatana.
The second decree. Darius I Hystaspes writes to Tettenai
commanding him to help the Jews.
Joshua the high priest crowned symbolically by Zechariah to
symbolize the priest-king anointing of the messiah.

516 Temple finished (February or March).

509 Roman republic founded.

493 An expedition, sent by Darius I Hystaspes against Greece, ends in
disaster.

490 A second expedition against Greece, sent by Darius I Hystaspes,
fails.

486 Xerxes becomes Persian emperor. He demands tribute from the Greeks. His demand is refused.

483 Vashti deposed.

480 Xerxes' army defeated by the Greeks at Thermopylae.
Xerxes' fleet defeated by the Greeks at Salamis.

479 The Greeks again defeat the Persian army and navy.

478 Esther becomes queen.

473 Feast of Purim established.

464 Artaxerxes becomes emperor.

458 Ezra receives a commission from Artaxerxes to go to Jerusalem and enact reforms.

447 Athenians begin building the Parthenon.

445 Nehemiah commissioned by Artaxerxes to go to Jerusalem and rebuild the walls of Jerusalem.

444 Nehemiah arrives in Jerusalem and rebuilds the walls of the city in the face of great opposition.

433 Nehemiah returns to Persia.

423 Artaxerxes succeeded by Darius II.

420 Nehemiah returns to Jerusalem.

397 Malachi prophesies. Old Testament canon closed.

359 Philip II becomes king of Macedonia.
Artaxerxes III Ochus becomes Persian emperor.

356 Alexander born in Pella.

343 Artaxerxes III conquers Egypt.
Aristotle invited to be Alexander's tutor.

339 Philip of Macedonia conquers Greece.

338 Arses becomes Persian emperor.

336 Darius III Codomannus becomes Persian emperor.
Assassination of Philip of Macedonia.
Alexander the Great becomes king of Macedonia.
He crushes a revolt by Athens, Thebes, and other Greek cities.

334 Alexander leads his army into Asia Minor, captures Miletus, and
marches through Lycia and Pamphilia. Defeats Darius III at the
river Granicus.

333 Alexander marches to the Cilician gates and reaches Tarsus.
Darius crosses Asia. The battle of Issus. Alexander captures the
Persian queen and her children. Refuses Darius's offer of ransom
and part of his empire.

332 Alexander captures Bybloc, Sidon, and Tyre.
Gaza captured. Darius again sues for peace in vain.
Alexander invades Greece. Is crowned as pharaoh. Founds
Alexandria.

331 Renewal of Persian crusade. Alexander crosses the Tigris.
Darius sues for peace for the third and last time.
Babylon falls to Alexander. Susa falls.

330 Alexander sacks Persepolis. Darius retreats toward Bactria.
Alexander pursues him via the Caspian gates.
Darius found murdered near Hecatompylus.
Bessus assumes the title of "the Great King" in Bactria.

329 Surrender of Bessus to Alexander.
Alexander marches to Maracanda (Samarkand).
Bessus executed.

327 Alexander marries Roxane. Invades India.

326 Alexander's army mutinies.

324 Alexander returns to Persepolis. Mass marriages at Susa.
Alexander deified.

323 Alexander falls ill and dies. His empire is carved up by his four
leading generals.

320 Ptolemy I Soter takes Egypt, Cyrus, and Palestine.

311 Seleucus I Nicator takes Babylon, adds Syria.

285 Ptolemy II rules Egypt.

281 Seleucus takes most of the empire except Egypt and Palestine. He is killed.
Antiochus I Soter rules in Syria.

275 First Syro-Egyptian war. Ptolemy invades Syria.

264 Rome's first Punic War against Carthage begins.

261 Antiochus II becomes "king of the north" (Syria).
Second Syro-Egyptian war.

252 Antiochus II marries Berenice, daughter of Ptolemy II.
She is later murdered (Daniel 11:6).

250 Translation of the Hebrew Bible into Greek begins about this time.

246 Ptolemy III Euergetes rules in Egypt.
Seleucus II Callinicus becomes king of Syria.

245 Ptolemy III invades Syria to avenge the murder of his sister Berenice (Daniel 11:6).

240 Seleucus II attacks Egypt (Daniel 11:9).

227 Rome adds Sicily, Sardinia, and Corsica to its budding empire.

225 Seleucus III becomes king of Syria.

223 Antiochus III the Great becomes king of Syria.

222 Ptolemy IV Philopator becomes king of Egypt.

221 The fourth Syro-Egyptian war.

219 Antiochus III invades Egypt (Daniel 11:10).

218 Hannibal crosses the Alps during Rome's second Punic War.

217 Ptolemy IV invades Syria and defeats Antiochus III at the battle of Raphia (Daniel 11:11-12).

215 Rome's first Macedonian war.

203 Ptolemy V Epiphanes becomes "child king" of Egypt.

202 War breaks out between Egypt and Syria lasting to 198 B.C.

200 Rome's second Macedonian War. Macedonia forced to secede Greece.

198 Battle of Panion. Antiochus supported by apostate Jews in Palestine. He invades and conquers Egypt. He takes control of Palestine and desolates the land (Daniel 11:13-16).

196 Ptolemy V Epiphanes is crowned in Egypt.

193 Ptolemy II Epiphanes marries Cleopatra, daughter of Antiochus III. Antiochus hopes his daughter will subvert her husband. She supports him against her father (Daniel 11:17).

192 Rome declares war on Syria and Antiochus III.

190 Battle of Magnesia. Romans defeat Antiochus III (Daniel 11:18-19).

187 Seleucus IV Philometor becomes king of Egypt.
Cleopatra, his mother, is queen regent until 174 B.C.

178 Seleucus IV poisoned by the tax collector Heliodorus who seizes the throne (Daniel 11:21).
Antiochus IV Epiphanes seizes the throne of Syria (Daniel 11:22-23).

175 Antiochus begins a series of campaigns against Egypt lasting until 168 B.C. (Daniel 11:22-28).

171 Rome's third Macedonian War.

170 Ptolemy VII Physcon (Euergetes)becomes co-regent of Egypt (Daniel 11:26-27).

169 Antiochus Epiphanes captures Jerusalem.

168 Antiochus Epiphanes defiles the temple and suspends the daily sacrifice (Daniel 11:28).

166 Revolt against Antiochus Epiphanes under Mattathias.
Reign of the Hasmoneans begins.

165 Reconsecration of the temple in Jerusalem.

164 Death of Antiochus Epiphanes. Antiochus IV become king of Syria.

162 Demetrius I Soter becomes king of Syria.

149 Rome's fourth Macedonian War.
Rome's third Punic War.

148 Macedonia becomes a Roman province.

146 Rome destroys Carthage.

139 Astrologers and Jews expelled from Rome.

135 Rome's first Servile War. Revolt of slaves crushed in Sicily.

133 Rome begins her eastern empire. Attalus, king of Pergamum, bequeaths his kingdom to Rome.

103 Rome's second Servile War.

100 Julius Caesar born.

88 Rome's first Mithridatic War (Rome against Mithridates IV Eupator, king of Pontus).

83 Rome's second Mithridatic War.

74 Rome's third Mithridatic War.

73 Spartacus lead a slave revolt.

65 Pompey invades Syria. Conquers Palestine.

63 Pompey captures Jerusalem, annexes Syria and Judea.

59 Julius Caesar becomes consul.

55 Julius Caesar raids Britain.

49 Julius Caesar crosses the Rubicon.

48 Julius Caesar defeats Pompey.

46 The Julian calendar inaugurated.

44 Julius Caesar assassinated.

37 Herod becomes king of Judea.

31 The battle of Actium, during which Octavian defeats Antony..

27 Octavian assumes the title of Augustus.

15 Roman empire reaches the Danube.

5 Probable year of birth of Christ.

4 Death of Herod.

COMPLETE OUTLINE*

PART ONE.   Daniel and His Personal Friends(Daniel 1:1–6:28)
I.   A KING'S DAINTIES (1:1-21)
   A. Daniel and His Destiny (1:1-7)
      1. The Captivity (1:1-2)
         a. Jehoiakim and His Depravity (1:1-2)
            (1) His Disobedience to the Word of God
            (2) His Departure from the Worship of God
         b. Nebuchadnezzar and His Cruelty (1:1-2)
         c. Jehovah and His Sovereignty (1:1-2)
      2. The Captives (1:3-4b)
         a. Their Nobility (1:3)
         b. Their Ability (1:4a,b)
      3. The Crisis (1:4c-7)
         a. An Authority Crisis (1:4c)
         b. A Morality Crisis (1:5)
         c. An Identity Crisis (1:6-7)
   B. Daniel and His Decisions (1:8-21)
      1. A Heart Decision (1:8a,b)
         a. Individual (1:8a)
         b. Influential (1:8b)
      2. A Humble Decision (1:8c-16)
         a. The Abstinence He Requested (1:8c-10)
         b. The Alternative He Suggested (1:11-16)
      3. An Honored Decision (1:17-21)
         a. Spiritual Revelation (1:17)
         b. Royal Elevation (1:18-20)
         c. Personal Continuation (1:21)
II.   A KING'S DESTINY (2:1-49)
   A. The Dream and Its Consequences (2:1-30)
      1. The King and His Distress (2:1-3)
         a. His Disturbance (2:1)
         b. His Demand (2:2-3)
      2. The Scholars and Their Dilemma (2:4-13

*Please note that not all outline points contained in the Complete Outline appear in the text.

a. Their Ignorance (2:4-9)
b. Their Arrogance (2:10-13)
3. The Prophet and His Desire (2:14-30)
   a. His Promise (2:14-16)
   b. His Prayer (2:17-18)
   c. His Praise (2:19-23)
   d. His Proclamation (2:24-30)
B. The Dream and Its Contents (2:31-49)
   1. Prophetic Truth (2:31-45)
      a. The Image Described (2:31-35)
      b. The Image Discussed (2:36-45)
         (1) Man's Kingdoms (2:36-43)
            (a) Babylon
            (b) Medo-Persia
            (c) Greece
            (d) Rome
         (2) Messiah's Kingdom (2:44-45)
            (a) The Supernatural Stone
            (b) The Stumbling Stone
            (c) The Salvation Stone
            (d) The Sovereign Stone
   2. Personal Triumph (2:46-49)
      a. Respect Given to Daniel (2:46-47)
      b. Rule Given to Daniel (2:48-49)
III.   A KING'S DEMANDS (3:1-30)
A. They Would Not Bow (3:1-12)
   1. Construction of the Image (3:1)
      a. Deification of Nebuchadnezzar
      b. Glorification of Man
      c. Unification of Religion
   2. Dedication of the Image (3:2-7)
      a. A Powerful Order (3:2-3)
      b. A Paid Orator (3:4-6)
      c. A Pathetic Ordeal (3:7)
   3. Repudiation of the Image (3:8-12)
      a. Consternation of the Majority (3:8-11)
      b. Determination of the Minority (3:12)
B. They Would Not Bend (3:13-18)
   1. Attitude of the King (3:13-15)
      a. Anger (3:13)
      b. Amazement (3:14)
      c. Antagonism (3:15)
   2. Answer of the Hebrews (3:16-18)
      a. Courage (3:16)
      b. Confidence (3:17)

(1) The Prophet's Preparation (9:3)
(2) The Prophet's Petition (9:4-19)
    (a) God and His Character (9:4-9)
        i. God's Person (9:4)
        a. His Might
        b. His Majesty
        c. His Mercy
        ii. God's Patience (9:5-6)
        a. What He Saw (9:5)
        b. What He Sent (9:6)
        iii. God's Punishment (9:7-8)
        a. Its Extent (9:7)
        b. Its Explanation (9:8)
        iv. God's Pity (9:9)
    (b) God and His Commandments (9:10-14)
        i. The Demands of the Law (9:10)
        *a.*Revealed in Its Precepts
        b. Reaffirmed by Its Prophets
        ii. The Doom of the Law (9:11-14)
        a. Curse Was Conveyed (9:11)
        b. Curse Was Confirmed (9:12)
        c. Curse Was Continued (9:13-14)
        1. The Reason (9:13)
        2. The Result (9:14)
    (c) God and His Covenant (9:15-17)
        i. The Exodus (9:15)
        ii. The Exile (9:16-17)
        a. Plight of the People (9:16)
        b. Plea of the Prophet (9:17)
    (d) God and His Compassion (9:18-19)
        i. God's Gracious Nature (9:18)
        ii. God's Great Name (9:19)
2. Daniel Received a New Prophecy (9:20-27)
  a. The Coming of the Messenger (9:20-23)
    (1) When He Came (9:20-21)
      (a) The Importunate Saint
      (b) The Immolated Sanctuary
    (2) Why He Came (9:22-23)
      (a) Daniel's Perplexity (9:22)
      (b) Daniel's Prayer (9:23a)
      (c) Daniel's Person (9:23b)
  b. The Content of the Message (9:24-27)
    (1) Seventy Weeks Are Decreed (9:24)
      (a) Focus of the Period (9:24)
      (b) Features of the Period (9:24)

        (a) Powerful Foes Who Hindered the Herald
        (b) Powerful Friend Who Helped the Herald
    (3) Imparted Response (10:14)
        (a) People Involved
        (b) Period Involved
  b. Reaction (10:15-19)
    (1) Daniel's Weakness Was Revealed (10:15-17)
        (a) He Was Overcome by the Message (10:15-16)
        (b) He Was Overwhelmed by the Messenger (10:17)
    (2) Daniel's Weakness Was Removed (10:18-19)
        (a) The Touch of a Loving Hand (10:18)
        (b) The Tenderness of a Loving Heart (10:19)
  c. Resolution (10:20-21)
    (1) Unseen War (10:20)
    (2) Unseen Warrior (10:21)
III. TWO COMPLETE DISCLOSURES (11:1–12:13)
  A. Specific Details about the Future (11:1-45)
    1. The Coming of Antiochus (11:1-35)
      a. The World of Alexander the Greek (11:1-9)
        (1) His Success (11:1-4)
          (a) The Concluding Period of Persia (11:1-2)
          (b) The Coming Punishment of Persia (11:3-4)
            i. His Conquests (11:3)
            ii. His Collapse (11:4)
        (2) His Successors (11:5-9)
          (a) The Egyptian Prince (11:5)
          (b) The Egyptian Princess (11:6)
          (c) The Egyptian Protest (11:7-9)
      b. The Wars of Antiochus the Great (11:10-20)
        (1) His First Campaign (11:10-12)
          (a) Victorious (11:10)
          (b) Vanquished (11:11-12)
        (2) His Further Campaign (11:13-17)
          (a) Mobilization (11:13-14)
          (b) Molestation (11:15-16)
            i. Pharoah Defeated (11:15)
            ii. Palestine Desolated (11:16)
          (c) Manipulation (11:17)
        (3) His Final Campaign (11:18-20)
          (a) His Vain Scheme (11:18-19)
          (b) His Vile Son (11:20)
      c. The Wickedness of Antiochus the God (11:21-35)
        (1) His Contemptibility (11:21-22)
          (a) His Coming to Power (11:21)
          (b) His Control of the Priesthood (11:22)
        (2) His Craftiness (11:23-24)
        (3) His Conquests (11:25-27)

(a) Entered the Egyptian Kingdom (11:25-26)
(b) Entertained the Egyptian King (11:27)
(4) His Cruelty (11:28)
(5) His Crimes (11:29-35)
(a) His Rebuff (11:29-30a)
(b) His Revenge (11:30b-35)
i. Invaded Jerusalem (11:30b)
ii. Insulted Jehovah (11:31)
iii. Inflamed Judea (11:32-35)
a. Those Who Deified Him (11:32a)
b. Those Who Deified Him (11:32b-35)
2. The Coming of Antichrist (11:36-45)
a. His Blasphemies (11:36-38)
(1) Royal Pride (11:36)
(2) Religious Policy (11:37)
(3) Real Purpose (11:38)
b. His Battles (11:39-45)
(1) His Great Powers (11:39)
(2) His Great Problems (11:40-45)
(a) His Rivals (11:40a)
(b) His Revenge (11:40b-43)
(c) His Rage (11:44)
(d) His Ruin (11:45)
B. Specific Dates about the Future (12:1-13)
1. The Tribulation (12:1)
2. The Tomb (12:2-3)
a. Resurrection (12:2)
b. Rewards (12:3)
3. The Times (12:4-7)
a. The Sealed Book (12:4)
b. The Spirit Beings (12:5-7)
(1) Their Coming (12:5)
(2) Their Conversation (12:6-7)
(a) Question Asked (12:6)
(b) Question Answered (12:7)
4. The Truth (12:8-13)
a. Request by the Prophet (12:8)
b. Reply to the Prophet (12:9-12)
(1) Why (12:9)
(2) What (12:10)
(3) When (12:11-12)
c. Rest for the Prophet (12:13)